Thinking: Objects
Contemporary approaches to product design

Tim Parsons

academia

An AVA Book

Published by AVA Publishing SA
Rue des Fontenailles 16
Case Postale
1000 Lausanne 6
Switzerland
T +41 786 005 109
enquiries@avabooks.ch

Distributed by

Thames & Hudson
(ex-North America)
181a High Holborn
London WC1V 7QX
United Kingdom
T +44 20 7845 5000
F +44 20 7845 5055
sales@thameshudson.co.uk
www.thamesandhudson.com

Distributed in the USA &
Canada by:
Ingram Publisher Services Inc.
1 Ingram Blvd.
La Vergne, TN 37086
USA
T +1 866 400 5351
F +1 800 838 1149
customer.service@
ingrampublisherservices.com

**English Language
Support Office**

AVA Publishing (UK) Ltd.
T +44 1903 204 455
enquiries@avabooks.ch

©AVA Publishing SA 2009

ISBN 978-2-940373-74-1

10 9 8 7 6 5 4 3 2 1

Design by
EMMI / www.emmi.co.uk

Production by
AVA Book Production Pte. Ltd.,
Singapore
T +65 6334 8173
F +65 6259 9830
production@avabooks.com.sg

All reasonable attempts have
been made to trace, clear and
credit the copyright holders
of the images reproduced
in this book. However, if any
credits have been inadvertently
omitted, the publisher will
endeavour to incorporate
amendments in future editions.

Thinking: Objects
Contemporary approaches to product design

Tim Parsons

an AVA Academia advanced title

Contents

HOW TO GET THE MOST OUT OF THIS BOOK

The book has four chapters, each based upon an essential theme within product design: perception, motivation, process and context.

PERCEPTION
This chapter discusses the way product design is perceived in relation to societal constructs, such as politics and value.

MOTIVATION
This chapter attempts to answer the question: Beyond the need to earn a living for themselves and their clients, what drives designers to do what they do? It focuses upon the creative rationale behind projects and suggests that a recognisable (although not exclusive) series of approaches are being taken to product design today.

PROCESS
Perhaps the most difficult part of design to adequately quantify, this chapter attempts to grapple with the elusive nature of the design process. By calling upon philosophical viewpoints, a picture of the cognitive process is built up. The nature of creativity and insight is discussed and a range of working tools introduced, which designers can use to enrich their own process.

CONTEXT
This final chapter examines the working contexts of designers. It also looks at the rules of engagement with clients and illustrates how speculative work presents the opportunity for radical independent voices.

Fig. 1 Chapter openers Each chapter starts with a chapter opener. Each of the chapters are given a specific colour, which runs throughout.

Fig. 2 Section breaks and navigation Each chapter is broken down into further sections. The start of each of these sections is marked by a coloured box at the top of the left-hand page. Every left-hand page also contains a navigation bar, displaying previous, present and future sections, and the present chapter.

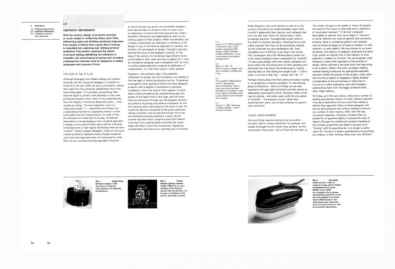

Fig. 3 Grey boxes
Some sections have additional
information displayed in grey
boxes. These explain a concept
or theory further.

Fig. 4 Margin notes
Additional references and notes
are shown in the margins.
Image captions are displayed
below horizontal lines at the
bottom of each page.

Fig. 5 Sources
The back pages of the book
work as a further information
and reference section.

INTRODUCTION

This book aims to present information, insight and argument concerning the thoughts and theories behind contemporary product design. But what does it mean to be a product designer in the early twenty-first century? Is it simply a job or must it be a consuming passion? Is it to follow a brief or create your own? Is it to be a household name or a vital but unseen cog in a vast machine? Is it to be an inventor or a stylist? Artist or businessman? Hero or villain?

Since it developed as a profession in its own right around 100 years ago, product design (or industrial design – the terms are compatible although imply a different focus) has broadened in scope to encompass a vast range of specialisms. Co-opting knowledge from the fields of psychology and the social sciences, product designers can be found exhibiting in art galleries, working for fashion labels, speculating on the future of biotechnology and programming computers to generate products autonomously. Yet away from the glare of the ever-increasing media interest in "extraordinary" projects, the mundane objects of everyday life are still conceived, drawn up and manufactured on a mass scale.

Hence the most pressing challenge for those new to the profession lies in deciding where to focus their creative energies. What is product design? What can it be? What do we want it to be? In the past, these questions were largely answered for us if we aligned ourselves with the thinking of one of the major design movements. Manifestos set out the purpose of design and, in some cases, the language of form that was considered "good". Any type of design could be measured against these rules and results reached that were considered definitive. Through questioning the validity of these rules by designers and theorists, the

notion of a collective concept of "good design" has been eroded, leaving behind fragmented bodies of opinion. Consequently, designers themselves can be found promoting their particular view of what design is:

"'Design' means how something works, not how it looks – the design should evolve from the function." (1)

"[Design is] the act of imposing one's will on materials to perform a function." (2)

"Design is about creatively exploiting constraint." (3)

To James Dyson, designer of the cyclonic vacuum cleaner, design starts with an engineering innovation and the form is secondary (fig. 1, page 08). To Ron Arad, renowned furniture designer, the innovative manipulation of materials is his focus (fig. 2, page 08) and for Nick Crosbie, whose company Inflate has developed a vast range of products with the manufacturing process used to make plastic inflatables, the challenge of limited resources is what drives the creative process (fig. 3, page 09).

Not one of the designers quoted is wrong – product design is all these things and more – but it would be futile for any of them to suggest that theirs is the only valid approach. Pluralism is here to stay and it is up to designers, their clients and collaborators, to make their own rules. The search for "good design" therefore becomes the search for definitive results identified according to the designer's own intentions and the specific conditions of each project. If we are to judge products holistically, we therefore need access to this information, along with some insight into the social fabric into which they are introduced.

[1]
Dyson, J. In:
<www.dyson.co.uk>

[2.]
Arad, R. In: Fairs, M. 2004. "What is design?" 'Icon' magazine No.18

[3.]
Crosbie, N. In: Fiell, C. and P. 2001. 'Designing the 21st Century'

Fig. 1   Dyson DC01 Vacuum Cleaner The aesthetic of James Dyson's cyclonic vacuum cleaners fetishises industrial components to reinforce his view that engineering must be considered ahead of form.

Fig. 2   Ron Arad Big Easy Chair Ron Arad's early work contained pieces such as Big Easy, wrought from stainless steel sheets by welding and polishing with hand tools.

Sadly, little background knowledge is imparted when products are launched. With some designers unwilling to explain their work, and press interest often confined to the shopping pages, there is a scarcity of in-depth education about design reaching the general public. It is left to design historians to build a picture of the significance of objects, but this often focuses entirely upon the designer's perspective rather than attempting to look at the object's wider impact. (4) With this information staying largely within the confines of specialist publications (this one being no exception), the public can be forgiven for the misapprehension that "design is for designers". It is therefore vital that consumers, as well as designers, are encouraged to hone their skills at reading objects to see if this information can be gleaned directly.

The wealth of avenues of design activity now open, combined with the increasing awareness of the damage caused by socially and environmentally irresponsible design means that now, more than ever, designers have a bewildering array of decisions to make and issues to face. Many choose to avoid the more difficult questions. However, those to whom design feels more like a calling than simply a way to earn a crust revel in the challenges it presents: "Design is not a discipline but a stance born as a result of a personal formation based on humanistic, technological, economic and political criticism." (5)

Achille Castiglioni, the grand master of Italian post-war industrial design, underlines the fact that design inescapably implies ideology. Yet the capacity of designers to express a coherent set of values and to pursue these to create meaningful change has been hampered by the confines of their role. As Adrian Forty explains in his book, 'Objects of Desire' (6), although designers tend to present themselves as the prime movers behind the existence of objects, in reality it is the entrepreneurs and managers of production companies who decide what reaches the market. According to Forty, the paradox of designers claiming omnipotence and yet experiencing relative impotence has led many to ignore the task of articulating a philosophy and to instead concentrate on building the myth that they are indeed masters of their own destiny.

This sense of helplessness among designers, combined with a reticence from British industry to engage their services during the 1980s led to the gradual increase in so-called "self-production", designer-maker activity and craft-based design work. Many practitioners have made their names designing, making (or outsourcing) and selling their products direct to retailers or to commission, as opposed to working directly for the manufacturing industry. Some have used this as a springboard to enable them and their work to achieve public recognition, while to others it has been a necessary step to entice industrial clients. The parallel explosion of media interest in design has largely bypassed the "traditional" design consultancies and in-house design teams (who continue to design the majority of consumer products that come on to the market) in favour of publishing the work of this new band of independent designers. While this has brought a glut of gimmicky products into the public eye, the increase in self-production has also led to a greater awareness of singular visions and of the poetic possibilities of the design object.

[4.] -
Forty, A. 1995. 'Objects of Desire.' London: Thames & Hudson

[5.] -
Castiglioni A. In: Asensio Cerver F. 1997. 'Home Product Design.' Hove: Rotovision

[6.] -
Forty, A. 1995. 'Objects of Desire'. London: Thames & Hudson
-

Fig. 3   **Egg cup by Inflate** Nick Crosbie and his partners set up Inflate to market a range of products made by a process called high frequency welding, normally used to make seaside inflatables such as rubber rings and dinghies.

Fig. 4   **Van den Puup** IKEA's fictitious "star designer" was an attempt to distance the company from any association with designers who were seen as prima donnas.

[7.] -
Papanek V. 1972. 'Design
for the Real World'. London:
Thames & Hudson
-

With our increasing knowledge of the environmental crisis that we currently face and the constant reminders of how the manufacturing industry is adding to this, designers are under growing pressure to apply their skills ethically as well as aesthetically. Some of the most vehement criticism of product designers over the years has been aimed at their apparently uncritical stance, particularly when asked to work on products of dubious merit. "There are professions more harmful than industrial design", wrote Victor Papanek in 1972, "but only a few of them. And possibly only one is phonier. Advertising design, in persuading people to buy things they don't need, with money they don't have, in order to impress others who don't care, is probably the phoniest field in existence today. Industrial design, by concocting the tawdry idiocies hawked by advertisers, comes a close second. Never before in history have grown men sat down and seriously designed electric hairbrushes, rhinestone-covered file boxes, and mink carpeting for bathrooms, and then drawn up elaborate plans to make and sell these gadgets to millions of people". (7)

Although a lack of moral backbone can be blamed for accepting such jobs without challenging their underlying motives, it is important to recognise why such requests have arisen. As products evolve through the attentions of numerous designers, many reach a settled form that is accepted as being appropriate. Over time, changes in behaviour and the application of new materials, technologies or other such advances may cause a shift in this settled form, but until then radical redesigns are generally considered unnecessary and even damaging to a company's market-share. Hence, designers are encouraged to find other methods of differentiating products within these received limitations, in order to generate appeal.

The time designers and manufacturers spend bringing a new product to market (the "lead time") has shortened as competition has increased. This has resulted in less time being available for research that may bring to light new and valuable discoveries. While these factors do not excuse designers from their part in filling the planet with the "tawdry idiocies" Papanek talked of, they at least illustrate that designers work within a system of constraints. At worst, designers are simply the pencil-wielders of business, neither exercising conscience nor creative input. At best, they encourage their employers into meaningful dialogue, challenging them to ensure what is brought to the market is of genuine worth.

Feelings as to whether a product deserves to exist or not can only be based on our personal reaction to the values it offers. Consequently, we should have no reason to presume others will share our reactions. Product concepts contain the latent possibility of offering several different kinds of value. Beyond the use-value of the product itself lies its value as a signifier of identity and status. We are all fearful of appearing to lack style, wealth, hygiene, virility or fertility and products appearing to grant us these "riches" boost our self-esteem. By selling design changes as part of a story based in the fantasy world of advertising rather than the practical reality of the everyday, designers contribute to the individual's "cultural capital".

Fig. 5 **Sponsored Food by Martí Guixé** Spanish self-styled "ex-designer" Martí Guixé conceived Sponsored Food as a way of allowing his artist friends to eat for free. Paid for by corporate sponsorship, the free food would mean that they would no longer need to sell work or undertake paid labour.

Fig. 6 **Air Chair by Jasper Morrison** Morrison's approach owes a debt to modernist pioneers such as Jean Prouvé (for honest use of materials) and Dieter Rams (for aesthetic cleanliness), but compared to these forebears some of his work exhibits a more playful, warmer touch.

PLURALISM, MODERNISM AND POSTMODERNISM

While having several broader meanings when applied to design, the term 'pluralism' refers to the diverse nature of objects produced by designers today, their thinking characterised, as it is, by its adherence to not one but many different approaches, theories, standards and aesthetic preferences (hence 'plural' as in more than one).

The last and most determined attempt to establish a universal ideology for designers to work within emerged around the turn of the twentieth century. Rising to prominence in Europe as a theoretical framework affecting the arts and architecture as well as design, modernism pursued human progress through social, cultural and technological innovations and is still hugely influential today. The harnessing of the machine and manufacture to democratic ends was a central theme, as was the assertion that pure geometric forms and undecorated materials embodied superior moral as well as aesthetic values. Such principles were considered absolute and not determined by the preferences of one culture or society, let alone the designer. (Yet modernism's preferences, although spreading over time, had emerged from the opinions of one group and this hypocrisy was not lost on its detractors.) Hence, according to modernist principles, objects could be designed to be 'timeless' and continuously desirable.

Postmodernism, the most direct rebuttal of modernist values, drew its strength from modernism's failures and contradictions. These rebuttals included:

1) the belief that the famous modernist axiom "form follows function" was flawed in a number of respects. It implied designers were giving form to products independently of their own aesthetic preferences. It also suggested that the form should always follow function as opposed to, as was later espoused, ease of use, poetic metaphor or other equally valid criteria.

2) the fact that the pure geometric forms modernism's followers praised were not always easily and efficiently reproducible using the manufacturing technology it wished to employ;

3) the insistence on a link between purity of form and morality could not be proven;

4) the utopian vision of generating complete social harmony through architecture and design simply didn't materialise; and

5) its elitist attitude failed to acknowledge the preferences of the mass audience.

'A dining table of the period,' wrote design educator Victor Papanek 'might have a top, well proportioned in glistening white marble, the legs carefully nurtured for maximum strength with minimum materials in gleaming stainless steel. And the first reaction on encountering such a table is to lie down on it and have your appendix extracted'. (i) Throughout the previous century various self-appointed arbiters of taste (Augustus Pugin, William Morris, Henry Cole to name but three (ii)) had harangued 'the masses' with their opinions on what was correct and appropriate and modernism continued in this tradition albeit with some differing and opposing views.

As postmodern theory became accepted in the 1980s many designers warmed to the notion that different forms could be considered appropriate in different contexts. However, it also unleashed the unfettered curiosity of some designers, resulting in an 'anything goes' approach that many found unpalatable and which stuck in the consciousness of some critics as postmodernism's main legacy.

Postmodern thinking, as design historian Andrew Jackson points out, considers that "an object is not able to speak for itself, but is in fact 'spoken for' by its social and political context. The values associated with the object are determined by the position from which the object is viewed and aesthetic appeal is regarded not as a universal value, outside of history, but rather as an ever-changing quality relative to the circumstance within which the object is consumed". (iii)

[i.]
Papanek, V. 1970. 'Design for the real world; human ecology and social change'. New York: Pantheon Books

[ii.]
Bayley, S. In: Bayley, S. and Conran, T. 2007. 'Intelligence Made Visible'. London: Conran Octopus

[iii.]
Jackson, A. Designing Britain, 1945–1975 [online]. Accessed 4th March 2009. Available from World Wide Web: <http://vads.ahds.ac.uk/learning/designingbritain/html/crd_postmodern.html>

Coined by French sociologist Pierre Bourdieu, cultural capital is one of a number of forms of capital (wealth) that an individual may acquire and use within a system of exchange. It consists of, among other things, knowledge and understanding of culture, cultural groups and the figures of authority and authenticity within those groups. In design terms, it is the knowledge behind the goods bought: what they signify and to whom, and the status conferred by them.

One particular strain of cultural capital that designers and their clients have been criticised for fostering is that of the "design signature". In contrast with the majority of design work that is undertaken anonymously, some designers are asserting their right to be recognised. In doing so, many are tempted into adopting the fine artist's myth-making around the value associated with the hand of the maker. A "design

world" has emerged in which "in-the-know" consumers drop the names of star designers, some of whom have become valuable brands in their own right. Glitz, gloss and glamour accompany the launch of a new chair, kitchen or bathroom suite. Yet it can sometimes be hard to see what all the fuss is about – are we looking at a work of genius or the emperor's new clothes? In an attempt to lampoon the scene and distance themselves from the negative connotations of the designer as prima donna, the furniture manufacturer IKEA created its own fictitious star designer, Van Den Puup (fig. 4, page 09) who appeared in their commercials, lambasting the company's products for their cheapness and lack of "soul"– a strangely double-edged campaign considering their own designers are named and photographed in their catalogue. However, what it revealed was that IKEA felt that the popular view of designers was one of suspicion at their elitism and style over substance. (8)

While the cult of the personality has invaded the psyche of certain product designers, plenty are nevertheless involved in advancing the profession into new

Fig. 7 Banana juice carton by Naoto Fukasawa for Takeo Paper Show "HAPTIC", 2004 One of a series of fruit carton designs that took colour and texture from the skin of the fruit from which the juice was made, Fukasawa's banana juice carton is particularly effective – the waxy carton paper and octagonal shape prompting a sensory double-take.

Fig. 8 Packaging for Waitrose by Goodwin Hartshorn These ring-pull cans were designed to make the process of opening cans easier for everyone, but particularly those with reduced finger dexterity. The large ring pulls are easier to grasp – and are a good example of "inclusive design".

territory. Those featured in this book have developed contemporary approaches that are widely considered to deliver significant results. Some have found ways to reconcile anti-consumerist, pro-ethical views with their role as conceivers of objects by challenging conventional behaviour (fig. 5, page 10). Some update past movements such as modernism, adopting its utopian optimism and aesthetic cleanliness, while sidestepping its tendency towards social engineering (fig. 6, page 11). Others look for poetic and appropriate connections between a product's form and its function that inject rational thinking with new life (fig. 7, page 12). Also covered are those who focus on genuine advancements in usability and functionality, improving the experience of using a product for all, regardless of age or physical ability (fig. 8, page 12). Another cohort takes the opposing view that increasing user friendliness contributes to a banal interaction with products, promoting the "on-demand" culture. They feel that by building in ambiguities, our experience with certain objects can be enriched (fig. 9, page 13). As Western economies continue to shift from providing discrete products to providing services, some design firms have moved their input "upstream" to help shape the business models and organisational structures of their clients. Design firms wishing to engage with these companies have defined a field – "service design" – that focuses on the "touch-points" where people interact with the employees and fabric of the service provider.

Finally, the book recognises the increasing level of collaboration between designers and the public and the changing nature of this relationship. Facilitated by the networking power of the Internet, consumers are becoming "prosumers" (9), taking a pro-active role in commissioning and specifying their own products.

An examination of these different approaches can be found in Chapter 2, but the book is structured around the proposition that there are three other elements of product design that require theoretical scrutiny: our perception of the profession, the design process itself, and the contexts within which it occurs. The book takes each element as a chapter. Chapter 1, "Perception", examines design in relation to political stances, types of value and the meanings of form. Chapter 2, "Motivation", discusses "design as personal ideology", uncovering what the designer is trying to achieve, and illustrates the wide range of approaches taken to product design today. Chapter 3, "Process" asks, "What does the design process look like?" in terms of a methodology and a mental model. It attempts to clarify the confusion as to what constitutes a design process and observes how practical tools such as drawing and model-making aid decision-making. Finally, Chapter 4, "Context", examines typical circumstances in which designers find themselves working and charts the key differences between them.

Although this is a "theory book" on product design, it is to be remembered that theory must go hand-in-hand with practice. Our ability to discuss the ideas behind the work presented here is due to them being translated into models, prototypes and finished products through commitment, skill and, often a good deal of hard work. The adaptation of these theories, and their application to new and worthwhile products, is up to you.

[8.]　-
Sudjic, D. 2004. 'The Strange Case of Van Den Puup: Design in the Age of Celebrity, the Death of the Object and the China Crisis.' RSA Bicentenary Medallist's Address, at the RSA, London, November 2004.
　-
[9.]　-
Derived by merging the word "producer" (and later the word "professional") with the word "consumer", the term "prosumer" was coined by Alvin Tofler in his book, 'The Third Wave' (1980, New York: Bantham Books).
　-

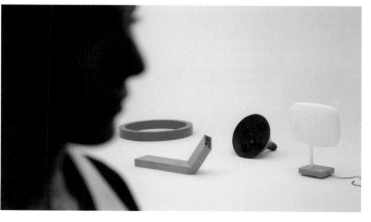

Fig. 9　　Technological Dream Series No. 1 Robots by Anthony Dunne and Fiona Raby Dunne and Raby prompt us to question the received wisdom that robots, and indeed any electronic object, should be a servant, offering on-demand functionality. Their robots have skills and traits, some of the purposes of which are unclear.

01 Perception

[1.]
Gordon, G. 2002. 'Advocacy Toolkit: Understanding Advocacy.' Teddington: Tearfund. Available from World Wide Web:
<http://tilz.tearfund.org>

[2.]
Mari, E. In: Burkhardt, F. 1997. 'Why Write a Book on Enzo Mari?' Milan: Federico Motta Editore

1.1

DESIGN AND POLITICS

Since the 1900s, product design has come of age, gone to seek its fortune, found fame and developed a conscience. Throughout this time, the more worldly designers have wrestled with how to reconcile their political views with their design output. Should we choose to do so, we can try to predict their political stances from who their clients are, what they design, how they design it, how it is sold and to whom. However, the design world is not a hotbed of political debate. Most designers neither wear their political agendas on their sleeves, nor make them explicit in their portfolios. Yet design and politics are, as I hope to demonstrate, undeniably linked.

DESIGN AND THE POLITICS OF STATE

"The broad definition of politics (with a small "p") considers the interaction of all forms of power, which happens wherever there is a relationship. Everyone is therefore political and has the potential to influence what happens in their lives, their communities and their countries." (1)

As Graham Gordon explains, the word "politics" does not relate only to matters of government (Politics with a large "P") but to the use of power on any scale. If design is used to influence or change anything, or even to maintain things as they are, it is exerting power and is therefore a political tool.

"Everything we do is politics. The difference is whether we are aware of this or not." (2)

Design that involves production is intrinsically politicised whether, as Enzo Mari (fig. 1, page 16), one of Italy's most cerebral industrial designers points out, we recognise the fact or not. Designers, while not directly in control, are nonetheless in the business of negotiating with industry about the ways in which production is applied, and the choices possible within this role can be made with particular goals in mind. Those goals may be political with a large or small "p", that is, they may or may not be part of a "big picture" of how a country or a society should operate. Mari's point is that many designers act out their role without ever considering these political ramifications.

To unearth the roots of the link between product design and the politics of the state, we have only to look as far as the dictionary definitions of communism, socialism and capitalism; they are differentiated by who controls the means of production and how it is operated.

THE POLITICS OF THE DESIGNER

Through their work, designers serve, comment on or attempt to change the political systems within which they are born and from this we can infer (rightly or wrongly) compliance with, or criticism of, that system. Translating the politics of the state to the individual, our society has generated stereotypes of political beliefs that imply different behaviour. As a simplistic illustration, socialists believe in the sharing of personal wealth, whereas capitalists believe in the right to keep what they have earned (hence the constant political battles over paying more or less tax

Fig. 1   Enzo Mari at work Enzo Mari, one of Italy's "grand masters" of product and furniture design, has wrestled more than most with the contradictions of trying to design definitive forms in a consumer environment, driven in part by novelty. Here, he is seen working on a project about the nature of value, the vehicle being detergent bottles re-modelled as vases.

to fund public services). In terms of possessions, this suggests that "true" socialists will never own items of conspicuous consumption (anything purchased to elevate social status through an overt display of wealth) as to do so would show they had chosen to keep rather than share their income. Conversely, to those believing in capitalism, conspicuous consumption is a useful mark of their right to ownership. In reality, consumer behaviour is murkier. We may accept the adverse connotations of an object if it serves our needs. However, as designers, it follows that to keep our political ideals we ought not to design objects that represent an opposing model of thought to our own.

POLITICS AND STYLE

The political connotations of a piece of product design can be considered on three levels; as well as the signals the object itself sends us, we can take into account its wider impact (the way it is discussed, marketed, sold, used or misused and disposed of or recycled) and the way the design process was seen to be carried out. So what political signals might an object send and how do we correctly interpret them?

Particular styles of design do not intrinsically belong to particular political belief systems. They have been linked by choice for the political ends of those concerned. As the late Peter Dormer points out in his book 'Meanings of Modern Design: Towards the Twenty-First Century', modernism and its aesthetic rules such as "form follows function" (see page 23) were adopted by those with socialist political leanings because it suited them:

"If the dominant style of the old, non-socialist establishment had been plain and functional, then I am sure that the aesthetic riposte of the socialist or democratically inclined designers would have been towards elaboration, figuration and decoration. The point is that you can argue either style both ways: both can be seen as oppressive, both can be seen as democratic. You can say you are being honest about the object's role, or that you are bringing decoration and metaphor to the people. You can almost toss a coin." (3)

While there used to be a practical explanation as to why decorative objects were the preserve of the rich – decoration takes workmanship, which takes time, which means the craftsman will need to be paid more than for an undecorated item – with the arrival of mass manufacturing processes such as printing, casting and press-forming, complex decorative surfaces could be reproduced quickly and inexpensively using machine tools. Once mechanised production emerged the designer could choose his aesthetic and, as Dormer points out, could argue the reason for his choice from his own political standpoint, regardless of whether his object was plain or decorative.

Whether or not the designer's choice of style has a political motive, an object may imply a political leaning by the effect it has upon us. Objects can liberate or channel behaviour and this is a key political weapon (this phenomenon is discussed in more depth on page 120). It is therefore important to be aware when an object appears to be applying political pressure upon us, whether that comes from the experience we have with it directly, or via learned association with its style.

[3.]
Dormer, P. 1990. 'Meanings of Modern Design: Towards the Twenty-First Century.' London: Thames & Hudson

FROM THE MACHINE AESTHETIC TO THE AESTHETICS OF USE

For the reasons so far discussed, it is dangerous to attempt a reading of the political persuasions of a designer purely from the aesthetics of an object they have designed because the reasons for applying that style can come from either side of the political spectrum. Alternatively, they may have been arrived at naively.

However, we cannot avoid the associations of history and Dormer rightly reminds us that the pared-down, undecorated, geometric purity characteristic of modernism came to be associated with socialist views. This followed a period where the dominant taste aspired to the decadence of the wealthy establishment, hence goods for "the common man" tended to have pretensions of ostentation even when inexpensively made (fig. 2, page 18). Modernism and the "machine aesthetic" – the appearance of an undecorated, machine-made object (fig. 3, page 18) – aimed to change this and had the potential to differentiate inexpensive goods sufficiently to represent a stance against the bourgeoisie. Yet these intentions were hindered because many of the early objects of modernism, although entering the design lexicon as classics, were either (ironically) expensive to manufacture (purity of form and ease of production do not automatically go hand in hand) or were unappealing to the wider public, many of whom still favoured decoration. Although many modernist principles have been extensively adopted since, they were slow to "trickle down".

The political location of a product is therefore defined not just by its image (or indeed its purpose) but by a variety of factors, including to whom it is financially available and by whom it is actually consumed. With the gradual dismantling of class barriers, the converging of left and right in mainstream politics, and emergence of postmodern views, these old aesthetic signposts have become historical relics. Where, for example, should we politically locate Apple's iPod (fig. 4, page 19)? Its clean lines, uniform radii and undecorated surfaces, not to mention its harnessing of new technology, place it in a historical line that leads us back through Dieter Rams (fig. 5, page 19 – Braun's influential chief designer from 1965–1995) to the socialist modernism of Germany's Bauhaus School. Yet, with its bright white earphone wire, shiny case and high price tag (US$400 or around £280 when first released) it is a potent sign of capitalist conspicuous consumption.

Observing the products of consumer culture provides us with the opportunity to make subjective judgements on many levels. The connotations of their use may be towards selfless or indulgent ends. They may express the desire for practicality or frivolity, modesty or ostentation, engagement or aloofness, with advertising and branding helping to shape our verdicts. This "aesthetic of use" extends to the product's effect on its users and those around them, on its environment and the environment in the wider sense. The most vilified consumers are therefore those who excite criticism on all of these levels – owners of sports utility vehicles who use them for short school runs being an example, with detractors attacking not only the aesthetics of the vehicles but the indulgence of the unused off-road specification, the anti-social elevation and disconnection from other road users and the high fuel consumption and emissions. This illustrates how views on products are often influenced by political views on the limits of personal freedom and technological progress. It also raises such questions as, "to what extent should our freedom to design, manufacture and consume be restricted for the good of society? Is it the role of governments to constrain damaging behaviour, or should the people (including designers) be given autonomy?" (4)

Fig. 2   **Portland Vase by Josiah Wedgwood** Wedgwood's vase was a copy of a famous Roman artefact owned by the Duke of Portland and showed that despite pioneering new manufacturing techniques, design of the time still aspired to the tastes of the aristocracy.

Fig. 3   **MT8 table lamp designed at the Bauhaus by Wilhelm Wagenfeld and K.J.Jucker** An example of what became known as "the machine aesthetic", Wagenfeld and Jucker's lamp is entirely devoid of any decorative flourishes.

FASCIST AND DEMOCRATIC DESIGN

The never-ending debate between the "top down" imposition of decisions and the "bottom up" consultation of the audience is one held on macro and micro levels – in the design of the state and the design of products – and ought to be a fundamental consideration of any project. A state is "designed" by policy makers although the execution of this design, in democratic countries, relies on consensus with other politicians and, to a certain extent, the public at large. In dictatorships, these barriers are quashed.

When The National Socialist (Nazi) Party in 1930s Germany "designed" The Third Reich, it put in place architecture, products and systems to help fulfil its view of the ideal society. The atrocities it generated were planned, the tools sketched, drawn up and manufactured. Fascist design – forcing one view of how the visual and built environment should look upon others, regardless of their opinion of it – exists but is made impotent under democratic regimes. The free market acts like a democratic government in that the objects of design, like politicians, rely on a certain level of support (consumption) for their survival. Design that is not in tune with the general public's desires and expectations may continue to exist but will remain niche (unless those desires change). Designers, realising this, have been taking note of what consumers think and building this into their products for many years (see 2.3 Aesthetic refinement).

Recently, designers have gone far beyond simple market research. New design methodologies are apparently making design more democratic by engaging the public in the design process. Charles Leadbeater, journalist and author of 'The Pro-Am Revolution' (see 2.10 Participation) and a leading authority on creativity, has written: "Design used to be done by specialists for users. From now on, in a growing number of fields, design will be done with users and by them. In this context the designer is becoming the facilitator, the enabler, rather than the dictator of what people themselves want to do" (5).

However, just as in the political sphere, over-emphasis on shaping design decisions by focus groups can be interpreted as a tangible lack of leadership, while design by committee can often lack potency. Compare automobiles designed by visionary Italian coach builders Pininfarina, Bertone and Guigiaro with the lacklustre output of British companies in the late 1980s and early 1990s when focus groups became popular (figs 6 and 7, page 20). Criticism of Blairite politics struck upon the apparent preoccupation with the focus-grouping of style to the detriment of meaningful discussion of issues. It may well be that, in matters of style a singular vision is beneficial, but in matters of use an inclusive survey may indeed be constructive, especially when the scope of the project falls outside of the designer's experience. "Spin" and "styling"– the packaging of ideas and objects – are correlated, and in some quarters regarded as pejoratives implying shallowness and lack of substance. Both need to be backed up with results in order for either a policy or product to be accepted as successful.

[4.]
Ambasz, E. 1972. 'Italy: The New Domestic Landscape', New York: MOMA. Page 21: "To the traditional preoccupation with aesthetic objects, these contemporary designers have therefore added a concern for an aesthetic of the uses made of these objects."

[5.]
Leadbeater, C. "Design Your Own Revolution". 2005. 'The Observer', 19 June

Fig. 4   **Apple iPod** Beautiful, pure minimalism or a vulgar sign of conspicuous consumption? The Apple iPod follows many modernist principles.

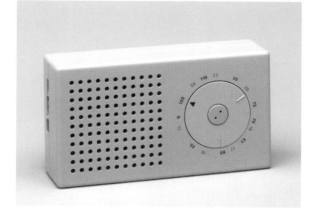

Fig. 5   **T3 Pocket Radio by Dieter Rams and Ulm Hochschule fur Gestaltung** Rams radio looks familiar. Its cleanliness of form and balance of proportion appear to have given rise to the i-Pod some four decades later.

DESIGN AS POLITICAL ACTIVISM

"For many designers it is no longer enough to fulfil the demands of commercial clients. They wish their art to be something more than "useful". Through critical and polemical projects, they signal the readiness to play a more transformative role in society". (6)

As "matter" that we must negotiate, products can literally shape our daily experience in ways that spark particular thoughts, and designers can therefore influence what these thoughts are. In addition, objects have the ability to be the locus of discussion about our potential futures; to explore through objects, the logical conclusions to certain models of thought, be they politically partisan, positive (utopian) or negative (dystopian). For these two reasons, design is a powerful tool for the band of designer-activists Hugh Aldersey-Williams pinpoints.

Graphic design has a long history of turning the persuasive skills of advertising to political ends. However, it is less common to see product designers making objects specifically to raise political points. As we have discussed, political ideologies can be read into everyday objects but the communication of these political views is rarely the central rationale behind their design. Yet, as its boundaries expand, product design is emerging as an overtly political tool, both to actively effect change and to raise awareness of where it is needed.

With product designers broadening their remit to include services and offering advice at boardroom level, they are increasingly being called upon to shape the implementation of government policies. In 2002, the UK Home Office commissioned architects and theorists to develop a model for a twenty-first-century prison. The design reflected the government's agenda of "rehabilitation as citizenship training". The proposed prison, like a neighbourhood, was literally divided into houses, each equipped with online learning facilities. Similarly, designers and design students are currently involved in the Building Schools for the Future programme that aims "to rebuild or renew nearly every secondary school in England". (7) While it may be relatively straightforward to agree upon what constitutes a humane prison and an effective schooling environment, when government policy comes closer to home it can become more contentious. The Design Council's Design of the Times (DOTT) project looked at sustainability in the north east of England and included community projects such as Low Carb Lane, in which residents were encouraged to monitor their own energy usage. A television-based Home Energy Dashboard showed energy and emission levels and included targets that, if kept within, would earn users financial rebates. However, critics of the project have suggested such systems would generate anxiety among homeowners and that they would shift the focus away from the government's responsibility to tackle climate change at the level of power generation. "Why should designers join a finger-wagging campaign to tell the working classes that their lives are contaminating?" (8) asks James Woudhuysen, Professor of Forecasting and Innovation at Leicester's De Montfort University. The debate highlights the need for designers to consider their political positions on such issues before diving in with product-based solutions.

Products have long been a means of expressing support for various causes. They appear to be essential trappings of political campaigning (t-shirts, badges, flags, mugs) and no charity worth its salt is without its talisman of support (paper poppies, ribbons, wristbands, etc.). Thankfully, some product designers have begun to look beyond the artless translation of slogans and images and are investigating ways in which products can express views in a more cerebral way. Students from London Metropolitan University highlighted the plight of the Saharawi people of

[6.]
Aldersey-Williams, H. 2008. 'Design and the Elastic Mind', New York: MOMA

[7.]
'teachernet'. 2009 [online]. Accessed 26th January 2009. Available from World Wide Web: <www.teachernet.gov.uk>

[8.]
Woudhuysen, J. 2007. 'The Limits of Design', a keynote address to the intersections 2007 conference, the Baltic Centre, Gateshead, UK

Fig. 6   Volkswagen Golf Cars like the Golf by Italian stylist Giorgetto Guigiaro are examples of the vision of an individual providing aesthetic integrity to the form of a vehicle.

Fig. 7   Austin-Rover Montego The Montego was produced at a time when Austin Rover and other British car companies were known for using "customer clinics" – focus groups that would critique the design of a vehicle, the results of which could seriously affect the final design.

Fig. 8   Sahara
Water by Amos Field Reid Part
of a series of objects designed
by students of London
Metropolitan University to
raise awareness of Morocco's
30-year occupation of Western
Sahara, the project is a rare
example of product design
being used to communicate
an overtly political message.

Fig. 9 / 10   Sahara
Jigsaw by Jess Corteen /
Sahara Sand Globe by
Rhian Jones

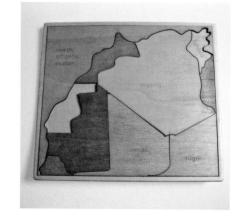

[9.]
Thomas, M. In: 'UHC Press
Archive'. 2007 [online].
[Accessed 26th January 2009].
Available from the World
Wide Web: <http://uhcpress.
blogspot.com>

Western Sahara through an exhibition of "guerrilla-style awareness objects". Displaced by Morocco's illegal occupation of Western Sahara over 30 years ago, nearly 200,000 of the Saharawi have become refugees in the Algerian desert. The objects, exhibited in a London shop window, act as metaphors for their lost land and the hope of its future re-inhabitation. (figs 8, 9, 10, page 21).

Another new breed of designer is projecting current scientific practices through the lens of product design, presenting speculative products and scenarios specifically to elicit debate. Unlike the political work above, many of these projects are presented from a neutral standpoint so that any adverse reaction to them is our own. The 2008 exhibition at the Museum of Modern Art in New York, Design and the Elastic Mind showcased many such projects including some by British designers James Auger and Jimmy Loizeau. One of Auger–Loizeau's projects describes the fictitious development of an Audio Tooth Implant (fig. 11, page 22) – essentially a mobile phone implanted in a tooth that can receive calls by translating vibrations through the jawbone to the inner ear. The notion that individuals could be receiving information invisibly raises considerable ethical dilemmas. The proposal sparked widespread media coverage, fuelled by the designers' caginess about the reality of them releasing such a product – necessary, Auger and Loizeau claim, in order to create genuine debate. What better way to shock us into concerned discussion than by tricking us into thinking that some immoral designers have already created our worst nightmares and are presenting them for our approval? The work encourages us to think about the moral and ethical problems the new sciences are throwing up (see 2.8 Ethics and 2.12 Design for debate).

Finally, product design touches upon activism through direct action. Manchester-based, socially conscious design studio, The Ultimate Holding Company (UHC) were commissioned by activist and comedian Mark Thomas to produce 100 "Spring Shrouds", (fig. 12, page 23) – fabric covers tailored to fit over pavement advertising hoardings. The shrouds, bearing an illustration of a tree and the slogan "trees breathe – adverts suck", were slipped over the hoardings around Manchester early one morning. "It was a gift that we could give to Manchester's commuters. To give them a temporary respite from the barrage of advertising that everybody who comes into the city suffers from" (9), said Thomas. The project demonstrates that just as governments wield the designed products of war in conflicts, designers can create objects with which to fight their own battles closer to home.

Fig. 11 **Audio Tooth Implant by James Auger and Jimmy Loizeau** Emerging from a project exploring the implications of electronics entering the body, Auger–Loizeau's Audio Tooth Implant made national news when it was presented as a near-future reality in development rather than a piece of critical commentary.

FORM FOLLOWS FUNCTION

Attributed to American architect Louis Sullivan, "form follows function" is one of a number of famous modernist axioms. The idea that the form of an object should follow its function required a product's function to signal a "correct" form. In making an object fit for its purpose, the designer embodied those signals as purely as possible to create an "honest" product. Widely adopted, at first by socialist designers in Germany promoting a progressive language of form and later more broadly as a means of making objects "user friendly", the notion was undermined in the mid 1960s by David Pye in his book 'The Nature of Design' (later reprinted as 'The Nature and Aesthetics of Design'). (i)

Pye contends that although the form of an object will have an effect on its ability to function (measurable in results), there is significantly more freedom in what this shape could be than is often presumed. If function is the primary purpose we assign to an object, then Pye reminded us that "purpose exists in men's minds, [whereas] 'results' exist in things". (ii) The purpose we assign to objects is variable and highly personal and not as singular or straightforward as the word "function" implies. An object may have tertiary roles that will differ from person to person. It may have dual or multi-functions or may be misused creatively. Pye argues the notion that a product's function can signal or determine a singular, "correct" form is therefore nonsense. A designer can predict the primary purpose to which an object is likely to be put and can choose appropriate forms to fulfil that purpose, but these are not predetermined and nor do they intrinsically "belong" to the functions they aim to fulfil.

An analysis of Dutch Designer Joris Laarman's Heatwave radiator, a recent hit with the design press, can illustrate this (fig. 13, page 23). Laarman argues that its baroque form makes it more functional than "sober conventional radiators" due to its greater surface area. He wishes to present the paradox that "functionalists are also sinners of styling, and that soberness is not always more functional than highly decorative form". (iii) However, radiators with equal or greater surface area to Laarman's – those with lines of geometric fins – already exist. The ability of the radiator to function well comes not from the choice of baroque or geometric form – either is suitable – but from the extent to which the chosen form is designed to achieve the necessary physical results.

[i.]
Pye, D. 2000. 'The Nature and Aesthetics of Design'. London: A & C Black Ltd

[ii.]
Dormer, P. Paraphrasing Pye, D. 1990. 'Meanings of Modern Design: Towards the Twenty-First Century'. London: Thames & Hudson

[iii.]
Laarman, J. 2007. <www.jorislaarman.com/heatwave.htm> [Website no longer available]

Fig. 12 **Spring Shrouds by UHC** Tailored covers for pavement advertising hoardings were designed by UHC to give city dwellers temporary respite from the daily barrage of commercial messages.

Fig. 13 **Heatwave radiator by Joris Laarman manufactured by Jaga and Droog Design** Laarman chose to use baroque forms to create the large surface area required from a radiator in contrast to the traditional lines of fins.

VALUE AND THE OBJECT

Design is sometimes described as "adding value". This is unfortunate because, although this is precisely what design does, it encourages the view that design is an optional extra – the icing on the cake rather than, as it should be, an ingredient that permeates the whole cake. Before considering individual approaches to product design that, in their own way, imbue objects with value, it is perhaps worth considering the ways in which value as a concept has been explained and how these relate to objects.

DESCRIBING VALUE

Value held and exchanged by individuals or groups is also known as "capital", particularly in the fields of economics and sociology. The traditional usage of the term in economics held that financial capital – money – was exchanged for assets.

Besides financial, many other forms of capital have been identified. These include:

> physical, manufactured or infrastructural capital, which denotes man-made assets such as the tools used in production;

> natural capital, which is the natural resources of the planet and basic necessities of life including raw materials, energy sources, clean air and water;

human, knowledge or intellectual capital, which indicates the skills or knowledge held by people, in particular within a company's workforce;

cultural capital (described in the Introduction), which encompasses aspects of human capital but, as well as denoting knowledge used in work, includes knowledge of culture, including artefacts and products;

social capital, which is the value of social networks such as friends or business contacts;

symbolic capital, which is the value of status bestowed upon objects or people by those in recognised positions of authority – for example, an object bought by a respected collector gains symbolic capital.

As an illustration of how these forms of capital may be used, one can imagine that the ability to access certain clubs or societies may come from any of four types of capital:

> you may buy membership (using your economic capital);

> you may be asked to join by a friend (using your social capital);

> you may have sufficient knowledge of a subject as to be accepted (using your cultural capital);

> you may have been honoured similarly to other members (using your symbolic capital).

Fig. 1   Mods
Icons of Italian post-war reconstruction such as Vespa and Lambretta motor scooters became staples of British mod culture.

FIELDS OF VALUE

A design object recognised as being "classic" has had status bestowed upon it by those "in the know" (the "cognoscenti"). Consequently, it has gained symbolic capital in the same way that its designer will have done for the recognition of having designed it. Symbolic capital requires people to have sufficient knowledge (cultural capital) to be able to identify it. They may also make a conscious decision not to recognise it, deciding it has no value to them. French sociologist Pierre Bourdieu (who coined the terms cultural and symbolic capital) describes "fields" of capital, each "having its own laws of functioning independent of those of politics and the economy". (1) The boundaries of these fields therefore denote where appreciation of their value ends. Hence an object may be recognised as having value in one field but not in another.

This is particularly apparent when considering products associated with subcultures. The visual integrity of a subculture relies on its members consuming products with limited and defined aesthetics and meanings. These preferences work to generate the fields Bourdieu refers to. Mod and rocker subcultures in 1960s Britain displayed affinity towards products, fashion and music in direct contrast with those of the other, thereby making their members easily recognisable (fig. 1, page 24 and fig. 2, page 25). Mods rode motor scooters and wore suits – aspiring to an image of smartness and sophistication – whereas rockers rode motorcycles, wore leather jackets and denim – highlighting their gritty working class credentials.

This differentiation has become so highly nuanced that it has gone from defining distinct societal groups to allowing individuals to feel they are defining specific aspects of their own personality through the objects with which they choose to surround themselves. Our products simultaneously allow us to "belong" to groups of our choosing and to differentiate ourselves from others within those groups. These small differences are, according to design historian Stephen Bayley,

a form of "one-upmanship": "With the spread of materialism, consumerism and commodity fetishism (see page 26), minute aesthetic criteria are being established as the basis for general social competition for the first time in civilisation." (2)

PERFORMANCE

Critics of consumerism pick up on the way that we are increasingly being trained by advertising to notice, and consider important, the minute variations between products. With so many similar products on our shelves, performance claims have become a key factor in providing this differentiation. High performance has become a sign of prestige even among the most mundane of products. However, the performance of many products has reached a point where their incremental improvement is indiscernible to us. Yet these "improvements" continue to form the rationale behind new designs and their subsequent advertising campaigns. For example, of what value to the gentleman shaver are the microns of difference between the cut of the three-bladed razor and the four-bladed razor?

New products, we are told, have been made more comfortable, convenient, time-saving, longer-lasting, efficient, effective, safer, stronger...but beyond the marketing bluster we must ask to what extent are these forms of "better" an illusion? New products expand our choice, yet it has been shown that more choice often makes us less satisfied, as we become anxious that we may not have made the best choice from the many similar options on offer (3). Substantial and genuine improvements in usability are of course to be welcomed, but we must be aware that there is a considerable amount of "smoke and mirrors" being used to sell spurious innovations on the grounds of increased performance. Designers can either become implicated in this game or can steer clear and investigate alternative ways of connecting with the consumer.

[1.]
Bourdieu, P. 1993. 'The Field of Cultural Production – Essays on Art and Literature'. Cambridge: Polity Press

[2.]
Bayley, S. 2000. 'General Knowledge'. London: Booth Clibborn Editions

[3.]
Schwartz, B. 2004. 'The Paradox of Choice – Why More Is Less'. New York: Harper Collins

Fig. 2   Rockers
Emerging from the Teddy Boy scene, the rockers favoured the image of the macho leather and denim clad biker.

COMMODITY FETISHISM

Karl Marx, political economist and primary author of the 'The Communist Manifesto', described goods as having a use-value – the value to their owner of using or consuming them – as well as an exchange-value (price). For example, the use-value of a bicycle is that of providing travel, with little or no maintenance costs, for as long as it remains serviceable. Hence two different bicycles can be said to have the same use-value (barring differences in performance). This use-value will be roughly quantifiable (through comparison to alternative methods of achieving the same outcome) and may differ considerably from the actual price of the bicycle.

Commodity fetishism is the situation that exists in capitalist societies whereby the value of goods, including designed products, is made abstract by the separation of their use-value from their exchange-value. Therefore, products with no practical use (such as jewellery) may gain greater value (as symbols of taste and status, for example) than items designed to perform a utilitarian function. In addition, products designed for use can become more valuable than others for the same use when their design goes beyond the utilitarian and appeals on other levels (as they become "fetishised").

What Marx termed the "fetishism of the object" is what many product designers today are in the business of providing – that which, beyond the practical functioning of it, gives us the reason to desire, purchase, keep and cherish it. Even when an apparently new and utilitarian invention is brought to the market – such as Trevor Baylis's clockwork radio (fig. 3, page 26) – once product designers are involved, the resulting object is ripe to be embellished in such a way as to meet perceived expectations of a particular target audience (fig. 4, page 26). This fetishising of the object by its designers, while attracting customers can also violate an apparent honesty in the original. This is clear when comparing anonymously designed archetypal products with their "designer" cousins (figs 5 and 6, page 27).

Conversely, the designer's "fetishising" can transform objects from being crude, unsafe, overly complex, and otherwise alienating to being seamlessly efficient and pleasurable. Clearly many prudent design improvements that Marx would have branded as "fetishes" bring quality to our lives beyond vainly displaying our status. His choice of the term "fetishism" – negatively loaded with the implication of an irrational obsession – was, of course, calculated to enhance his communist arguments. In capitalist society, it is more usefully applied to products where this irrationality is in evidence – where moderation has been overturned by the pursuit of the extreme.

Fig. 3   Freeplay **radio by Trevor Baylis manufactured by Baygen**
Baylis's original clockwork radio, designed for use in Africa, communicates robustness through its thick sections and chunky dials.

Fig. 4   Freeplay **FRP2 radio by Syzygy manufactured by Baygen**
Designed by South African firm Syzygy, the second version of the Freeplay radio was aimed at Western audiences. In an attempt at refinement, the chunky black case has been replaced with an asymmetrical, translucent polycarbonate creation, thereby losing any connection with the radio's original utilitarian context.

[i.]
Baudrillard, J. 1996. 'The System of Objects'. London: Verso Books

[ii.]
Baudrillard, J. 1981. 'For a Critique of the Political Economy'. St Louis: Telos Press

SIGN-VALUE

In his 1968 book, 'The System of Objects' (i), French social theorist Jean Baudrillard proposed that the ways that consumer products are differentiated from one another forms a system of signs with which all objects are encoded. To Baudrillard, our knowledge of the use and exchange-values of objects proved insufficient to explain our ongoing fascination with consuming the new. Applying the study of signs – semiotics, (which had developed from linguistics, the study of language) – to objects, Baudrillard proposed that our culture had become driven by the analysis of these signs that denoted the relative status and meaning of objects. By casting objects as participants in this ever-changing and evolving system, many new reasons to consume (and hence for designers to create) were revealed.

Though Baudrillard was critical of consumerism, his theory revealed how an individual's possessions could be used to paint complex pictures of their tastes and desires. Baudrillard coined the term "sign-value" to describe this attribute of communicating an object's prestige. He also used the term "symbolic exchange" to explain the role of objects, such as the wedding ring, in symbolising a particular event or connection with its owner. (ii)

Fig. 5 **Archetypal corkscrew** The archetypal two-armed corkscrew has character by the nature of the layout of its components.

Fig. 6 **Anna G corkscrew by Alessandro Mendini manufactured by Alessi** Alessandro Mendini highlighted the corkscrew's character, yet in doing so created an object that feels more self-conscious than the original.

PRODUCT STORIES

In 1997, a group of designers and theorists in The Netherlands called The Eternally Yours Foundation convened a conference to examine methods of effectively extending the life of products. The published proceedings revealed a number of ways in which we become emotionally attached to products. Furthermore, they proposed that by being aware of how these emotional bonds are formed, designers may be able to build in the possibility of products becoming cherished and therefore kept for longer. One of the main tools for engagement is the power of product stories or "narratives": "Products need to express through design a story that one can identify with and explain to others. That is what makes them personal." (4)

Allowing potential consumers to know about the creation of a product could be the first chapter in such a narrative, but one that is often overlooked by manufacturers in favour of an often-fictional advertising scenario. Those companies (and designers) who are willing to be open about their methods increase the possibility of consumers becoming attached to their products. Learning about a company's ideology, people, heritage, skills, materials, processes, service etc. gives us the chance to connect with them. The factory tour, although not appealing to everyone, provides this opportunity and, if done well, brings willing customers into the factory shop (similar displays of appreciation through consumption can be seen in gallery and museum shops and in theme parks, where layouts are commonly designed so that customers "exit through retail"). Any retailer used to be expected to know and be able to expound the virtues of their merchandise but, as the shopping experience has become less

personal, such education is increasingly becoming an indulgence of the well-to-do. This lack of input from the retailer denies many customers the opportunity of confirming via an experienced, if biased, source that they have bought the right product for their needs. It is also a way of products of dubious heritage being sold without attracting scrutiny. Some Internet shopping sites have attempted to fill this knowledge gap by providing previous customers with the opportunity to leave feedback on their experiences of purchasing and using products. However, by relying on the layman, such information lacks the authority associated with expert opinion.

Eternally Yours believes that by extending contact with customers beyond the point of sale to a series of events throughout the life of the product, experiences could be designed to bolster its perceived value. Although difficult in markets driven by new technology, such interventions could counteract a product's otherwise inevitable decline in value as we become aware of newer and "better" versions coming on to the market. We should, they say, not be "product designers" but "product career designers". (5) So what can we learn from existing product narratives that might be co-opted? According to Eternally Yours, there are three ways in which narratives become associated with products. (6) The first is through advertisements and endorsements; the second is through users' collective appreciation of products, culminating in "cult" status; and the third is through individual events that turn products into mementoes or souvenirs.

Advertising is the most obvious and powerful creator of narratives around products. By associating their products with aspirational lifestyles, scenarios and glamorous celebrities, companies seek value through association. Perfumes and watches are often advertised as worn by famous – apparently discerning – individuals. Sporting goods are sold on their connection with professionals who have supposedly achieved success whilst using them. If we are lucky enough to own the product when the display of excellence with it is publicised, the value still transfers on to it and consequently, on to us (this appears to work even when the reason for success clearly ought to be attributed to the skill of the professional rather than the features of the product). Of course, the credibility of this value depends upon the often foggy details of these relationships. For example, if the endorsement given by the professional or celebrity resulted from a sponsorship deal or advertising contract, it is not based on an unbiased choice. The only value that remains is that which we place in the fact that the professional or celebrity is not ashamed to be associated with the product.

As we become versed in the strategies of advertising, we are less liable to be swayed by the narratives they present. Hence the everyday experience of using products becomes more important in determining their relevance to us. As their newness fades and they become part of our everyday lives, we discover their true colours. Those that remain tolerable company – like people – will be retained, and relationships allowed to develop. Over time they may come to be regarded as having a special place among our possessions. It is these products that are most commonly repaired rather than disposed of – as we repay their service by extending their life. Sadly, the economy of repair is often false, with items costing more to repair than to replace. Worse still, repair in many cases has ceased to be offered at all outside of guarantee periods. When undertaken, it marks an important moment in a product's story, signifying the point at which we nursed it back to health.

[4. 5. 6.]
Van Hinte, E. (ed.) 1997.
'Eternally Yours – Visions on Product Endurance'. Rotterdam: 010 Publishers

COLLECTIVE APPRECIATION

The most cherished objects bring people together in admiration for them. Vehicle owners' clubs are the most prominent example and the Internet has facilitated the spread of owners' clubs and fan sites (official and unofficial) for everything from vacuum cleaners (www.kirby-vacuum-owners-club.co.uk) to Jaffa Cakes (www.jafferygoodness.com) allowing small groups of aficionados a repository for their devotion. Even if you are not a member, if you own a product that has a visible owners club, the collective appreciation it represents has a value that rubs off. In recent years, the Austin/Morris Mini, VW Beetle and Fiat 500 cars have been celebrated with the release of new "retro" designs referencing their aesthetics (see fig. 7, page 29). This would not have been viable had the original vehicles not been taken to consumers' hearts with passion, thereby generating value for them as brands. In the case of the Beetle, becoming associated with a particular subculture – that of surfing – added further value to its brand. The film 'The Italian Job' along with a well-publicised string of celebrity owners did the same for the Mini.

SOUVENIRS

The nature of souvenirs differs from these objects of collective affection. By contrast, their value emerges largely by personal association – based upon the memories of the activities undertaken in the place to which they refer – and is determined to a lesser extent by the intrinsic qualities of the objects themselves. Such personally held value may not be recognisable by others and is akin to that of family heirlooms where memories external to the object's design produce value that transcends the monetary. Along with Eternally Yours, designer Constantin Boym has argued that "The

Fig. 7 **Original and "retro" Beetles manufactured by Volkswagen** A recent phenomenon, retro remakes of popular cars have been appearing, borrowing aesthetic cues from their well-loved namesakes. However, it could be argued that the sense of utility apparent in the originals has been somewhat lost in translation.

world needs a lot of new souvenirs — for culture's sake" (7), seeing the harnessing of associative value as a means of increasing the user-product bond. He explains that, "unlike many 'serious' products or appliances, the souvenir always contains a built-in emotional value, such as a memory of a past journey or the affection of a far-away friend." Discovering ways of applying this kind of value to "serious" products may open a door to us having a far more engaging relationship with objects.

INCONSPICUOUS CONSUMPTION

With the growing concern at the world's over-production and resource use there is a migration beginning towards the inconspicuous, the lightweight and the immaterial. Products may mesh with owners' concerns by not being seen. Designers at Industrial Facility use a strategy they have termed "voluntary simplicity", which they describe as "a conscious revolt against conspicuous consumption", adding that "owning and displaying luxury as a status symbol is passé, superseded by an urge to make meaningful, relevant and sustainable choices as consumers" (8). Objects converge or disappear into software (the mobile phone has swallowed the music player, diary, watch, calculator, hand-held video-game and, with the arrival of Internet-enabled mobiles, encyclopaedias, maps and a lot more besides). Products become embedded in services where we hire rather than own them. Here the infrastructure that surrounds the product gives us value — we no longer have the burden of storing, maintaining and upgrading them. However, hiring denies us not only the pleasure and convenience of ownership, but also the opportunity to form a connection with a specific object, personalising or customising it to reflect our taste and show our identity.

[7.]
Boym, C. 2002. 'Curious Boym'. New York: Princeton Architectural Press

[8.]
Hecht, S. and Colin, K. 2005. 'Product as Landscape'. London: Industrial Facility

SALES VALUE

Returning to the economic value of objects, although many kinds of value are relative and fluid, price is fixed, albeit momentarily, by a sale. Knowledge of a number of sales at a similar price provides a collective notion of what something is worth. Different kinds of selling determine price in various ways. The retail price displayed in shops is based on what the retailer bought the product for (the wholesale price), plus their mark-up. The wholesale price is based upon what the item cost the manufacturer to make (the cost price), plus their mark-up. If the product is sold through a distributor, another layer of marking-up will occur. This mechanism, necessary to cover the costs of those involved (to pay staff, to cover overheads and designer's royalties, etc.) and provide a profit, produces the situation whereby the actual cost of making a product (the cost price) is a small fraction of the price at which it is available in shops (the retail price). Prices are fixed at each stage (or a negotiated price confirmed). Some mark-ups will be disproportionate in relation to others, based on what the manufacturer/wholesaler/retailer feels they can charge, but each participant in the supply chain uses an equation to ensure they do not lose money on a sale. The financial value of a new object is largely determined by whether or not the object sells at its retail price without that being reduced. However, the object generally "depreciates" (loses value) as soon as it is bought, unless it is a limited edition or is subject to a waiting list, in which case its rarity value may counteract or reverse this depreciation.

Value is more fluid with auction sales. Whether for high-priced artworks and antiques, or for inexpensive items sold over the Internet, price is set locally by those taking part in the auction (one phenomenon of online auctioning is the ability to see what a huge number of second-hand objects might be worth —

information that was previously hard to determine). The seller decides the minimum for which they are willing to sell the item by setting a reserve price. Bidders will then express how much they feel it is worth. Publicity of the value of the winning bid affects the wider collective notion of the value of that object and those similar to it. Auctions may sell items for many times their previously perceived value or a fraction of it, raising or lowering their expected value at subsequent auctions. Hence, the value of an object may be dramatically affected by the changing desires of a small number of collectors.

While these circumstances traditionally belong to the world of art and antique collectables, designers have become involved in a new crossover phenomenon labelled "Design Art". One-off or limited batch-produced items, usually furniture or lighting, have begun to be sold at auction for huge sums, granting designers' work a new financial price tag far higher than when it was set within the retail system (fig. 8, page 31). The "ceiling-less" nature of this value is no longer related to the material or manufacturing costs of the item and the percentage mark-ups of those involved, but is based instead on the perceived status of the designer and their work among collectors. This in turn is driven largely by the mythical value of the "hand of the creator" – the last vestiges of design's arts and crafts heritage. As well as being crucial to the design-art market, the notion that the hand of a famous creator has "touched" the work – or that their mind originated it – is central to the marketing of mass produced "design" products, where the designer is named on the product and its packaging. With computers and rapid prototyping interjecting in the once very physical sculpting of product form, nowadays the "hand of the creator" may touch little more than a computer mouse, yet this seems to have done nothing to diminish the perceived value of their output. The new breed of design-artists have fully embraced this new technology rather than shying away from it, using it to manufacture spectacular one-offs – a state of affairs that could hardly be further from the social project of harnessing production methods to provide quality goods for all.

Fig. 8   **Aqua Table by Zaha Hadid manufactured by Established & Sons** Made in production versions, limited editions and in red for the AIDS awareness campaign fronted by Bono, one of the prototypes for Hadid's table sold at auction for just short of US$300,000.

READING FORM

This section deals with our perception of form and some of the tools designers use to imbue their products with meaning. Products communicate to us through visual language. Like spoken and written words and sentences, this language can be split into units and studied. On their own these signs would be meaningless. They only become comprehensible when compared with other signs within a system. The study of these signs, and the systems in which they operate, is called "semiotics". It is a field of which few product designers are fully aware, yet it is one that all, to some degree, operate within. Consciously understanding its theories can help pin down exactly from where meaning emerges and, as Sara Ilstedt Hjelm (Professor of Product and Service Design at KTH, Stockholm's Royal Institute of Technology) points out, be more alert to its implications: "Studying semiotics can assist us to become more aware of reality as a construction and of the roles played by ourselves constructing or designing it." (1)

SEMIOTICS AND PRODUCT SEMANTICS

Rather than attempting a full dissection of semiotics (2), this section tries to introduce the structures most useful to product designers. Although emerging from the study of language (linguistics), semiotics has come to provide the theoretical underpinning for art and design. In 1957, French critic and theorist Roland Barthes applied semiotic theories to the interrogation of popular culture in his writings on products such as soap powder, toys and the Citroën DS. In the volume 'Mythologies' in which these essays were collected, Barthes wrote: "We shall therefore take language, discourse, speech etc., to mean any significant unit or synthesis, whether verbal or visual: a photograph will be a kind of speech for us in the same way as a newspaper article; even objects will become speech, if they mean something." (3) As its name suggests, Barthes' book was concerned with the myths that society had built and in semiotic analysis he found a means of revealing a sense of truth. Since Barthes, Jean Baudrillard has been the most celebrated theorist working on the analysis of products as signs. Baudrillard focused on consumer society, arguing that sign-value was central to our purchasing of all products, regardless of the apparent need they fulfilled.

In the 1980s, Reinhardt Butter and Klaus Krippendorf applied semiotic theories to the field of product design. They coined the term "product semantics" to describe the study of meaning in man-made objects and its application in new designs, "semantics" being the branch of semiotics that deals with the study of meaning in communication. Butter and Krippendorf's studies can be seen as an attempt to give theoretical structure to the misgivings among product designers towards continuing their application of modernist rules, in particular, "form follows function". By focusing primarily on the product as a sign, product semantics suggests that a multitude of meanings can rightfully be presented for the same object type, a theory that cuts directly across modernism's search for singular definitive forms. As one interpretation of modernism led electronic product design up the stylistic cul-de-sac of the black box (fig. 1, page 32), an appetite emerged for change. By the time Butter and Krippendorf's article on the subject had appeared in the journal of the Industrial Designers' Society of America (4), the Italian radical design group Memphis had already opened the door to postmodernism in product design, with their startling exhibitions of furniture and accessories (fig. 2, page 33). Led by architect and designer Ettore Sottsass, the work of the Memphis group encouraged people to question many of modernism's rules, allowing

[1.]
Istedt Hjelm, S. 2002. 'Semiotics in Product Design'. Stockholm: Royal Institute of Technology

[2.]
For a more thorough understanding of how visual communication works, see Crow, D. 2003. 'Visible Signs'. Lausanne: AVA Publishing SA

[3.]
Barthes, R. 2000. 'Mythologies'. London: Vintage (Random House)

[4.]
Krippendorff, K. and Butter, R. 1984. "Product Semantics: Exploring the Symbolic Qualities of Form". 'The Journal of the Industrial Designers Society of America, 2' (3)

Fig. 1   **Black 201 Television by Marco Zanuso and Richard Sapper manufactured by Brionvega** Sapper and Zanuso's approach to this television set was to hide the curvature of the screen behind a dark but translucent flat panel so that when turned off, it resembled a sculpture of pure rectilinear black plastic.

Fig. 2 Carlton
**Bookcase by Ettore Sottsass
for Memphis** An example of
postmodernism in design,
Sottsass's bookcase neither
conformed to typical notions
of layout nor materials. Its
totemic stature and riotous
coloured laminates still
polarise opinion.

[5.]
Sottsass E. In: Silva, H.
"Memphis Has Left The
Building". 2002. 'New York
Times', 14 April

designers the confidence to break new ground. Sottsass talked of "opening a window upon a new landscape" (5), hinting at the poetic possibilities he wanted designers to explore. Memphis also reaffirmed the desperate need for mainstream product design to have a lively avant-garde that is at once in opposition to it and yet provides it with a source of inspiration.

SEMIOTIC STRUCTURES

The most useful description of the relationship between signs, objects and our interpretation of them came from the American father of semiotics, Charles Sanders Pierce. Pierce proposed that there was a triangular relationship between "sign", "object" and "interpretant". The sign is the actual thing being viewed (be that a word, image or product), the object is the article referred to by the sign and the interpretant is the viewer's individual concept of the sign. Seeing the word "cup" (the sign), we think of a cup (the object) and we think of our interpretation of what a cup means to us (the interpretant). Seeing a picture of a cup is a different experience. The picture (the sign) makes us think of the specific cup depicted (the object) and again we interpret that through the filter of our personal experience (the interpretant).

How we see signs – the means by which they are delivered – has an effect on our interpretation of them. When focusing on objects, there are subtle differences in meaning that come from experiencing the same object described in different ways – through words, images, or by seeing the object itself (this is the familiar difference experienced by reading a story in a book as opposed to watching it on film). When looking at a product, we experience both the sign, and the object to which the sign refers. However, if we are looking at a prototype, it is the sign that we experience, but the object it refers to is the final product.

Semiotics describes three ways by which meaning is communicated by signs. These are "denotation", "connotation" and "myth". In terms of objects, these can be described as follows: denotation covers the literal reading of it and includes recognition of the object and anything it literally reminds us of, how it should be used, and how it may be misused (see pages 39–41). For example, most of the plastic products manufactured by Alessi (fig. 3, page 35) denote characters we might expect to find in cartoons. Connotation refers to an object's associative meaning. This includes what its form, material, construction, colour and texture might remind us of beyond the literal. This includes what social and cultural associations they suggest. A simple case would be that a tall, wooden pepper grinder connotes its owner's aptitude for, particularly Italian, cooking. Finally, myth concerns the beliefs surrounding the object. These may include stories surrounding its creation, who may have owned it or others like it, and what it has been used for. Myths are also created or perpetuated by advertising and may or may not contain an element of truth. For example, the popular Moleskine notebook comes with a small text containing information about the famous writers and artists who previously used them, said to include Van Gogh, Matisse, Picasso and Hemingway. Yet the company that currently produces them has no direct link (other than producing an identical-looking notebook) with a manufacturer who would have produced the books used by these famous individuals. The notebooks sell at a higher price than their competitors thanks to this apparent provenance.

A product is a sign, but the features of that product and its individual components (and, in turn, their features) are also signs. We access the meaning of signs by comparing them to other signs within the same system. Consequently, if a sign changes, this has a knock-on effect on the meaning of other signs. If we see the same product for sale in a high-end retailer and subsequently, a budget retailer, the perceived value

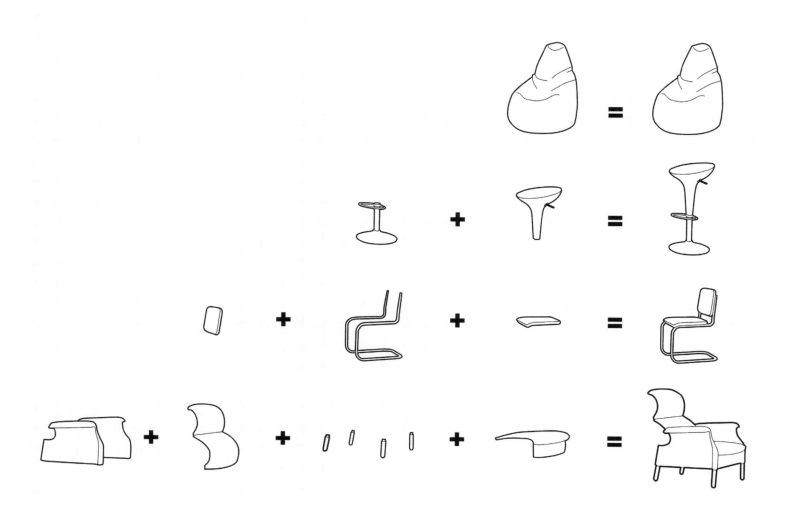

Fig. 3 Lilliput
salt and pepper shakers
These plastic products
manufactured by Alessi have
an overt, cartoon character-
like appearance, which could
be read as a postmodern
attempt to bring the brashness
of toys to the "serious" world
of kitchen and tabletop
accessories.

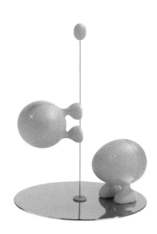

Fig. 4 Syntagmatic
and paradigmatic relation-
ships Using types of products
for sitting as an example, this
diagram shows some different
paradigms on the right-hand
column (bean bag, bar stool,
dining chair, arm chair) and
the syntagems that define
them (seat, legs, back, arms).
The diagram implies that
adding or removing a synta-
gem from an existing paradigm
can create a new one.

Fig. 5 Red and
Blue Chair by Gerrit Rietveld
This chair emerged from
Rietveld's involvement with
the De Stijl movement that
restricted the palette for
works of art and design to
a minimum, concentrating
upon horizontal and vertical
arrangements of black, white
and primary colours.

Fig. 6 Speed
camera sign The icon
used to signify speed limit
enforcement cameras on
Britain's roads is oddly
anachronistic, referencing
a medium-format camera.

of it is liable to drop simply through the associations we make with its surroundings. Our senses or prior knowledge tell us when two signs are the same, completely different or different examples of the same type. Semiotics identifies the "same/different" comparator as "syntagmatic" and the "examples of type" comparator as "paradigmatic". With these tools designers (often intuitively) assemble the elements of their creations (fig. 4, page 35).

The most explicit example of artists and designers intentionally cutting down their palette of formal options was the work of the Dutch De Stijl movement. Meaning "the style" and surfacing in 1917, the movement's leading lights were painter Piet Mondrian and designer and architect Gerrit Rietveld. Their work is markedly similar, with Rietveld's famous Red and Blue chair (fig. 5, page 36) being a Mondrian painting in three dimensions. Only its angled seat and back deviate from the grid of horizontal and vertical black or primary coloured elements – a small concession towards use.

ARCHETYPES, ICONS AND DIFFERENTIATION

An "archetype" – a standard or classic example conjured in the mind when an object type is mentioned – is rarely, if ever, based on one specific object but is formed through amalgamating experiences of seeing many of the same kind. These are distilled into a collective "architecture of the typical". We are also aware of a set of icons that denote object types. The most common ones that appear on public signage can bear little or no resemblance to the actual devices to which they refer. This is because although these icons evolve, they often do so more slowly than the products they signify. For example, the icon used to denote the telephone is still modelled on the layout designed by Henry Dreyfuss in 1937, despite both public and private telephones changing their form substantially since. The icon chosen to represent the roadside speed camera in the UK was out of date as soon as it was introduced. The use of an icon depicting an old-fashioned medium format camera is almost enough to conjure up the image of a man with a top hat appearing from under a black cloth as offending cars speed by (fig. 6, page 36). This mismatch between sign and product is due to the fact that some contemporary products do not have a commonly recognised "archetypal" form and the sign designer therefore looked into history for the last example.

Products incorporating new technology, while often first appearing in the form of other objects (radios, gramophones and television sets were built into pieces of fine wooden furniture, mimicking drinks cabinets and the like) are particularly susceptible to reconfiguration (fig. 7, page 37). However, such is the tight hold of marketing upon the design of many products that boldness is often downplayed and blandness prevails. "Showing originality so as to win the marketing race is a favourite refrain," says designer Naoto Fukasawa, "but the fixation with keeping a close eye on other products lined up on the store shelves results in the same kind of things being generated". The approach of designing "different but not too different" products is justified by the alibi of recognition. On the one hand designers can underestimate the public's intelligence and curiosity, producing banal, patronising objects. On the other, in their desire to reinvent and innovate, they are in danger of overestimating consumer understanding and changing the fundamental signs that allow us to recognise products.

Fig. 7 **Spot the odd one out** Insufficient differentiation can cause frustration as we reach for the wrong remote or discover we've picked up our mobile instead.

[9.]   -
Levien, R. 2008. [Personal
communication]. 26 March
           -
[10.]   -
Norman, D. 2002. 'The Design
of Everyday Things'. New York:
Basic Books
           -

Designer Robin Levien describes this balance as one of finding "the extraordinary within the framework of the ordinary." What a designer thinks is patently obvious may not be so in the eyes of the consumer. Levien cites some pebble-shaped dining plates he designed that were not immediately recognised as such (fig. 8, page 38): "You have to remember we've had 12,000 years of round plates – there's quite a precedent for them. When you make one that's a funny shape people don't really understand it's a plate. We depend upon the consumer to understand what it is that we're doing… We can get it wrong sometimes by pushing things 'too extraordinary' within the framework of the ordinary. I suppose we'd rather be there than at the ordinary end. But if you push the extraordinary at the expense of marketability you would have to close up shop. You've got to get this balance going on." (9) In the sale of tabletop homewares, Levien points out that there's rarely someone explaining the products, so they must speak for themselves. A product has to appear close enough to what the buyer is expecting for them to feel comfortable that they are looking at the right object. If the product sits outside of this framework of the ordinary, recognition is under threat. Once the boundaries of that framework are understood, the designers can work on ideas that will be appealing without breaking out from it.

Sadly, much product design fails to deliver anything of value, even within the framework of the ordinary. Far from defining archetypes, bland products shift form gradually, each borrowing and differentiating within tight bounds. The iconic nature of archetypal forms and the clarity and directness with which they communicate can cut through this reciprocal pastiche (fig. 9, page 39). Designers at Industrial Facility

achieved this in their design for a DVD projector for Epson. By using the icon of an old reel-to-reel cine-projector rather than contemporary projector layouts, IF were able to communicate the product's purpose instantly while still styling the product to feel contemporary. The design avoids being "retro" because it is not a literal replica of a cine-projector. Instead of its form following function, it follows understanding through the collective memory of the archetype.

-            -

AFFORDANCE

In negotiating spaces and using objects, physicality channels behaviour. While references to archetypal form help us to identify products, our ability to navigate unaided how objects are used is driven by "affordances". The term "affordance" was coined by psychologist James Gibson and refers to the clues with which an object reveals its use: "Plates are for pushing. Knobs are for turning. Slots are for inserting things into. Balls are for throwing or bouncing," as Donald Norman explains in 'The Design of Everyday Things', "When affordances are taken advantage of, the user knows what to do just by looking: no picture or instruction is required…When simple things need pictures, labels, or instructions, the design has failed." (10)

Affordances are provided both by what the product allows us to do, and what it reminds us of having done. That is, they are derived from what Norman calls "knowledge in the world" and "knowledge in the head". The designer Jasper Morrison explains thus: "The instinctive knowledge of how to use something can be suggested in a design, through shape most often, but also through memory of other things that looked or behaved similarly, even if the end result is

Fig. 8   Isola
tableware range by Studio
Levien for Costa Verde
Designer Robin Levien
describes a fine balance
between what, to the designer,
may appear to be small
changes (going from a round
to a pebble-shaped dining
plate) and something that is
enough to plant doubt in the
mind of the customer.

different." (11) As the form of an object affords us the understanding of its use, by borrowing form from recognisable places, the way to use new products can be made clear and a resonance set up.

Affordance is one of a number of concepts useful to designers that emerge from understanding how the brain makes decisions, the study of which is part of "cognitive science". Another is the provision of feedback – notification that once an action has been taken, it has had an effect. In simple mechanical devices, feedback is often clear (we turn a handle, a door opens), but electronic products (the area of design upon which cognitive science has focused most attention) actions can produce invisible results, and feedback must be specifically built in. For example, the pressing of a button that sends an electronic pulse around a circuit board requires visible or audible feedback to register that our command has been actioned.

IMPROVISATION AND APPROPRIATION

As well as allowing us to understand how objects are used, affordances can enable their intentional misuse. When we are looking for a solution to a problem presented by our daily activities, we look at the forms around us and see if they afford us an answer. These images by James Bartlett (fig. 10, page 40), inspired by the photography of artist Richard Wentworth (fig. 11, page 41), show the ways in which people have improvised to solve bicycle-related problems. The carrier – by luck rather than intention – provides the perfect fit for a cup of coffee. The cables offer themselves as a newspaper holder. A shopping basket is appropriated to become a bicycle basket, a torch is taped on for lighting and a plastic bottle is fashioned into a mudguard. These latter three examples are

more purposeful than simply discovering and misusing what was already there, requiring the appropriation of another object. The final image of a CD used as a reflector raises the question, "from which direction was the problem tackled?" Rather than seeing the problem and looking for an object to solve it, it is perhaps more likely that upon discovering a scuffed CD, the person considered to what use it could best be put. This highlights the potential of objects themselves to inspire designers. All the examples display the observation of objects, consideration of their properties, and a projection of their possible uses – the three most essential tools of a design education.

The fact that much design activity comprises of choosing from catalogues of existing components, rather than shaping them anew, is often overlooked. There is, after all, no point in reinventing the wheel. The same rigour that goes into considering form, structure, use, meaning etc. of newly designed components must go into the choice of those selected "off-the-shelf." While not implying a make-do-and-mend approach, this activity is nonetheless improvisation of a sort.

Both at home and in the factory, when resources are tight, improvisation increases. Wartime rationing brought a wealth of creative solutions to the resulting shortages supporting the axiom, "necessity is the mother of invention". The "ad-hoc" – meaning "for this" (specific need or purpose) – could even be the central tool in a philosophy of life according to writer Charles Jencks and architect Nathan Silver. Their book 'Adhocism – The Case for Improvisation' charts the history and potential of tackling problems using whatever is to hand, and in the most direct way, in art, design and architecture. It presents improvisation as

[11.]
Morrison, J. In: Fukasawa, N. 2007. 'Naoto Fukasawa'. London: Phaidon

[12.]
Jencks, S. and Silver, N. 1973. 'Adhocism – The Case for Improvisation'. New York: Anchor Books

Fig. 9 DVD projector by Industrial Facility for Epson IF's projector avoids associations with typical office projectors by using an upright layout that borrows from the archeytpe of the cine-projector.

Fig. 10 **Bicycle Adhocism photographed by James Bartlett** These images show improvisation with the bicycle itself (to hold coffee and a newspaper) and bicycle accessories improvised from other objects.

a tool for social liberation. By shunning bureaucratic organisations and the red tape they create, change, they say, can be wrought through direct action. "Shaping the local environment towards desired ends is a key to mental health; the present environment, blank and unresponsive, is a key to idiocy and brainwashing." (12)

Improvisation has its aesthetic qualities and these have been used variously to contrast opulence and express dissent. Surrealist art and the youth cultures of hippies and punks are just a few examples. In art and design, the component knowingly selected to contribute significantly to the character of the end result becomes elevated to the status of the "ready-made" (see pages 64–65). It has become most used as a means of prompting connections between the object's original use and its new context, exercising within the viewer the same creativity with which they themselves improvise. Rather than simply denoting their original purpose, ready-mades, like other means of constructing form, have the potential for representation, as this Picasso anecdote concerning his best known ready-made piece Tête de Taureau (Bull's Head) (fig. 12, page 41) illustrates: "One day I found in a pile of jumble an old bicycle saddle next to some rusted handlebars. I put one on top of the other and I made a bull's head. Well and good. But what I should have done was to throw away the bull's head... Then a worker would have passed by. He'd have picked it up. And he'd have found that, perhaps, he could make a bicycle seat and handlebars with that bull's head. And he'd have done it. That would have been magnificent. That's the gift of metamorphosis." (13)

The project by designer Antonio Cos entitled Embouteillage (fig. 13, page 42) shows both pragmatic and poetic improvisations using a standard wine bottle. Of the project he says: "The wine bottle "bordelaise" is a common object that everybody knows about... More than its contents, I'm interested in the container. What is a bottle? Which geometrical characteristics does it have? What is it used for? When we don't have a rolling pin at home, we generally use a bottle; it's one of those "clichés" where an object is used in a manner different to its real purpose. From a container, it becomes a roller to flatten the dough. I used, on the one hand, the physical characteristics of the bottle to re-propose different types of rolling pins. On the other hand, I explored the expressive and geometrical characteristic of the "bordelaise" proposing a typical ready-made and conserving the icon of the bottle." (14)

[13.] -
Picasso, P. In: Golding Dr. J. and Penrose, Sir R. 1973. 'Picasso in Retrospect.' New York: Praeger and Picasso, P. In: Ashton, D. 1972. 'Picasso on Art. A Selection of Views.' London: Thames & Hudson

[14.] -
Cos, A. 2008. [Personal communication] 10 February
-

Fig. 11 Islington, London, 1976 by Richard Wentworth Wentworth's ongoing series of photographs 'Making Do and Getting By' have influenced many designers to look more closely at the way objects are misused, recognising the freedom this expresses.

Fig. 12 Tête de Taureau by Pablo Picasso Picasso's bull's head shows the representational possibilities of the ready-made – what do you see first – bicycle components or horns and a head?

Fig. 13
Embouteillage The project
Embouteillage by Antonio Cos
explores the popular misuse
of a wine bottle as a rolling
pin and other ways in which
it may be co-opted.

METAPHOR

Although common in art and the niche markets of high design, it is rare to find ready-mades in mass production. However, it is common for components to be redesigned in their image. More common still is the strategy of designing "otherness" into new products – metaphors that reshape them away from the archetype. While the machine aesthetic was in effect a metaphor for technological progress, as was "streamlining", it was not until the postmodern era and the exploration of product semantics that metaphor took centre stage. As the skin of a product broke free from its working parts it became acceptable for designers to explore representative possibilities directed by lifestyle as well as usability. Alessi in Italy branded themselves "the dream factory" while students of the design department of Cranbrook Academy near Detroit produced the most celebrated examples under the tutelage of Michael and Katherine McCoy. The Book Computer (fig. 14, page 43) by D.M. Gresham powerfully symbolised the importance of computing to Corporate America with its skyscraper-like façade, while Lisa Krohn's Phonebook telephone answering machine (fig. 15, page 43) merged with its instruction manual to promote ease of use. In spite of this, the approach is not without its critics. "Such literal use of analogy results in metaphors with a single meaning" explains Anthony Dunne, head of Design Interactions at London's Royal College of Art. "Products depict what they do, limiting the viewer's interpretation of the electronic object to the designer's and although sometimes the link made between groups of objects is ingenious, the power of these borrowed images to sustain interest is weak – they are the material equivalent of one-liners. Once the viewer has grasped the connection there is little else to engage with." (15)

Although chiefly aimed at those dealing with the electronic object, Dunne's criticism sounds a valid note of caution to all product designers. We must ask whether the metaphors we are considering are "appropriate" and remain open enough to allow individual interpretation. Will products such as Alessi's Lilliput cruet set (see page 35) in which the salt and pepper characters "cry" their ingredients, and the Woofer speakers by Sander Mulder (fig. 16, page 44) in which sound emanates from the severed heads of ceramic dogs, offer a sustained sense of connection or will our initial smile wear off?

Used with care and intelligence, the metaphor has its place in product design. When working for Thompson Multimedia in France, designer Matali Crasset set about redesigning their range of audio and audio-visual equipment under the art direction of Philippe Starck. Their approach was radical, steering away from traditional forms, layouts and colours. Most of Crasset's designs avoided literal translation in exchange for metaphorical forms such as the cone used in the Soundstation radio alarm to represent a blast of sound (fig. 17, page 44). Their bold approach produced some classic designs still on sale today, but it wasn't without its problems. Crasset remembers the team's attempts to reference high culture with a radio influenced by a sculpture of a head by Constantin Brancusi. When the reference was missed by Thompson employees (the prototype was nicknamed "the mouse"), Crasset realised it was a step too far. "The problem was we were pushing a little bit too fast. The market was not yet ready for products like this. At the time, everything else was black boxes. Sales staff... were used to speaking about the picture and the sound. They had to start speaking about the design, so they were lost." (16)

[15.]
Dunne, A. 1999. 'Hertzian Tales: Electronic products, aesthetic experience and critical design.' London: RCA Computer Related Design Research

[16.]
Crasset, M. 2006. 'Matali Crasset' in 'Icon' magazine October p.165

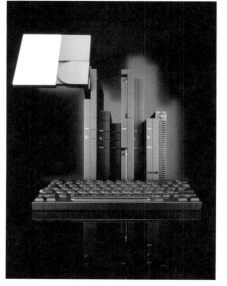

Fig. 14   **Book Computer by D.M. Gresham with Hel Rinkleib** Gresham's computer literally celebrates the corporate structures it is intended to serve.

Fig. 15   **Phonebook telephone answering machine by Lisa Krohn with Tucker Viemeister** Krohn's answering machine uses metaphor to explain its use, each page offering instructions. However, it has been noted that such heavily applied analogies discourage our own interpretations.

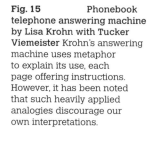

THE IMPORTANCE AND UNIMPORTANCE OF FORM

Concentration upon meaning must not come at the expense of ensuring effectiveness in the multifarious roles in which the object must perform. Peter Dormer has written that: "More and more debate about design has turned into a debate analogous to literary criticism; we ask ourselves 'what does a design mean' and not 'what does it do'. And in concentrating on meaning we lose ourselves in words; the actual object is left behind and it escapes a proper audit on matters such as how well it wears, what it feels like, even how safe it is." (17)

"The formal appearance of an object need not be the result of hours of careful analysis of the problem or pages of drawings" says Jasper Morrison (18). "It could be the visual consequence of an idea, a process, a material, a function or a feeling. Then again, it could arrive in the shape of a borrowed form or a stolen object. There can be no moral objection to this if the result contains something that wasn't there before...So describing the designer as a form-giver is inaccurate; he may be this but not only this and the less he concerns himself with creating form the better for all of us."

In the media frenzy surrounding design, this advice has fallen upon deaf ears and form has become a tool some designers are using to generate recognition for themselves as brands. By feeding the press with images of consistently similar-looking products designed for different manufacturers, they define a set of forms that become identified as their own. Although far from being alone, New York-based Karim Rashid is an example – the voluptuous, waisted form of his successful Garbo waste-paper basket (fig. 18, page 45) reappearing in salt and pepper shakers, vases, sinks and keepsake urns, all for different clients.

From wherever it is derived, the importance of form as the chief communicating element in design cannot be denied. Most significantly, it is a research medium in which designers engage in dialogue with the public and with other designers. A fervent avant-garde investigating the most appropriate form for the products of our time is a vital life force coursing through the profession, even if its ideas are slow to reach a mass audience (if they ever do). The problem is not so much the over-concentration upon form, but that so much of it is unadventurous. We are yet to explore fully the ways in which forms and materials can reflect our fragile reality rather than our fictional perfection. As new high-tech materials replace the old we are losing enduring qualities of wear and patina. Rapid prototyping technologies – initially used to aid product development – are being turned towards producing finished products. Yet some of these techniques produce a stilted materiality, which offers nothing of the dynamism of many industrial production methods and some designers are still overcoming their desire to make previously impossible shapes simply because technology now enables them to do so.

[17.]
Dormer, P. 1990. 'Meaning of Modern Design'. London: Thames & Hudson

[18.]
Morrison, J. 1991. The "Unimportance of Form", 'Ottagono' No. 100

Fig. 16   Woofer speakers by Sander Mulder Although its designer claims to have transformed a grotesque object into a desirable one through the addition of a function, the image presented by this speaker is, nevertheless, a dog with a severed head.

Fig. 17   Soundstation radio alarm by Matali Crasset manufactured by Thompson Multimedia Less literal than many of the designs pictured, Soundstation redefines the typology around a three dimensional blast of sound.

Fig. 18 Garbo
waste-paper basket by Karim
Rashid, manufactured by
Umbra The shape of Garbo
has become something of a
signature for Karim Rashid, its
"waisted" form appearing in a
number of his other products.

02 Motivation

2.1

CONFORMING, REFORMING OR CONTESTING

"That creativity is the foundation of their work is the faith that motivates all designers. To exist at all as a designer, a belief in at least a modicum of personally possessed creative ability is as necessary as it is for a bricklayer to have confidence in his capability of laying a straight course of bricks." (1)

Beyond this core belief in creative ability, the motivations of individual designers vary considerably. A fog of intertwining factors, both selfish and selfless, contributes to the behaviour. The practical need to earn a living and the altruistic wish to improve society mingle in the mind with the desire for recognition and, in some cases, for fame. However, specific sets of ideas and principles also have a defining effect on particular designers' work and this chapter examines how these shape the objects they bring into the world.

In his introduction to the catalogue for the 1972 New York Museum of Modern Art exhibition, 'Italy: The New Domestic Landscape', its curator Emilio Ambasz wrote: "Italy has become a micro-model in which a wide range of the possibilities, limitations and critical issues of contemporary design are brought into sharp focus." (2) Ambasz described this model as revealing three ways in which designers approach their subject. He proposed they either conform to, wish to reform, or utterly contest the systems that have shaped society thus far. These descriptors are still useful for discerning differences between practitioners' ideologies today.

Conformists "do not question the sociocultural context in which they work [or if they do, they choose not to challenge it], but instead continue to refine already established forms and functions. Their work...is mainly concerned with exploring the aesthetic quality of single objects...that answer the traditional needs of domestic life." (3) Within these acts of product refinement, designers may well propose innovative solutions in function, form or use of materials and technologies, but these remain within the traditional confines of the consumer product – that it is recognisable, appealing and hence marketable, and able to be manufactured at the right price.

Reformists, Ambasz says, are "motivated by a profound concern for the designer's role in a society that fosters consumption as one means of inducing individual happiness, thereby ensuring social stability."

However, they are, he suggests, "unable to reconcile the conflicts between their social concerns and their professional practices". Ambasz paints a picture of a somewhat disaffected group who use irony and rhetoric in "recharging known forms with altered meanings". Rather than being the refuge of the defeatist, this category should also include those who design optimistically, while fully aware that their individual actions are unlikely to bring about wholesale change. Their active and pointed practice is aimed at fighting certain injustices or inequalities through engagement with industry and the marketplace. By tackling emerging issues such as the ageing population or sustainability, some reformists have picked up the gauntlet thrown down by critics like Victor Papanek. Others try to engage the public in subtle and charming ways with products that use poetic metaphor and celebratory or witty gestures – methods adopted from literature for an audience used to "ad-speak".

Those in the final category ("in contest" with the system) share the concerns of the reformists but do not wish to participate in making change "from within". They react not by generating products to be consumed, but by proposing alternative models of behaviour, through written or visual communication. (4) Objects may form part of an exhibit describing a new way of living, acting like props in an unseen performance, but are not intended to be purchased.

Where the lines are drawn between these categories – in particular between conformists and reformists – will be a matter of irresolvable debate. The notion that to innovate might be considered "conformist" will, no doubt, upset some designers. However, it can be argued that "the norm" is the continual incremental development of everyday objects (what remains of modernism's pursuit of progress) and that, if innovation stays within certain limits, it ought to be viewed that way. Some conformists naturally try to promote their innovations as being radical because it suits their profile to do so. To be truly reformist is to innovate in ways not usually attempted by the mainstream, or to take intentionally "off message" approaches in order to explore new territory.

The reader may like to consider the design work in this chapter in the light of these descriptors – I will leave it to you to consider which labels best suit the work you find here.

[1.]
Black, M. In: Heskett, J. 1980. 'Industrial Design'. Oxford: Oxford University Press

[2. 3.]
Ambasz, E. 1972. 'Italy: The New Domestic Landscape'. New York: MOMA

[4.]
Ambasz's description actually split the "in contest" group into two: those who flatly refuse to engage with the market and those who undertake what he called "active critical participation", but here, for the sake of clarity, those whose contesting is played out through the market are considered reformist.

DEFINING APPROACHES

The remainder of this chapter on designers' motivation offers an overview of prevalent and emerging approaches to product design. It is not a taxonomy of all approaches currently or historically in use, focusing instead on contemporary ones considered worthy of note. It does not favour commercial achievement as it is felt this would exclude new approaches yet to make their mark or those that do not judge themselves upon their success in the market. Instead, the choice of approaches discussed here aims to level the playing field of intellectual engagement in the profession – to give equal weight to ways of working that do not share equal commercial potential, media coverage or promotion within education, yet have much to offer in terms of their cultural, ethical and intellectual input.

Rather than considering design for different types of products separately, approaches to design are recognised and discussed in order to show that they are often transferable across genres of products. For example, one might take the approach of examining material, process and technological innovation in the design of homewares, but this would be equally applicable to vehicle design.

Any form of categorisation is liable to offend, and designers – those who so often enjoy thinking "outside the box" – are particularly loath to be put in one. To do so tends to focus on only one area of their work, while seemingly ignoring others. Some designers are specialists, exploring and refining one approach whereas others are generalists, acquainting themselves with many genres of design and product types, and attacking them from different angles. Even suggesting that their work emerges from an ideology is too fixed for some, fearing inference of a closed-minded approach to new methods or an insidious political undercurrent. By way of a disclaimer, it is therefore important to stress that work featured here under a particular heading by no means implies that the designer works solely in this way. The proposed categories are also not necessarily mutually exclusive and may overlap like a Venn diagram. For example, one may combine material, process and technological innovation with an ethical and sustainable approach, despite the two being discussed separately here.

There has been, since industrial design began as a profession, a gradual maturing of conceptual ideas, analogous to that which has occurred in the art world. As art has developed beyond figuration, exploring deeper and more challenging territory, designers have gone from being the packagers of engineering to developing a holistic understanding of products. They have acquired human-centred perspectives, embraced cognitive science and warned us of the potential applications for technologies beyond our control. Design has stepped into the envisioning of new business directions and ways in which consumers can become more involved in shaping their surroundings. Through all these changes, design has not lost touch with the physical substance of the object itself and the refinement and exploration of new forms.

Again, like art, design has an avant-garde that is ahead of the public's understanding, appearing mysterious. (1) Like the record-head of a tape deck, designers lay down new ideas, breaking new ground. From the play-head alongside it, the public pick up and assimilate those ideas. But unlike a tape deck, the record and play-heads of culture can become separated. Ideas can be "ahead of their time", meaning insufficient knowledge exists among the general public to interpret them confidently. Many people are not used to looking for culture in domestic products – it is as if they are conscious of art, music, theatre etc yet the signals sent by our everyday objects are only absorbed subconsciously. Few fully grasp the notion that a new product can be a mini essay

on a new way of living and fewer still pursue this as a brief. That design is increasingly being shown in art galleries as well as on the high street is met in some quarters with bemusement or derision. In short, as a society, we are yet to make the leap of faith that design does not require a translator – a mouthpiece, be they journalist, critic or curator – to validate its role. Objects themselves communicate their creator's views on society and culture. All we need to do is to meet what they offer with open and questioning minds.

Author's note: In the following section, along with examples of work from others, I occasionally use examples of products I have designed myself. In doing so, I make no special claim for their importance as design objects. They are shown because they illustrate the approaches being discussed and, as the designer, they provide a primary source of reference I am most equipped to explain.

-          -

[1.]   -
Dormer, P. 1990. 'Meanings of Modern Design'. London: Thames & Hudson
          -

2.3

AESTHETIC REFINEMENT

With the exterior design of products carrying so much weight in conferring status upon them, influencing sales and eliciting emotional responses from people, it follows that a great deal of energy is chanelled into exploring and refining product aesthetics. This section examines the nature of product styling, identifying the influence of scientific and technological progress and revealing contemporary theories used by designers to define languages and nuances of form.

THE RISE OF THE STYLIST

Although emerging from theatre design and window dressing, the first industrial designers to practice in America in the late 1920s set up as consultants, taking their lead from the previously established role of the advertising agent. It is perhaps unsurprising, then, that the figure to attract most attention to this new profession became known more for his salesmanship than his integrity. Frenchman Raymond Loewy – once quoted as saying: "The most beautiful curve is a rising sales graph" (1) – beautified everything from a duplicating machine to a spaceship interior via the Coke bottle and the Greyhound bus. In spite of this, the followers of modernism in Europe, considered themselves to be developing a more cerebral approach to design, and so did not hold Loewy and his American contemporaries in high regard, dismissing them as mere "stylists". These European designers, many of who were trained architects, believed product design should be more than skin-deep and were not impressed by what they saw as a surface-oriented approach. However,

as the profession has grown and stratified, designers have become able to choose to work in areas (such as tableware, furniture and home accessories) where aesthetic refinement can legitimately be seen as the central aspect of their projects. When functionality and complex components are reduced to a minimum in the design of, say, a fruit bowl as opposed to a camera, the intuitive, formal aspects of design ("styling") naturally become the focus of the designer's activity. In the case of the camera, its functional requirements (to be comfortable to hold, clear and easy to adjust etc.) must be considered alongside, and in sympathy with, its form. A surface-based approach would be an abdication of responsibility. It is this that Loewy's critics sensed.

Designers, who primarily deal in the aesthetic refinement of simple, low-tech products, are unlikely to find the label of stylist particularly hurtful. It becomes a derogative when applied to those who have designed products with a degree of functional or technical complexity, where the exterior form appears to have taken undue precedence. By concentrating upon the aspect of the object that is first seen, and not those that are discovered through use, the designer attracts accusations of putting style before substance. As this first viewing often takes place at the point of sale, the stylist has become compared to the pushy salesman, hoping customers will be seduced enough not to ask any awkward practical questions. Loewy, like his present-day heirs Ross Lovegrove and Karim Rashid (who have most appropriately attracted the stylist label) did little to avoid this comparison, displaying considerable charisma but an alarming lack of humility.

Fig. 1   Kodak Baby Brownie camera, 1928 The forms of Teague's Baby Brownie are distinctly architectural.

Fig. 2   Kodak Bantam Special camera (1936–1948) The art deco detailing of the Bantam Special, like the Brownie, can be seen in buildings of the period, especially cinemas.

[1.]
Loewy, R. In: Official Website of Raymond Loewy. 2003 [online]. [Accessed 26th January 2009]. Available on World Wide Web: <www. raymondloewy.com/about/ quotesby.html>

[2.]
Bierut, M. 2007. 79 'Short Essays on Design'. New York: Princeton Architectural Press

[3.]
The quotation "Talking about music is like dancing about architecture" has no clear source and has been attributed to a number of well-known figures including artist Laurie Anderson and musician Elvis Costello.

[4.]
Dormer, P. 1990. 'Meanings of Modern Design.' London: Thames & Hudson

While designers who work beyond as well as on the surface of products are understandably upset when a stylist's apparently less rigorous work eclipses their own, the skill with which the stylist talks is often grudgingly admired. The legitimate stylist works in the realm of intuitive decisions, inflecting forms with subtle nuances that may not be consciously noticed by the consumer but are nonetheless felt. Such intangible work is difficult to pin down with words. This, as designer and critic Michael Bierut points out, is the reason designers have a reputation for "bullshit": "In discussing design with their clients, designers are direct about the functional parts of their solutions and obfuscate like mad about the intuitive parts, having learned early on that telling the simple truth – 'I don't know, I just like it that way' – simply won't do." (2)

Perhaps talking about the finer points of product styling is, to paraphrase a famous quotation (3), like dancing about architecture – there are things we can only experience through sight and touch and that cannot be adequately expressed in words. However, while words may be lacking – and when used, invite the accusation of "bullshit" – the eloquent stylist, rather than deceiving their client, can at least attempt to capture their intentions.

VISUAL GOOD MANNERS

Not everything requires styling to be successful – the tools used in various industries, for example, will largely be bought on the results they achieve, not the impressions they evoke – but as Peter Dormer tells us,

"the closer one gets to the public or home, the greater the need for the stylist to intercede with a repertoire of visual good manners." (4) Dormer's eloquent description of exterior form as an object's "manners" is useful. Manners are culture-specific and constantly evolving. What is considered polite in one situation may be embarrassingly out of place in another. As with manners, so with objects. We may choose to surround ourselves with objects of pedigree, displaying the latest style, prefer an eclectic mix or find matters of style pedantic in relation to function. The same applies when designers choose their approach to the practice of design. Some cultivate a personal style that they bring to all projects. Others find such a prospect stifling, instead looking to discover an appropriate aesthetic direction within the journey of the project; while some still find the prospect of engaging in highly detailed consideration of the correctness or otherwise of a curve or a radius obsessive, even self-indulgent, sidetracking them from the bigger problems their skills might address.

Yet today, as in the last century, there are a number of leading practitioners known for their refined treatment of product aesthetics who are more than willing to defend their approach. Many of these designers will also be acting beyond the surface, looking to improve any number of other factors, often with the help of product engineers. However, primarily they are lauded for an apparent ability to elevate the value of objects through the studied and sensitive handling of the concept, proportion and detail of product form. "Styling", with its pejorative air, is no longer a useful catch-all. The best of today's aestheticians are anything but shallow in their thinking. Many have very different

Fig. 3   Smoothie travel iron by C. Kerr, N. Lucas, E. Lucas, and H. Holder, manufactured by Lucas Holder & Co (1946)
As a metaphor for progress, streamlining entered the home and was applied to products where effectiveness in the wind tunnel was redundant, such as in this travel iron with its locomotive-like styling.

[5.]
The Biomimicry Institute.
2008 [online]. [Accessed 26th
January 2009]. Available
from World Wide Web: <www.
biomimicryinstitute.org>

ideas about how product aesthetics should be defined. This prompts us to ask, "On what grounds do these designers justify their choice of formal language?" and "How do they define beauty in everyday objects?"

THE AESTHETICS OF PROGRESS

It is possible to pinpoint a number of methodologies in use by those designers adept at aesthetic refinement. The most common is to construct a design language from visual cues mined from contemporary symbols of progress. In the 1930s, when the skyscraper was considered the height of technological advance, its vertical lines began appearing in products. The art deco period also brought horizontal detailing and both styles can be seen in cameras designed for Kodak by Loewy's contemporary, Walter Dorwin Teague (figs 1 and 2, page 52). Loewy himself rode the next wave of influence as long-distance train travel and intercontinental flight became de rigueur and he helped define what became known as "Stream-form". Streamlined forms derived from the science of the wind tunnel were applied to products, many of which were going nowhere fast, such as the travel iron (fig. 3, page 53). The splitting of the atom and the prospect of space travel were among the formal influences of the 1950s through to the 1970s. Televisions were styled on astronauts' helmets and lunar landing pad feet appeared on furniture.

More recently, the discovery and mapping of DNA and other advances in biological science have proved influential with designers applying human, animal or molecular forms to products. This was not a new source; the art nouveau of the 1920s – characterised by the work of Hector Guimard and Louis Comfort Tiffany (figs 4 and 5, page 54) – drew its inspiration from nature, but tended to be more decorative and heavily detailed than its more recent incarnation. However, just as there was a difference between using streamlining to improve efficiency (by reducing drag on vehicles) and using it purely for stylistic effect, a similar distinction exists here. The discipline of borrowing structures and processes from nature to solve man's problems (of which streamlining was an early example) is called biomimicry. (5) However, many product designers working with natural form appear to be doing so largely for aesthetic reasons.

The most visible figures in this field are German-born Luigi Colani and his acknowledged protégé, Welshman Ross Lovegrove. Both have named their approaches (Colani "Biodesign" and Lovegrove "Organic Essentialism") and express deference to nature's skill at building economical and beautiful forms. Nevertheless, in the way those forms are applied – to televisions, chaise-longues, tea services, (fig. 6, page 55), water bottles, chairs, lighting – it is difficult to see how they offer more efficient solutions than the geometric. Lovegrove's Go chair (fig. 7, page 55), besides its elegance, is sold on its use of magnesium rather than aluminium, thereby cutting its weight by 40 per cent, is in fact a similar weight to the die-cast

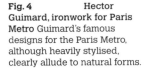

Fig. 4   Hector Guimard, ironwork for Paris Metro Guimard's famous designs for the Paris Metro, although heavily stylised, clearly allude to natural forms.

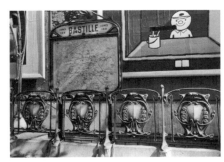

Fig. 5   Jack-in-the-pulpit vase by Louis Comfort Tiffany Son of the founder of Tiffany & Company and designer of the Tiffany lamp, Louis Comfort Tiffany became renowned for his use of stained glass.

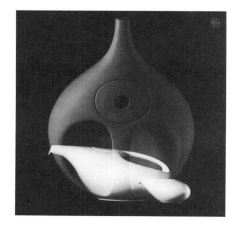

Fig. 6   Drop tea service by Luigi Colani manufactured by Rosenthal
The teardrop form of Luigi Colani's teapot for Rosenthal is a typical example of his "biodesign" style.

Fig. 7   Go chair by Ross Lovegrove manufactured by Bernhardt
Like Colani, Ross Lovegrove favours organic forms over the geometric as an underlying approach running throughout his work.

Fig. 8   Chair
One by Konstantin Grcic
manufactured by Magis
After designing Chair One,
its angular aesthetic was
interpreted as Grcic's "style",
although later projects have
proved this is not the case, the
designer instead allowing the
aesthetic of each project to
emerge as appropriate to its
various requirements.

aluminium Chair One by Konstantin Grcic (fig. 8, page 56). In Lovegrove's chair, the form itself is not sparing enough in its use of material for the magnesium to make it significantly lighter than its competitor. Grcic's efficient use of material happened to be applied to geometric form, rather than organic, but this is incidental. Just as in the "baroque versus geometric form" debate explained on page 23, either treatment could be used – to argue that one style is functionally better is a red herring. If the aim were weight reduction – as was apparently the case here – the results are measurable in kilograms. This begs the question, if geometric form can be used just as effectively as organic form in the design of products, can either be argued as being intrinsically "correct"?

The key argument for organic style is that we have innate empathy with it. Theoretical physicist John D. Barrow demonstrates that our survival instincts still affect our first aesthetic preferences (very young children, given the choice of images of different landscapes, consistently chose the African savannah, from where humans are said to have emerged). (6) Yet Barrow also reveals that as we get older and we experience other environments, this affects our choice: "Our aesthetic preferences are a fusion of instinct and experience...A taste for the avant-garde or the abstract is a fruit of experience overriding instinct." (7) It appears we are able to override an instinctive desire towards the organic should we so choose.

Without additional criteria upon which to base decisions, or a specific object under discussion, talking hypothetically about style preferences gets us nowhere. However, it is important to recognise that style has a practical relationship to manufacturing. For example, with certain manufacturing processes, the

production of organic form is difficult and expensive compared to the production of the geometric – unless guided otherwise, saws like to cut straight lines, milling machines mill straight slots and so on. In other cases there is little difference and in others still, such as when using glass and ceramics, the organic form is easier to produce. Such realities point to an approach whereby style could be determined, at least in part, by the tools to be used. A style in tune with its manufacture can emerge, rather than being predetermined. However, there will always be personal preferences among designers and Colani and Lovegrove have faith in the notion that we must remake our surroundings in nature's image: "The earth is round, all the heavenly bodies are round; they all move on round or elliptical orbits. This same image of circular, globe-shaped, mini-worlds orbiting around each other follows us right down to the microcosmos. We are even aroused by round forms in species propagation-related eroticism. Why should I join the straying mass who want to make everything angular? I am going to pursue Galileo Galilei's philosophy: my world is also round." (8)

IN SEARCH OF AUTHENTICITY

There is a difference in approach between those designers who fully accept, embrace and explore the abstraction of the object from its technical, functional and manufacturing roots, and those who search for a sense of authenticity. Even if this authenticity can be viewed as an artificial construct, the illusion of it can be valuable. Modernist theories and the rationalising of manufacture provide us with some of the tools of this authenticity, in particular the harnessing of geometric form. Proportional systems such as the golden section, (fig. 9, page 57) described by Greek mathematician Euclid in 300BC and used in painting for centuries, appeared in modernist architect Le Corbusier's working

[6. 7.]
Barrow, J. D. 1997. 'The Artful Universe'. London: Penguin Books

[8.]
Colani, L. In: 'Colani Trading AG.' 2007 [online]. [Accessed 26th January 2009]. Available from World Wide Web: <www.colani.ch/historie.html>

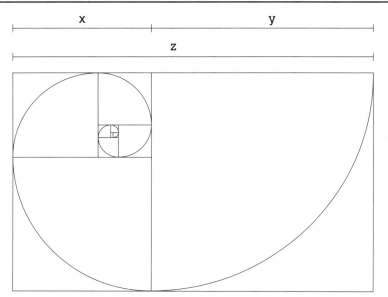

Fig. 9 The Golden Section/Mean/Ratio When splitting a line at the Golden Section, the ratio between the shorter part (X), and the longer part (Y) is the same as the ratio between the longer part (Y), and the complete line (Z). To create a rectangle using the Golden Section the same system is applied where the shorter line is used for width and the longer for height or vice versa. By splitting such a rectangle along its longer axis at the Golden Section, a square and another smaller Golden Section rectangle are created.

[9.]   -
'Horizon: Little Boxes.' TV,
BBC1, 1980 September 9.
                        -
[10.]   -
Hecht, S and Colin, K. 2005.
'Things That Go Unseen.'
London: Industrial Facility
                        -

method as "The Modulor" in the 1940s. The ratio is found throughout nature, including the human body, but whether its use creates intrinsically beautiful proportions or we have simply become subconsciously accustomed to seeing it, is contested. Nevertheless, its legacy was to give designers a justifiable framework on to which a product's boundaries, features, and components could be fixed.

The most renowned and influential product designer to work with such grid systems is Dieter Rams. With the history of German modernism propelling them, Rams and his team at Braun combined mathematical precision with the sculptor's eye to produce highly regarded designs for home electrical equipment (fig. 10, page 58). Rams established a philosophy that was to be applied to all Braun products that focused on providing clarity of function by avoiding superfluous detail. What detail remained was considered with great care. Purity of form and a reduced palette of colours (primarily black and white) gave the products a severe, clinical and occasionally monolithic appearance that placed them on a cultural pedestal, above more pandering competition. Consequently, numerous Braun products can be found in the permanent collections of design museums around the world and are on permanent display at New York's Museum of Modern Art.

Various followers of Rams have tried to carry his mantle but few have managed to achieve the same exacting aesthetic rigour without compromising usability. Many electronic products of the 1980s and 1990s hid controls behind doors and sliding panels, literally reducing the object to a sinister black or silver box. (9) Jonathan Ive, after making the computer homely with the original Apple iMac, has successfully slid into Rams's shoes by directing the designs for the G4 Powerbook, iPod and iPhone (fig. 11, page 59). Ive and his team have applied geometric lines (no "swoop"), uniform radii and keen attention to the proportional grid that holds the product's features in harmony. Combining this with simple, intuitive interfaces and generous touches (such as paying attention to the design of transformers and plugs, providing built-in cable storage) has won Apple a new generation of fanatical fans. Ive's detractors, like those of Rams before him, flag up the dictatorial nature of such singular visions of "good taste"; the way that one product can appear to "preach" to those around it a sermon of abstinence from frivolity, from historical reference or applied narrative.

There is an ideological schism between designers whose goal is to elicit our positive reflex response to their object's beauty and those who see aesthetic refinement as a means to a less subjective end. For Rams and Ive, the sparse look of their objects has a function – that of providing clarity of use. Sam Hecht and Kim Colin of Industrial Facility share this view stating: "Form is a mechanism for use, rather than an aesthetic (or a surface upon which choice is played out). It is something that needs to be evolved and not applied". (10) To them, aesthetic refinement as an end in itself is not a valid starting point. With products often discussed in terms of image alone rather than with the benefit of the experience of use, designers are encouraged into a surface-deep design process that fails to expose the valuable thinking that creates the "evolved" forms Hecht describes. Paradoxically, Industrial Facility and others such as Konstantin Grcic, have become so adept at creating refined aesthetics that the underlying logic of evolution in their products sometimes fails to reveal itself without explanation.

Fig. 10 **D5 Slide Projector by Dieter Rams and the Braun Design Team manufactured by Braun**
Sometimes the product's interior component layout suggested a geometric approach to the casing. The dividing line between the two parts of the plastic casing (the "split line") on the D5 projector lines up with the direction of the lens and the entry point of the electrical flex.

FORMALISM

A term used in various fields including art, "formalism" considers the technique, form and structure of a work as being of greater importance than its content or meaning. A formalist approach to design – typical of designers labelled "stylists" – therefore focuses on the external form of an object to a greater extent than on other considerations.

A formalist designer will explore form as an end in itself, and while accepted in products of minimal complexity, this surface-centric approach becomes redundant when applied to products that require deeper investigation. Nevertheless, the emergence of photo-realistic imagery produced by advanced rendering software has enabled designers who wish to adopt a formalist approach to readily explore a myriad of forms within the virtual world of the computer.

MINIMALISM

The term "minimalism" refers to a tendency within various creative genres to reduce complexity in the work such as to reveal dramatically its essential qualities. Minimalism's influence in design has come largely from art and architecture where it is more clearly recognised as a movement (minimalist artist Donald Judd has produced numerous furniture collections while architect John Pawson, known for his minimalist approach to architecture and interiors, has designed ranges of domestic products including tableware, accessories and door furniture).

As the reductive ethos already existed in modernist thinking, many objects emerging from this tradition have qualities now associated with minimalism. However, while modernism placed emphasis upon improving the object in a number of ways, embracing manufacturing processes and new materials, minimalism is narrower in scope, placing greater emphasis upon visual purity. As a result, many designers regard it as a style choice rather than an embodiment of loftier ideals.

Fig. 11 iPod and iPhone by Jonathan Ive and the Apple design team
Apple's recent products designed under the direction of Jonathan Ive have an aesthetic rigor akin to those produced under Rams at Braun.

Another outcome of this surface reading of objects is that it encourages designers and their clients into attention-grabbing tricks (fig. 12, page 60). As products compete to be noticed, lined up on the shelves of stores with their features listed beside them, what shouts loudest may not be the most pleasant to live with in the long term. Railing against this, in Industrial Facility's design for a telephone to supplement the main home phone, they stripped away many attributes previously considered sacrosanct (fig. 13, page 61). As it was intended for short calls, an ergonomic, soft form was not needed. Number storage was eliminated and even the conventional base unit was done away with, allowing the surface the handset rests upon to depress the "end call" button. At first sight, Second Phone looks mysterious – like one of Rams's radios for Braun it has been reduced to a carefully radiused block – but once picked up, it reveals the familiar layout of buttons. Ultimately, it treats the consumer as intelligent and able to recognise common-sense thinking as well as minimalist beauty; to be sold less when more is superfluous.

Critics describing Industrial Facility and Grcic's work tend to focus upon its clinical exterior, describing it as minimalist. While this might be a fair observation of general appearance, it implies that look is the foremost criteria in the designer's mind; something both contest. As Grcic states: "I am never interested in showing how good I am at joining two bits of wood together or in drawing beautiful lines. For me, the most important thing in a design project is its conception." (11) "I have an abiding interest in very essential things. But this doesn't only refer to how things look...I am primarily interested in the ways an object is used, and I believe that aesthetics will naturally develop from that. I don't want to deny that design has a lot to do with giving form to something, creating structures and, let's be honest, making things beautiful. But the most beautiful design never comes from a formalistic approach, but from a process of observing, paring down and focusing information during the process of development." (12)

[11.]
Grcic, K. In: Picchi, F. 1999. Konstantin Grcic. 'Domus.' 820, p.47

[12.]
Grcic, K. interviewed by Bullivant, L. 2000. 'Interieur'

Fig. 12 IF4000 **knife sharpener by Industrial Facility manufactured by Taylor's Eye Witness** Industrial Facility's knife sharpener was developed through addressing considerations of stability, portability and safety. However, its clinical exterior is its most striking feature.

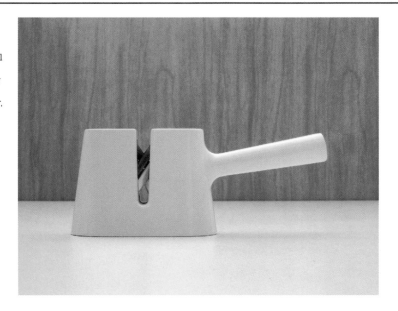

Fig. 13 Second
Phone by Industrial Facility
manufactured by Muji Second
Phone bravely does away
with many features that had
crept into telephone handsets,
but were an unnecessary
distraction. The phone uses
the surface it is put down on
to depress the button that
ends the call.

COLLECTIVE MEMORY AND BEHAVIOUR

One of the most powerful tools for generating emotionally durable products is to look beyond attempting to embody "progress" with form and instead make connections based upon memory and behaviour (1). The following section describes a number of ways of achieving this that could be adopted when tackling new work. What links designers featured here is a belief that the power of observation is the most important tool they possess. Without it they would be doomed to repeat past mistakes but, by refining it, their minds can be primed to facilitate countless creative opportunities. It is these practitioners who see design almost as a branch of anthropology. They study "why things are the way they are" with archaeological rigour, and investigate the effect that the form of objects has upon our behaviour toward them.

[1.]
Popularised by Jonathan Chapman in his book 'Emotionally Durable Design: Objects, Experiences and Empathy' (2005, London: Earthscan) the term refers to Chapman's vision of a future filled with objects consciously designed to create meaningful emotional links with people as a means of counteracting the prevailing throwaway society.

SUMMARISING FORM

Although there are many who find beauty in pure geometry, there are practitioners who are trying to augment this with an additional flavour. One of these is the British designer Jasper Morrison. He has written: "It would be ridiculous if everyone kept looking for a beautiful new form. It can be more interesting to look at what is already there and apply it in a different way" (2). In his early work, Morrison literally used existing recognisable objects (ready-mades – see page 76) and assembled them to create "new" pieces (fig. 1, page 62). Since then, his approach has evolved whereby rather than using ready-mades, he tries to "summarise" designs from the past in new products (fig. 2, page 62). By distilling the essence of anonymous, unselfconsciously designed objects,

Morrison tries to capture an aesthetic to which we can relate and with which we can feel immediately comfortable. Precedent can be found in designs by Italians of an earlier generation such as Achille Castiglioni and Vico Magistretti – fellow celebrators of vernacular objects – but much has changed since their heyday. In a climate in which design is, more often than not, expected to provide the different and the unusual, Morrison's work goes against the grain. He has described this approach in an exhibition and book compiled with fellow designer Naoto Fukasawa, entitled 'Super Normal' (fig. 3, page 63). It is, they say, an attempt to keep hold of something essential that design is losing – the "normalness" of the anonymously-designed object: "For me it's a reaction, a reaction to noticing how much better most normal things are than most design things. I think design is in danger of becoming something false and out of tune with real life, when it could be doing something worthwhile. It's degenerating into a marketing tool to promote the identity of companies and to sell magazines. That's not the profession I admired as a student. There's a lot of good design going on, maybe more than when I was a student, but unfortunately it's heavily outweighed by what can only be described as visual pollution, atmospheric interference, design with nothing more in mind than getting noticed, and on balance I'd have to say we would be better off without it. 'Super Normal' is a reminder of more genuine motives for designing something." (3)

Fig. 1   Flower pot table by Jasper Morrison
Although aware of artists who had used ready-mades, such as Duchamp and Picasso, Jasper Morrison used them as a means of emulating the qualities of industrial production. His Flower Pot Table, inspired by seeing a stack of the upturned pots, was later manufactured by Cappellini.

Fig. 2
Knifeforkspoon cutlery set for Alessi by Jasper Morrison
The approach of summarising form can be seen in Morrison's cutlery for Alessi that, rather than mould the pieces to the hand or embellish them with decorative detail, draws their users into a subtle sense of familiarity.

[2.]

Morrison, J. In: Ramakers, R. 1998. 'Droog Design - Spirit of the Nineties'. Rotterdam: 010

[3.]

Morrison J. In: Fukasawa, N and Morrison, J. 2007. 'Super Normal: Sensations of the Ordinary'. Baden: Lars Müller Publishers

[4.]

Morrison, J. 2002. 'Everything But The Walls'. Baden: Lars Müller Publishers

[5.]

Duchamp, M. In: Bailly, J.C. 1986. 'Duchamp'. Basingstoke: Palgrave Macmillan

[6.]

Hecht, S. 2008. [Personal communication]. 24 January

Morrison and others who have studied anonymously-designed artefacts from the past have discovered that "progress" has forced into obscurity some that seem perfectly suited to today's market. By making few if any changes, these out-of-production designs have been re-released, celebrating the original product and giving it a new lease of life. If these objects fulfil their role at least as effectively as their newer counterparts, then, rather than being anachronistic, this approach can enrich a typology of objects and raise awareness of the notion of the timeless. Morrison's Socrates corkscrew for Alessi is a case in point (fig. 4, page 63). Of the design he says: "I have had a corkscrew similar to this one for about 20 years. It's an old typology but a good one, which seems to have more or less disappeared. The pantograph lever action makes it much easier to take corks out and as there are so many bad corkscrews around I decided it was my duty to re-introduce it to the world!" (4) While some may see this as lacking originality, its justification is analogous to the nomination of manufactured objects as art by Marcel Duchamp and others in the early twentieth century. Just as an artist can select a mass-produced object, display it in a gallery and call it art, so a designer can select an out-of-production object and, barring intellectual property claims, release it under their own name. The "design" lies in the nomination of the right object, rather than the authorship of its form; as Duchamp put it, the intention being "...to relate notions of aesthetic worth to a decision of the intellect and not to a facility or cleverness of the hand" (5).

To those who have been conditioned to expect the element of design in a new product to manifest itself overtly – to show its value through eye-catching difference and to be entertaining – the understatement of the 'Super Normal' object will bemuse. Sam Hecht recounts an anecdote that highlights the problem:

"We've just done a project for LaCie and when it came out there was an enormous amount of criticism because 'it was just a box' and 'it wasn't design', that 'you could have designed that in five minutes. Why did it take two years?' I find that fascinating...It was a real shocker for me because it means that a designer can't make the simplest of solutions because 'that's not design'. [It implies that] the simplest, most enduring, most honest of solutions is out of bounds because 'anyone can do it'. Whereas if something looks quite complicated or it's fashioned in a way that looks styled, has got fancy materials or interesting sprays and all these sorts of things, then that's seen as something that is more worthy – 'that's design'...if you negate all of that and if you put that to one side, then 'you're not dealing with design'." (6)

Although on this occasion it was not the client who voiced the criticism – LaCie were happy and the products have sold well – Hecht admits this approach relies upon clients being capable of seeing good design in terms of providing products people will find enduring in the long term, rather than looking for a quick thrill, and this sometimes requires "education". He encourages companies to think about the life of the product beyond the point of purchase, especially the experience of using it day to day.

Super Normal

Sensations
of the Ordinary

Naoto Fukasawa & Jasper Morrison

Lars Müller Publishers

Fig. 3 Super Normal book cover Although stated through reasoned explanation and a collection of objects rather than dogmatic demands, Super Normal is nonetheless that most unfashionable of things, a manifesto.

Fig. 4 Socrates corkscrew for Alessi by Jasper Morrison In the spirit of Duchampian nomination, Morrison "re-introduced" this corkscrew he had owned for years, which had stood the test of time and use.

THE AURA OF THE READY-MADE

French artist Marcel Duchamp shook the art world in the early part of the twentieth century by displaying mass-produced products in galleries, challenging the previous tautology that to have value, works must show the artist's manual skill with media. Duchamp argued that an artwork could be entirely about the intellect and hence nominating an object was as valid as sculpting one with clay or depicting one on canvas. In doing so he heavily influenced the Dadaist and surrealist movements and paved the way for the recognition of what is now known as conceptual art. He called these nominated objects "ready-mades" (fig. 5, page 64).

German literary critic and writer, Walter Benjamin, coined the term "aura" to describe a certain elusive but valuable quality in artworks that we can assume is also present in mass-produced objects. Benjamin proposed that this aura "withered" in a reproduction compared to an original work (i), yet if we propose it exists in mass-produced objects, despite withering, it is something we ought to take into account. Product designers have talked of this "otherness" in various ways. British consultants Seymour Powell have called it the X-Factor (ii), while Deyan Sudjic, director of London's Design Museum, proposes that "consciously or unconsciously, we understand that everything around us has a personality". (iii) So how do ready-mades contribute to this sense of character?

To call something a ready-made as opposed to a component is to suggest its inherent importance as well as to illustrate that its origins lie elsewhere. Humble nuts and bolts would usually be considered mere components, yet when given centre stage in a product, they are elevated to the status of the ready-made, as in Massimo Varetto's Microservice dinner placecard holder (fig. 6, page 64). We may therefore conclude that in art and design, a ready-made is a component used out of context, knowingly selected to contribute significantly to the aura of work that it becomes part of, lending the result a certain charm, character or personality, expressing meaning.

When viewing these works, we are struck first by the fact that the ready-made is out of its expected context and we begin, if curious enough, to consider why. In an artwork we might ask first of all what the ready-made represents, whereas if we are looking at a piece of design, we will also be searching for its practical purpose. This thinking, Duchamp proposed, was the viewer's contribution to the creative act (iv) and by deciphering the piece the viewer also allows it to become complete. Hence, the ready-made is a "device" that requires interpretation in its new context and actively engages the consumer in the creative act.

[i.]
Benjamin, W. 1973.
'Illuminations.' London:
Fontana Press

[ii.]
"It's what we as designers are always striving for. The X-factor in a product is its essential personality, its desirability quotient, if you like - those intangible, emotional features, over and above function and efficiency, that make one product better and more desirable than another." Richard Seymour of Seymour Powell in an interview by Carl Gardner (1989) for 'Car Styling Magazine', No. 70, p.110

[iii.]
Sudjic, D. 1999. Student Design Awards Review: Face Values – The Changing Shape of Design. London: RSA

Fig. 5   **Bottle rack by Marcel Duchamp** Although less well-known than the urinal entitled 'Fountain', the bottle rack that Duchamp reputedly bought from a Paris department store around 1914 was the first sculpture he described as a "ready-made".

Fig. 6   **Microservice dinner placecard holder by Massimo Varetto** Varetto's dinner place card holder, a modest assemblage of a clothes peg and some metal fastenings, offers us the chance to consider these components in a context where they are on display for their aesthetic as well as functional properties.

Achille Castiglioni, along with his brother Pier Giacomo, designed some of the most memorable products using ready-mades (figs 7 and 8, page 65 and fig. 12, page 67) describes this engagement thus: "Selecting a form that 'appears' to connect certain traditionally recognized meanings, while actually treating those forms as if they possessed a quality unrelated to the original meaning, is for us an act of communication with observers who attempt to read the meaning hidden beyond superficial forms. This relationship can perhaps be called 'reciprocal curiosity'". (v)

In observing the paraphernalia of material culture and the behaviour it elicits, Castiglioni and others have picked and reapplied particular objects and details so we may, in turn, be curious enough to wonder what they saw in them. Like solving a riddle or getting a joke, when we make the connection, our affection for the creator and their creation is brought forth. The joy of such an approach is that if this connection stands the test of time, it will prompt a smile every time we glance at the object.

[iv.]   -
"The creative act is not performed by the artist alone; the spectator brings the work in contact with the external world by deciphering and interpreting its inner qualifications and thus adds his contribution to the creative act." Duchamp, M. In: Sanouillet, M. & Peterson, E., 1975. 'The Essential Writings of Marcel Duchamp'. London: Thames & Hudson

[v.]   -
Castiglioni, A. In: Taki, I. 2004. The Origin Of Castiglioni Design – Observation and Curiosity. 'Axis Magazine.' August, p.131

Fig. 7   Toio standard lamp by Achille and Pier Giacomo Castiglioni manufactured by Flos
The utilitarian character of this lamp expressed in its exposed transformer, bent metal frame, headlamp light source and fishing rod rings for holding the flex, reflects its heritage as an assemblage of found components. However, each has been carefully considered for its functionality and not as a novelty device.

Fig. 8   Mezzandro stool by Achille and Pier Giacomo Castiglioni manufactured by Zanotta
Why create the new when something that works already exists elsewhere? With this sentiment in mind, the Castiglioni brothers saw the great economy with which a comfortable seat for tractors had been pressed from a single sheet of steel, supported by a springy steel bar, and thus built it into a stool for the home.

[7. 8.]
Hecht, S. 2008. [Personal communication]. 24 January

PROPORTIONAL ANALOGIES

The smallest of the LaCie drives (fig. 9, page 67) is reminiscent of a Zippo lighter and the next size up, a packet of cigarettes but, Hecht says, the designs are not literal translations of dimensions:

"[The Lacie hard disk] was originally provided to us more the size of a MiniDisc cassette (long, wide and thin). After much experiment with re-orientating the components we came up with something similar in size to a packet of cigarettes. People are already familiar with this proportion inside their top pockets – much more than an MD – as something compact. However, the dimensions are not governed by the cigarette packet. It's more a feeling." (7)

Using familiar dimensions is a tool Hecht and Fukasawa have both used in order for their work to connect with people's physical and visual memory of objects. Referring to his work with Industrial Facility, Hecht continues: "We do a lot of that with Muji, quite subversively. We made a notebook that is exactly the same size and amount of pages as a passport. We used all the passport colours. We don't express it but people really feel it even though they might not know where it came from. They generally become very big successes because they are already instilled in memory." (8)

Another of Industrial Facility's projects references the proportions of a packet of chewing gum in a series of USB devices (figs 10 and 11, page 67), while Naoto Fukasawa has created a lamp for Plusminuszero that is a facsimile of a ream of A4 photocopier paper (fig. 12, page 68). Such links might seem obscure at first but are explained by the context of use – the lamp is for the office while the USB devices will be carried in the pocket. This way of thinking takes the idea of products being in harmony with their surroundings to a new level,

their physical properties being uncannily familiar. When arbitrariness exists in a product's precise dimensions, these links provide a reason to pin them down (although it is worth remembering that the dimensions of the products being referenced were at one time also arbitrary).

Occasionally, we see similarities in product proportions that suggest they have been consciously borrowed, but it may also be true that in deciding upon certain dimensions designers subconsciously choose those that are most common to them (fig. 13, page 68).

TRANSPOSING FORM

While Hecht and Fukasawa's proportional analogies are so subtle they can go unnoticed – a fact the designers enjoy – the approach of noticeably transposing characteristics associated with one type of product into another has become commonplace, especially in the field of home accessories. Combinations of shape, material, colour and finish are translated to provide new objects with familiar properties, appearance and meaning. However, without an appropriate link this work can easily descend into kitsch (see page 73). To avoid this, designers conceive of logical and poetic connections between the "donor object" and the "receiver" of its attributes.

However, these links do not need to be obvious. Duchamp and the Dada and surrealist art movements, whose members relished making ironic and oblique references by using everyday objects out of context, inspired much of the work in this territory. The designer Achille Castiglioni, who has acknowledged Duchamp as a major influence, has said: "We should focus on

Fig. 9 Little Disk series of hard drives by Industrial Facility manufactured by LaCie Sam Hecht and his colleagues at Industrial Facility reoriented the electronics inside the series of LaCie portable drives so as to create compact forms that have similar (but not exactly the same) dimensions to other objects we might carry: a Zippo lighter and a pack of playing cards.

Fig. 10 Sound Gum, mp3 player by Industrial Facility

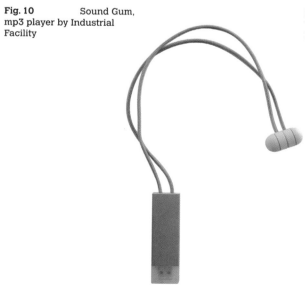

Fig. 11 Data Gum, USB data storage by Industrial Facility

being ironic, like Jacques Tati was, and not being so strict with design." (9) Tati, the acclaimed French comedy actor and filmmaker, was a master at using (or rather misusing) objects for comedic effect. The irony Castiglioni recognises is peppered throughout Tati's films. Objects are transformed – a car tyre inner tube covered in leaves is mistaken for a funeral wreath – while others cause havoc at the hands of the central character Monsieur Hulot. A naïve but likeable everyman, Hulot is unacquainted with, and therefore bemused by, anything remotely modern. Even the simplest of mechanisms can confound him. Hence, as he appears on screen with objects, we predict their behaviour long before he does, with, as they say, hilarious consequences.

However, Tati's comedy went far beyond mere slapstick, and built to form a heartfelt polemic against what he saw as the inhumanity of contemporary "progress". As Monsieur Hulot discovers in the film 'Mon Oncle' (1958), modernity that rejects common sense and collective memory is ridiculous. Here, Hulot's sister and brother-in-law live in a "modern" house full of the latest gadgets, yet it has a cold and clinical atmosphere. Thanks to Hulot's unintentionally amusing yet understandable actions, its dubious "innovations" are shown up as pure folly. By creating Hulot as a sympathetic character whose behaviour we relate to (despite its naïvety), Tati produced the perfect weapon for satirising "progressive" design and, by implication, its designers. The joy he uncovered by showing objects out of place, being misread or misused, has been emulated by Castiglioni and others in the world of design. Like Tati's films, these designs become an effective foil to po-faced, dogmatic modernism.

Although the components of some of these products are remade in the image of others, some are literally made from "ready-mades" (see pages 64–65) – components relocated from elsewhere and used out of their original context. This is often out of necessity rather than choice. Designer-makers not working for a manufacturing client who are developing batch production products tend to find many production techniques financially out of reach and the ready-made offers a solution with the aesthetic of production built in. However, this has practical drawbacks. Using an object for its original purpose but in a different context might be straightforward (for example, a bicycle seat brought indoors to be used as a stool – fig. 14, page 69) but changing its purpose can be problematic. Objects designed for one task are rarely found to be perfect for another. Unlike in the art gallery, ready-mades as design components cannot rely on their power to provoke alone. They are likely to have practical functions to perform; yet ready-mades often lack a necessary detail or contain some extraneous material that compromises the end product's ability to function as effectively as it would with a specially-designed part.

By creating specially made components, designers are able to design-out the elements of ready-mades that prevent them working in their new guises, while retaining familiar features that provide interest. If designers stick to using the ready-made, they must choose it carefully and ensure other components are designed in harmony.

Fig. 12
Plusminuszero / A4 lamp by Naoto Fukasawa Like IF's USB devices and hard drives, Fukasawa's lamp looks to its context for proportions to co-opt, in this case, the office and in particular, a ream of A4 paper.

Fig. 13   Canon Ixus **camera and cigarette packet** Coincidence, planning or subconscious borrowing of a familiar form? It is possible that designers may settle upon proportions that they find pleasing without necessarily knowing where these come from.

Although the meanings of some products rely upon their use of genuine ready-mades (for example, the re-configured chairs of Martino Gamper (fig. 15, page 70)), in many other cases, creating the impression of a familiar form is enough. For example, the Mayday lamp for Flos by Konstantin Grcic (fig. 16, page 71) clearly references a mechanic's inspection lamp, yet, with the obvious exception of the electrics, none of the components is literally borrowed. Instead, Grcic concentrated on how to get "garage lampness" into a product that was also refined enough to appear at home in the domestic interior. In doing so, he brought the flexibility of the inspection lamp indoors, providing a domestic light source that can be hung up or stood on a surface, its polypropylene skirt expressing the shaft of light from its ancestor. Mayday is an example of the designer recognising that the functionality existing in one kind of object could be usefully employed in another, and that the aesthetic reference would add a playful character. Rather than simply borrowing the form and functionality of the inspection lamp wholesale, Grcic "civilised" it, editing out its rawness. In doing so, he creates, in effect, a memento of the inspection lamp. This highlights one of the key reasons to transpose form – to elicit past memories.

Souvenirs, by associating themselves with the places we go to relax and enjoy ourselves, unsurprisingly become the carriers and transmitters of (hopefully) positive memories. Sadly, the design approach taken to most souvenirs is immature and the results are kitsch. Form is transposed but often in crass and obvious ways – onto dolls or soft toys, into snow-

domes, vials of sand and other charity-shop fillers. These archetypal blank canvasses of the souvenir merchant, once emblazoned with place names, shout for attention and once bought, continue shouting "look where we've been" with the subtlety of a megaphone. Exceptions are rare but satisfying. Mugs on sale at New York's Guggenheim Museum, rather than predictably displaying the name and photograph of the institution, subtly reference the building's shape. A channel gently winds its way up the mug's volume, mimicking Frank Lloyd Wright's famous rotunda (fig. 17, page 72). To those unfamiliar with the building (fig. 18, page 72), the mug, in plain white ceramic, would likely go unnoticed. And that's exactly the point. It subverts the "souvenir as show-off accessory" and directs its power to evoke memories towards their source.

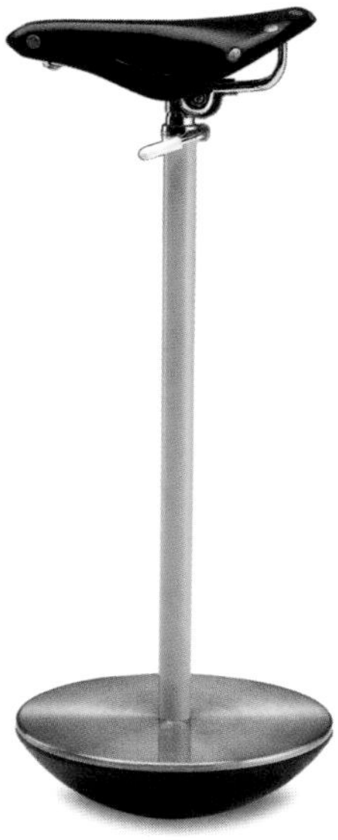

[9.]
Castiglioni, A. 2007. 'Design Interviews'. Mantova: Edizioni Corraini

Fig. 14   Sella Stool by Achille and Pier Giacomo Castiglioni, manufactured by Zanotta One of a number of products they designed using ready-mades, the Castiglioni brothers' Sella stool incorporates a Brooks bicycle saddle. It is intended for use while on the telephone.

Fig. 15   100 chairs in
100 days by Martino Gamper
Martino Gamper's project
creatively re-used well-known
and anonymous furniture
to make 100 new designs.
Although they could be seen
as three-dimensional sketch
models testing ideas, they are
also one-off finished pieces
assembled with directness
and ingenuity.

BEHAVIOURAL ANALOGIES

Much of Naoto Fukasawa's work focuses on analysing human nature to design sympathetic products. He wants us to be able to assimilate these objects into our lives so we may use them "without thought". Although we tend to think of ourselves as autonomous individuals, Fukasawa highlights that our environment, and the products in it, directs some of our actions. By carefully observing the ways objects and spaces channel behaviour, and by designing new products to take advantage of this, Fukasawa has generated an approach where his objects appear to fit naturally into certain environments and certain patterns of use – what he calls "design dissolving in behaviour". (10) Using recognisable forms and layouts outside of their original context, Fukasawa uses the affordances they carry (see pages 38–39) to help us comprehend the objects. Examples include transposing the layout of a kitchen fan into a wall-mounted CD player (fig. 19, page 72) – the pull chord replacing the play button – or his Sole Bag, a white cotton tote bag that can be put down on wet floors thanks to its rubber plimsoll base (fig. 20, page 73). Upon seeing these objects for the first time, their use is clear. Fukasawa's designs often have this equation-like elegance from which a sense of the authentic emerges. Even when he is unable to find a behavioural connection and he reverts to minimalism, his products seem not to alienate. They are examples of "designs you can describe over the telephone" – the best kind according to Italian maestro Vico Magistretti. (11)

Like Fukasawa, French designer Matali Crasset also has an interest in how traditional typologies of objects can be examined in order to reveal new possibilities. A product can influence how we feel about certain behaviour, making an action more or less desirable. Crasset has demonstrated how designers can give permission for a person to behave in ways that might otherwise have felt uncomfortable. Her Daily Starting Block legitimises the habit of polishing one's shoes on the backs of one's trouser legs by smuggling a brush in between (fig. 21, page 73) while her snoozing stool for the office unfurls into a bed with accompanying "do not disturb" sign (fig. 22, page 74). Normally taboo (yet known to increase efficiency), taking a short nap at work would become acceptable if such a bed were provided for us. In her designs for the Hi Hotel in Nice, various elements conspire to reverse the sensation that, as guests, you must be waited upon, instead empowering inquisitive individuals with the freedom to serve themselves. By removing conventions such as the mini-bar but making drinks available 24 hours a day in the main bar, Crasset surreptitiously encourages us to make new acquaintances.

Right from her early projects (such as the hospitality tower 'When Jim Comes to Paris' (fig. 23, page 74)) Crasset's work has been driven by her exploration of a set of principles and descriptors through which she frames the intentions of each project. These terms, which include "generosity", "autonomy", "hospitality", "empathy", "typology" and "ritual", act as a silent manifesto guiding her proposals for new ways of living.

Working products around behaviours is a way in which designers can reflect and encourage contemporary and emerging attitudes and, of course, express their own preferences. French design duo Ronan and Erwan Bouroullec, in their 'Joyn' office system for Vitra (fig. 24, page 75), tried to socialise the open-plan office by

[10.]
Title of a workshop run by Naoto Fukasawa at NTT InterCommunication Center [ICC], 2002.

[11.]
Magistretti, V. In: Finessi, B. 2003. 'Vico Magistretti.' Mantova: Edizioni Corraini

Fig. 16   **Mayday lamp for Flos manufactured by Konstantin Grcic** Mayday borrows the functionality of the garage inspection lamp but civilises it for the domestic interior.

bringing employees together round long tables, rather than giving them individual desks. By providing mini-screens that slide onto the table, workers can still define an area as their own, but the topology clearly implies that each table of employees works as a team. The design punctured a long established pretence that open-plan workstations are self-contained mini-offices.

Much of our new behaviour is the result of new technology entering our lives. As new formats of audio, visual and telecommunications equipment emerge and as existing functions such as clocks and radios have become embedded in new products, where and how we use these products changes. We either learn new skills – such as text messaging – or we cut ourselves off from their benefits. As well as bringing new "tech products" to the market, this creates an opportunity for designers to work with the knock-on effects these have upon existing product types.

While tackling a brief to design a wall or mantle clock I attempted to address this opportunity. With the ubiquity of wristwatches and mobile telephones, wall and mantle clocks have lost their primacy as the sources of time we habitually consult. Consequently, when we are used to "having the time on us" constantly, we become more acutely aware when we do not. The bathroom is one such context in which we may be without a source of time yet be anxious to know it – as we ready ourselves to go out. Contrarily, when using the bathroom as a place for relaxation, we would likely shun a clock, reminding us, as it would, of things to do, of schedules and appointments. Rather than destroying the idea of a bathroom clock, the duality proved to be the making of it when considered alongside potential bathroom typologies that the clock may adopt. The

two-sided pedestal mirror with its flip-able surface provided the "hide" and "reveal" states needed – denoting whether time was of the essence or to be forgotten (fig. 25, page 75). By concealing the clock mechanism between the mirrors and using mirrored hands, the surfaces remain functional and the object sits unobtrusively in its surroundings.

Designing based upon direct observations of user behaviour rather than predictions has spawned a field in itself – design ethnography – where information on user behaviour is collected, to be fed back into the design process. This method is closely linked to the notion of social inclusion in design (see 2.5 Social inclusion) and has its roots in the way we tend to "work around" problems caused by badly designed products. An example used by international design firm IDEO shows a receptionist who, on being unable to connect callers on two separate telephones, simply holds the two handsets together so the earpiece of one touches the mouthpiece of other. Seeing such behaviour clearly points to a need for clearer systems design.

PERVERTING MANUFACTURING

Rather than working with already domesticated forms or "civilising" industrial ones, some designers have tried to transpose unrefined industrial forms directly into the home, relying upon our affection for them. William Warren and Carl Clerkin worked together to turn the classic "barn" toolbox into a bathroom cabinet, celebrating the economy of its folded metal construction and simultaneously increasing its sales value (as a toolbox it sold for under £10 (US$15) but as a bathroom cabinet it could fetch upwards of £60 (US$95)). By attaching its base to the wall with a mirror inside and reconfiguring its innards, the toolbox becomes particularly effective in its new

Fig. 17 / 18 Guggenheim Museum souvenir mug / **Guggenheim Museum** Rather than predictably emblazoning it with images and text, the Guggenheim Museum's souvenir mug subtly reflects the form of Frank Lloyd Wright's famous rotunda.

Fig. 19 Muji / CD player by Naoto Fukasawa The typology of a kitchen fan provided the perfect analogy for Naoto Fukasawa's wall-mounted CD player, the pull-chord acting as the "on" switch, play button and power lead.

KITSCH

Kitsch, design-historian Stephen Bayley tells us (in the catalogue to the 1983 exhibition, 'Taste', that he curated at the Victoria and Albert Museum) "comes from the German expression 'verkitschen etwas' (to knock something off) and is used to describe a design where the form and the meaning are inappropriate to the purpose; thus Leonardo's Last Supper done in pokerwork on a coat hook is Kitsch, as is an inkwell shaped like a human breast." (i)

Most kitsch is the result of individuals following their interests, untrammelled by certain design principles. The designer mixes populist forms and basic functions to create the desired result. The value judgement that to do so is "inappropriate" is based upon modernist doctrine. Such was the influence of modernism on design education that its intellectual framework became the yardstick against which design was judged. "Good design' on modernists' terms became considered "good taste" and hence kitsch was regarded "bad taste". When postmodern thinkers began to debunk this, an intellectual rationale for kitsch emerged and it began to gain a measure of respectability, not least as a tool for thumbing one's nose at a stuffy establishment.

To committed modernists like Bayley this was beyond the pale. In the 'Taste' catalogue, he implied that an increase in kitsch was an indication of moral decline, citing Hitler's liking for it as an example. (ii)

Since the 1980s, designers have mixed the emotional and poetic possibilities that emerged from postmodern theory with the common-sense aspects of modernism to establish broader boundaries for "appropriate" aesthetics. While the arbitrary nature of kitsch is still condemned, designers have learned from its playfulness. The black-and-white opposites of kitsch and modernism have been augmented by a third way where appropriate form can be defined via poetic as well as pragmatic relationships. Andrew Stafford's Swiss door wedge (see pages 78–79), is one such example. To a dyed-in-the-wool modernist, it will be kitsch – surrealism and modernism are unconventional bedfellows – but one cannot avoid the deliciously appropriate way in which its form and material relate to its function.

[i. ii.]
Bayley, S. 1983. 'Taste – An Exhibition about Values in Design.' London: Victoria & Albert Museum

Fig. 20
Plusminuszero / Sole bag by Naoto Fukasawa Based on the white plimsoll shoes worn by Japanese schoolchildren, Naoto Fukasawa's bag combines this nostalgic reference with the practical utility of a tote bag with a waterproof rubber base.

Fig. 21   **Daily Starting Block by Matali Crasset** This product enables people to brush their shoes as if rubbing them on the backs of their trouser legs. A cartoon drawing on the product indicates how to use it.

Fig. 22 Teo from 2 to 3, snoozing stool by Matali Crasset Legitimising the often-taboo practice of napping at work, this office stool unfurls into a mattress with accompanying "do not disturb" sign.

Fig. 23 When Jim comes to Paris, hospitality tower by Matali Crasset This "hospitality tower" contains a mattress, a lamp and an alarm clock, making house guests feel welcomed and providing them with a sense of autonomy.

Fig. 24   Joyn Office
System for Vitra by Ronan
and Erwan Bouroullec
Overturning years of
individualism in the open-plan
office, the Bouroullec's Joyn
system proposed that teams
should be grouped together
around long tables with slide-
on partitions demarcating
individual spaces only where
necessary.

Fig. 25   Mirror
Pedestal Clock by Tim
Parsons This design for a
bathroom clock responds to
the dual nature of the room
as a place for relaxation
and hurried preparation
for going out, by fitting
hands to a reversible mirror.
The time can be shown or
hidden depending upon the
circumstances.

mirror inside and reconfiguring its innards, the toolbox becomes particularly effective in its new guise (fig. 26, page 76). The pair also worked with a woodworking tools manufacturer on a range of kitchen products that highlighted associations between the two contexts. Prototypes included a meat tenderiser based on a wooden mallet (fig. 27, page 76) and a breadboard that references a carpentry mitre, aiding parallel slicing and 45-degree sandwich cutting. Warren explains: "The associations between the two contexts are important for me. The toolbox is for maintenance, after all, and the kitchen utensils are tools by another name." (12)

In both cases, Clerkin and Warren approached the manufacturers of the "donor objects" in the hope that the firms would be happy to diversify into new market areas, especially as the proposed designs used existing tooling and celebrated their core products. Sadly, in both cases neither company sparked. I was equally disappointed when attempting to interest a music-stand manufacturer in the results of my graduation project (fig. 28, page 77). The archetypal metal stands, with their telescoping tubes and three-legged base, had provided inspiration for a series of lamps, side tables and coat stands and a company already making similar products seemed an obvious choice as a potential collaborator; yet my proposition was met with a guarded, even suspicious, response. Warren had more success with his Sleeping Rough bed – an archetypal wooden park bench, extended to become a bed base (fig. 29, page 77). This he puts down to the company being prepared to see itself as a service provider rather than a manufacturer of "fixed" products – they even engraved the back of each bed to order, in place of the conventional dedications.

Yet, on reflection, it was somewhat naïve to assume that these creations should have been met with open arms. When an object is wrested by the designer into a new context, its expected purpose altered, those in charge of companies who have been making the objects for many decades are apt to be perplexed. Sticking to what they know and not being distracted by the whims of fad and fashion is exactly what has led their products to be revered as archetypes. The approach of "perverting manufacturing", as William Warren calls it, turns the normal (or "Super Normal") into the special, providing knowing references for those tuned in to appreciate them. Even when done sensitively, such shifts tend to remove these objects from their workaday roots, into the self-conscious world of the design store – an environment entirely alien to their anonymous creators and current producers. Unless a particularly enlightened industrialist is at the helm, this elegant "catch 22" situation will most likely preclude any interloping designer from playing context-shifting games in collaboration with the makers of these vernacular objects.

[12.]
Warren, W. 2008. [Personal communication]. 15 February

Fig. 26   High Maintenance bathroom cabinet by William Warren and Carl Clerkin By cleverly redesigning its interior, Warren and Clerkin transformed the "barn" toolbox into a fully functioning bathroom cabinet.

Fig. 27   Meat tenderiser from Domestic Tools collection by Carl Clerkin and William Warren This meat tenderiser is one of a number of products where the designers drew parallels between the nature and use of woodworking tools and kitchen utensils.

Fig. 28 Music stand products by Tim Parsons
The foldability, lightness and clinical appearance of metal music stands was transposed into products for the home, re-engineered for their heavier duty tasks. The set comprises a coat stand, uplighter and side table.

Fig. 29 Sleeping Rough bed by William Warren
Warren's bed makes use of the design and making skills of an existing park bench manufacturer while presenting a poignant new product.

INTRODUCING NARRATIVE

As we have seen, in their wish to celebrate existing archetypal objects, designers often give them new uses, either as ready-mades, or by co-opting details and manufacturing methods into new products. Most of the examples so far have been driven by the designer spotting practical advantages to appropriating these elements, although some, like Warren's 'Sleeping Rough' bed, hint at something more. As well as being up to the job, the borrowed form has a connection with its new use that sparks thoughts (in this case, surrounding those to whom a standard park bench is their bed). By carefully choosing where a form is borrowed from, and the use to which it will be put, witty or poetic connections can be made and simple stories told.

In another of Warren's designs he approached a Japanese glass-blowing workshop initially hoping to buy lopsided "seconds" of their standard wine glasses. On being told "Japanese craftsmen don't produce seconds", he proposed the blowers be plied with wine before making his batch. The resulting Drunk wine glasses are indeed askew, their form being a direct result of the story of their creation (fig. 30, page 78). A delightful (albeit forced) circle of connections is drawn between the method of creation, the object and its eventual use that, although benefiting from explanation, is nonetheless hinted at through the object's form. Reflecting this storytelling through objects, Warren's Japanese client Trico named an exhibition of his work Alternative Folk Design.

Another example of a designer wishing to reveal something of the story behind an object's manufacture is one of Richard Hutten's contributions to a project for cigar-box manufacturer Picus on behalf of Droog Design. Rather than altering the form of the cigar box to change its function, Hutten proposed that each of the craftspeople involved in its construction apply a specially-designed name stamp to the piece of the box they had produced (fig. 31, page 78). Once complete, the object speaks of the people involved in its creation, but without the mannered "hand of the maker" visible in some craftwork.

Instead of telling a story, Andrew Stafford's Swiss Door Wedge uses collective memory to introduce an amusing piece of surrealism into our everyday lives (fig. 32, page 37). There is a clear and well-observed link between the material (plastic), the form (like cheese) and the function (door wedge). Although hardly moving poetry, the Swiss Door Wedge is a piece of product punning that transcends kitsch due to its designer having a knowing reason for applying what would conventionally be seen as "inappropriate" design language. Our collective experience of cheese with the consistency of plastic and the correlation between the shape of a segment of cheese and a door wedge makes sense, as well as giving us a joke-shop double-take on first sight. It is a concise, if whimsical, illustration of how meaning can be applied successfully to a mundane domestic object.

This narrative in the object is not to be confused with narrative that might surround the object – the way in which products are explained in presentations by designers or subsequently through advertising. Objects for consumption (as opposed to those to be viewed in art galleries) that aspire to express a narrative must do so on their own, without the need for additional explanation. A "back story" might complement the narrative embedded within the object, but if it is to succeed, the object itself must be able to tell enough

Fig. 30 **Drunk wine glass by William Warren** Japanese glass blowers are plied with wine prior to them blowing Warren's wayward wine glasses.

Fig. 31 **Trace Box by Richard Hutten as part of Droog Design's Pocket Furniture Project for Picus** Each maker involved in the construction of Richard Hutten's Trace Box applies a name stamp, emphasising the object's hand-made status.

of its own story to engage us. There may be "loose connections" that we can join up and, if judged well, this can be more alluring than overly literal works where meaning is hammered home. The doorbell by Peter Van Der Jagt for Droog Design that is made from two upturned wine glasses is at first glance a peculiar object. Its "Heath Robinson" (13) quality contrasts dramatically with the little white box we have come to expect a doorbell to look like, but by inspecting it closely it begins to reveal itself to us. The hammer mounted between the wine glasses rings each one in turn. We can see the glasses are different sizes and will therefore make different notes – the familiar "ding dong" of someone at the door. But more than simply working to recreate this noise, the glasses work symbolically – representing entertainment – and remind us that perhaps whoever is visiting may like to come in for a drink.

DESIGN POETICS

Designers are becoming more attuned to the ways in which meaning can be expressed through product form. Some see the exploration of narrative in products as an essential new focus for areas of design that appear to have lost their way. Designers and academics Ralph Ball and Maxine Naylor, in their book 'Form Follows Idea' observe that the mainstream furniture and lighting markets have become largely self-referential and creatively bereft. Rather than continuing to frame the design of these objects in the same way, Ball and Naylor propose poetic design as a genuine injection of life: "If there are now fewer material and manufacturing problems to solve in the general arena of furniture and lighting design, then we must find forms of expression where structure and material resolution are taken as

given and the designed object as cultural information can be contemplated...It is important to re-establish visual contemplation and communication: to put the brakes on unreflective proliferation and superficial replication. It is time to provide critical, ironic and playful commentary on our condition and our cultures of consumption of both material and information. It is time to play and play seriously. It is time to put the poetry back into design." (14)

Ball and Naylor define poetic design as "objects which are elevated above the pragmatic and formal requirement of the functional artefact, and deliver ambient observations in condensed form for reflection and contemplation." (15) Source material for poetic design is best found, the pair say, in what they call "mature typologies" – types of objects where the basic layout of form has settled over decades or even centuries and is unlikely to change radically with the application of new technology or the whims of fad or fashion. Such objects have a familiarity that "allow[s] formal investigation and questioning of cultural values, consumption, mass marketing, aspirational branding, and so on to be explored directly through the visual information within and associated with the objects themselves." (16)

[13.]
W. Heath Robinson was an English cartoonist and illustrator who came to prominence in the first half of the twentieth century. He became known chiefly for his caricaturing of the age of the machine and the way this impacted upon human behaviour. The humour in his cartoons often emanated from his drawings of ridiculously complex devices designed to do the simplest of things and hence such contraptions have come to bear his name.

[14. 15. 16.]
Ball, R. and Naylor, M. 2005. 'Form Follows Idea: An Introduction to Design Poetics'. London: Black Dog

Fig. 32   **Swiss Door Wedge by Andrew Stafford**
Stafford's door wedge offers a piece of surrealism that draws on memories of "plastic cheese" cut into wedges.

Fig. 33 One day
I'll design the perfect paper
lightshade by Ralph Ball
Blind, misplaced toil is evoked
in Ralph Ball's ironic lamp in
which screwed-up lampshade
designs inadvertently create
the lampshade around a bulb
mounted in the bottom of a
wire waste-paper basket.

Fig. 34 Chip Chop
Slice and Serve chopping
board by Michael Marriott
A chopping and serving
platter, which doubles up
as a ping pong bat. Sold
with a ping pong ball.

Ball and Naylor's desire for objects to transcend their formal and functional requirements is gradually emerging from avant-garde circles and into the mainstream. Ball's own 'One day I'll design the perfect paper lightshade', manufactured by Ligne Roset, is an illuminated waste-paper basket full of screwed-up design sketches (fig. 33, page 80). Michael Marriott has been known to mix elements such as word play with well-judged material choices that tend towards the utilitarian. His Chip Chop Slice and Serve is a chopping board for serving in more ways than one, and his candlesticks come with a cast iron guarantee (fig. 34, page 80 and fig. 35, page 81). Ian Roberts's clipboard finds a humane use for the mechanism used to trap mice (fig. 36, page 81) and Arnout Visser's glassware highlights simple scientific principles in everyday objects (fig. 37, page 81).

Finally, other design practitioners who explore how poetic narrative may be derived, not from the appearance of the object alone but from the ideas our interactions with it inspire. Professor Anthony Dunne has campaigned through research and design work for greater engagement by designers with the aesthetics of use as opposed to the aesthetics of surface. His first book, 'Hertzian Tales', reveals the untapped potential electronic objects have for creating meaningful user experiences – both pleasant and disturbing – that could enrich our lives. Along with historical examples, Dunne includes some of his own proposals in collaboration with Fiona Raby, including one called Tuneable Cities, where the car radio, instead of picking up commercial stations, is programmed to react to local signals (fig. 38, page 81). Dunne proposed a number of possibilities this could raise; in one, migrating birds tagged by scientists transmitted or reflected radio signals, creating ambient soundscapes through the car radio that would be site-specific and unique, re-connecting the passengers with the outside world.

-        -

Fig. 35 Cast iron candlesticks by Michael Marriott Word play and material choice work together in these candlesticks that highlight the attractive qualities of cast iron.

Fig. 36 Mousetrap clipboard by Ian Roberts The attractive qualities of the mousetrap mechanism are safely applied for holding paper in this clipboard, one of a range of small batch-produced products with a shared visual language using familiar but context-shifted components.

Fig. 37 Archimedes letter scale by Arnout Visser Using the principle of water displacement, as the weight of the letter pushes the glass plunger down, the level rises and the weight can be read from the scale.

Fig. 38 Tuneable Cities by Dunne and Raby This project proposed various ways by which the car radio could connect its users more directly to the cityscape by making available "leaked" sound from baby-coms and new site-specific soundscapes generated by birds and speed trap radar.

SOCIAL INCLUSION

One criticism of the way industrial design was carried out in its early days, particularly in America, was that although generating desirable products, design activity was primarily client- rather than user-centred. One of the pioneers of the profession, Henry Dreyfuss, made a concerted effort to change this through his design methods and his work on anthropometrics (the study of the measurements of the human body). Dreyfuss published an extensive book on the subject in 1960 – 'The Measure of Man: Human Factors in Design' (later reprinted as the politically correct 'The Measure of Man and Woman', (fig. 1, page 82)). It featured measurements of the human body and their relationship to the designed environment along with drawings that became an invaluable source for designers, paving the way for the field of ergonomics. The rigorous adherence to human dimensions can be seen in products such as the Aeron Chair by Herman Miller (fig. 2, page 83), which is both highly adjustable and comes in a variety of sizes.

While Dreyfuss's work made it easier for designers to attune the dimensions of their objects to their users, it did not stop them from choosing not to cater for a wide range of body types and levels of ability. This section looks at attempts to question such practices and establish awareness of socially inclusive design – a process that first aims to avoid marginalising individuals and, where possible, consult them during the creative process to ensure that their needs are met.

TOWARDS USER-CENTRED THINKING

"Any analysis of the object – outside of anthropology and its more recent offspring, Material Culture Studies – has traditionally concentrated on the production of things by industry. This analysis has taken the form of market research, target sampling, advertising and statistics. Such a particular representation tries to identify gaps for the profitable manufacture of commodities, to effectively locate, isolate and eventually stimulate demand. Clearly this is a warped perspective: it may account for what, or how many things are in circulation, but it does not begin to offer any understanding of how they are actually used." (1)

The location of demand that writer and sculptor Neil Cummings talks of has traditionally been undertaken through research questionnaires that use Freudian tactics to press the buttons of our subconscious fears and anxieties, in the hope of revealing how these may be overcome with the appropriate consumer product. Such probing has many problems, not least because some questions will be based upon hypothetical new products of which the person interviewed has no actual experience. In addition, if they feel that the truth reflects badly upon them, people are prone to giving false answers, throwing researchers off course. These difficulties have, of course, long since been highlighted and new methods developed, but the real problem is in the kind of information being sought. More often than not it focuses upon the signs that products present in-store rather than investigating how or why the user might be using the products and whether or not they are effective. Once money has changed hands, the realities of "post-purchase" have been of dwindling

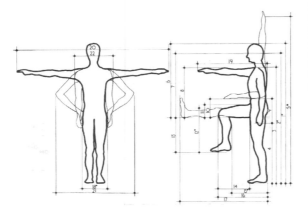

Fig. 1   Anthropo-metric drawing from the book Dreyfuss's book, and its successive editions, still provide useful reference material for designers wishing to check dimensions that relate to the human body.

interest to manufacturers, an example being fixed-length guarantees replacing repair services previously available for the life of products.

The more enlightened businesses are realising that a deeper, more sympathetic relationship with their customers can provide the inspiration for market-leading products and bolster a valuable commodity – "brand loyalty". An important part of this outlook is a change in how design is perceived by business. As Rama Gheerawo, Head of the Research Associate Programme at the Royal College of Art's Helen Hamlyn Centre explains: "If design is described as a purely aesthetic process, it makes for a one-dimensional relationship with business and society that weakens its effectiveness in both arenas. But if design is described as a way of thinking about and visualizing people's real needs and aspirations, it becomes a powerful tool for change." (2)

[1.]
Cummings, N. (ed.) 2003. 'Reading Things'. London: Chance Books

[2.]
Gheerawo, R. 2007. 'Vital Signs, Helen Hamlyn Research Associates Catalogue'. London: Royal College of Art

[3.]
Maslow, A.H. 1968. 'Toward a Psychology of Being'. New York: Van Nostrand Reinhold

[4.]
Lidwell, W., Holden, K., Butler, J. 2003. 'Universal Principles of Design'. Gloucester, MA: Rockport Publishers Inc.

PRIORITISING NEEDS

The most widely accepted attempt to categorise people's needs, not only in relation to design but to life itself, was made by American psychologist Abraham Maslow (3). His 'Hierarchy of Human Needs', typically illustrated as a triangle with five horizontal levels, proposes an order to our innate requirements exists, beginning at the bottom with the "physiological needs" such as air, food, water, sleep, stepping up through the "safety needs", such as security of body, property and employment; the "love needs" of intimacy and friendship; the "esteem needs" of achievement and respect and peaking at "self-actualisation" – a set of motivators rather than needs that drive humans towards fulfilling their potential. These include, among others, the desire to act morally, to be creative and to

solve problems. Maslow later added "cognitive needs" (experiencing knowledge) and "aesthetic needs" (experiencing beauty) to "self-actualisation".

In their book 'Universal Principles of Design' (4), authors Lidwell, Holden and Butler extrapolate Maslow's hierarchy into a model aimed at designers. Human need is considered in terms of what we require from our products. Just as Maslow's hierarchy implies, lower levels of need must be fulfilled before higher levels should be addressed and the same applies in the design model. Hence, functionality must be achieved first, followed by reliability, usability, proficiency and creativity (a level where all needs have been met and the user begins interacting with the product in their own way, for example through customisation).

By breaking down the elements requiring consideration in this way, it is possible to pinpoint where deficiency lies in genres of products or in specific objects. We can use the hierarchy to interrogate products, asking what level they have reached and what the next level suggests for their design. What Lidwell, Holden and Butler's model does not cover are the evocative and emotional elements of design. It also misses (perhaps intentionally) the obvious correlation between Maslow's aesthetic needs and the look of the product – often covered prematurely in design before more basic needs have been adequately fulfilled. Indeed, Maslow's "cognitive needs" may also have a place in a new model where the product can lead the user to the discovery of new knowledge. While a hierarchical model helps us avoid overlooking important essentials before becoming more ambitious, by continuing up, adding levels of achievement towards some kind of enlightenment through the object, we risk

Fig. 2 Aeron Chair by Bill Stumpf and Don Chadwick for Herman Miller On its release, the Aeron Chair was a tour-de-force of ergonomic design, being highly adjustable and available in different sizes.

Fig. 3 Wheel of options for product enhancement Rather than viewing the constituents to be considered in a product as a hierarchy, implying that all products are aspiring to the same ingredients, once fundamental aspects have been covered, it may be more useful to consider a wheel of further options that can enhance products in different ways.

overburdening products with unnecessary features that do not provide worthwhile benefit. In doing so, we can neglect the understated object that functions perfectly yet makes no claim to fame or high design. After the level of proficiency, a wheel of options could illustrate directions for enhancement (akin to Maslow's motivators), which broaden and deepen the human experience (fig. 3, page 83).

USABILITY

Useful though such models are, it remains for designers and their clients to decide, during the development process, when they consider they have fulfilled certain needs. This begs the question: to what standard have these needs been met, and on whose terms? With the rise of precise market targeting by client organisations, designers have often been channelled to think about the needs of a narrow band of, often young, fit consumers with 20/20 vision. Those who do not fit this model and find difficulties using products are either left high and dry or have to search out specialist products, although very few are actually available. Thanks to the work of many designers, researchers and campaigners, particularly in the USA, Scandinavia and the UK, there is now a growing awareness that products, services and experiences should be designed in such a way as to be enjoyed by a broad audience, regardless of age or ability.

Unlike disability language, which is black and white – you are either registered disabled or you are not – our capacity to use products is a graduated affair, ranging from a complete inability through ability with difficulties and frustrations, to relative or complete ease and pleasure. Society demographics show more of us than ever are living longer. As we experience the inevitable signs of ageing, there is an increasing market for products that maintain their ease of use in the face of our diminishing abilities.

While the need will always exist for products to help liberate those with specific disabilities (wheelchairs for example), by designing domestic consumer products for the mass market with less-able users in mind, they inadvertently cater for the supposedly able-bodied among us who might otherwise experience difficulties. Crucially, this approach allows less-able users access to products with a wide distribution that do not stigmatise them as "different". The Derby Kettle Tipper by Gordon Ellis Co. (fig. 4, page 84) is designed to aid those with low strength and coordination to pour hot water from their kettle. As a retrofit to work with existing kettles, it draws attention to the user's disability and would still require a carefully controlled pour to avoid spillage. In the face of this kind of ill-fitting solution, the thrust of inclusive design has been to turn the tables, and ask why mainstream design cannot change to accommodate a broader range of abilities. By re-orienting the product as a push-button dispenser (fig. 5, page 84) the kettle becomes easier and safer to use, as well as non-stigmatising. Similarly, Ben Wilson's design for a tricycle ingeniously incorporates pedal power by hand or foot, making it usable by a wide range of people with and without disabilities (fig. 6, page 85).

Two further examples show that considering marginalised users can produce mainstream successes. The enlarged buttons on the Big Button phones, designed by UK consultancy Alloy for British Telecom (fig. 7, page 86) would seem to single out its owners as being visually impaired, yet when polled, only 60

Fig. 4 Derby kettle tipper manufactured by Gordon Ellis & Co. **Home Healthcare Products** Companies such as Gordon Ellis produce products – such as this kettle tipper – specifically designed for older or disabled people. Although no doubt liberating for their users, products such as these often draw attention to the user's disability.

Fig. 5 Plusminuszero / Hot water dispenser by Naoto Fukasawa The act of pouring is eliminated in this hot water dispenser – an example of an inclusive design that does not stigmatise those with less strength and dexterity.

per cent said they had bought it for its accessibility features (5). The telephones in the range have numerous additional features to help the hard of hearing and visually impaired and have been a best seller for BT. Another popular case study looks at the OXO Good Grips ranges of kitchen utensils (fig. 8, page 86). After his wife developed arthritis and found the utensils on the market uncomfortable to use, Sam Farber looked into solving the problem himself. Together with Smart Design from New York, he developed the OXO Good Grips range. "The design incorporated plump, resilient handles for twist and push-pull tools like knives and peelers, while squeeze tools like can openers had hard handles. All handles were oval in cross section, to distribute forces on the hand and enhance grip, even for wet hands. The measuring cups and spoons featured large, high-contrast markings for visibility." (6) Since their launch, the products have been a hit with mainstream audiences and have picked up numerous design awards.

DISCOVERING INCLUSIVITY

The origins of the shift from designers targeting specific user groups to including as wide a range of potential user as possible have a number of different roots. In the United States, an almost evangelical movement emerged called Universal Design. It was formed by the convergence of two groups with similar goals: the researchers and producers of "assistive technology" – products designed to help disabled people function more independently, – and the Disability Rights and related Barrier Free movements of the 1950s and 1960s, which achieved legislative change regarding access to buildings. This later broadened to force manufacturers of business equipment not to marginalise older and disabled users. Presented as a

set of seven principles in 1997 by North Carolina State University's Center for Universal Design, its prescriptive nature has drawn criticism. However, its legislative achievements are to be applauded according to Roger Coleman, Professor of Inclusive Design at the Royal College of Art in London, and are favourable to leaving the market to its own devices.

"American Federal legislation obliges suppliers to meet accessibility criteria. The logic is simple in that if we have to be able to employ people of all abilities, so we have to have kit they can use. If you set performance requirements that are genuine then you leave industry to meet them, industry can compete to produce good designs. If you don't have that and you say it's got to be the cheapest, there's no incentive to improve the design. My belief is that the place for political effort is in putting in place the legislation that creates a level playing field for competition." (7)

In the UK, where it is known as inclusive design, The Helen Hamlyn Centre based at London's Royal College of Art has been at the forefront of research, practice and dissemination of knowledge on the subject. Coleman, a lynchpin in the centre since its inception, explains how the government structure in the UK has not benefited inclusive design: "In the UK, we lack a social cost accounting that allows one bit of government to be equated to another, so if you spent more money on providing housing that encouraged independent living, then you may need to spend less elsewhere on taking people out of their homes and into care environments. There's no proper cost benefit analysis guiding policy. If we had a government legislative and guidance framework, this would create the foundations of a market for inclusive design." (8)

[5.] -
'University of Cambridge Engineering Design Centre website'. 2005 [online]. [Accessed 27th January 2009]. Available from World Wide Web: <www.eng.cam.ac.uk/inclusivedesign>

[6.] -
'North Carolina State University, Center for Universal Design website'. 2008 [online]. [Accessed 27th January 2009]. Available from World Wide Web: <www.design.ncsu.edu/cud/projserv_ps/projects/case_studies/oxo.htm>

[7. 8.] -
Coleman, R. 2007. [Personal communication]. 10 December

Fig. 6 **Tilting trike** Rather than modifying a typical tricycle for those with restricted lower body movement, Ben Wilson created a new layout equally usable if pedalling with hands or feet, steered by leaning.

Fig. 7   BT Big
Button phone designed by
Alloy BT's Big Button phone
is known to have appealed
to users who did not need
its accessibility features.

Fig. 8   OXO Good
Grips kitchen products One
of a number of kitchen tools
manufactured under the OXO
Good Grips brand developed
with arthritis sufferers in mind,
but resulting in products that
the majority of customers find
comfortable to use.

Fig. 9   Gofer
electric screwdriver by
Matthew White manufactured
by B&Q Designed during a
Helen Hamlyn Centre research
associateship, the Gofer and
the Sandbug addressed the
needs of older users and
those with reduced grip.

By way of example, he flags up Sweden's impressive record, whereby the welfare system funded research and development into products for the disabled. This in turn seeded a culture of quality inclusive design led by influential consultancy Ergonomidesign.

TOOLS FOR INCLUSIVE DESIGN

In the design of domestic products as opposed to medical or business equipment, legislation is harder to achieve. Therefore, the focus has become the level of awareness of inclusive design principles among designers in business. Educational establishments have recognised the role that they can play in ensuring such awareness exists among their graduates. As well as engaging students in competitions, running graduate design research projects with live clients (fig. 9, page 86 and fig. 10, page 87) and conducting its own research, the team at the RCA's Helen Hamlyn Centre have developed tools to help designers and businesses adopt inclusive design practices. The Inclusive Design Toolkit (9) developed with British Telecom, and the Design Council's online resource (10) were followed in 2005 by the publication of the first British Standard on Inclusive Design (BS7000-6). Although not mandatory, the document provides businesses with practical guidance on managing inclusive design, from organisational level down to project level.

BT's online Inclusive Design Toolkit sets out a clear and detailed inclusive design process. It has four stages, each producing a specific output. These are described using a waterfall diagram (fig. 11, page 88). The first stage, "Discover", begins with the perceived needs, described as the impetus for the project, which may not necessarily include any altruistic goals and could simply be to increase turnover. This stage involves research of these needs in relation to the individual

stakeholders involved (the end users, purchaser, retailer, manufacturer and so on). The result should be a full picture of the real needs of the project. The second stage, "Translate", generates a "requirements specification" for the product from these needs. This sets constraints but ought not to "lead" designers by implying solutions, instead remaining objective and matter of fact. The third phase, "Create", is where design work begins. The toolkit suggests working in teams with thinking tools such as brainstorming (see page 173) in order to capture a broad range of ideas before filtering and ranking them. Potential users of differing abilities can also be involved at this stage where initial concepts are tested. Finally, once concepts have been firmed up and trialled, the "Develop" phase delivers the solution, verifying it against the initial requirements specification and its ability to fulfil real needs based upon actual evidence of use.

The online toolkit, available to all for reference, helps students as well as professionals check the rigour of their development process against inclusive design principles. Naturally, such a process has time and cost implications. If designers wish to create an inclusive product they can either rely upon their predictive skills to empathise with users of varying abilities, or they can seek out such users for first-hand consultation. Some advocates of the inclusive design methods will say that the latter is essential, although in reality each project must be assessed individually based on its own context. The more complex the product, and the further away from the designer's own experience, the more important it is to conduct (or obtain) research into its usability. It is no surprise, therefore, that those involved in designing interactions with computers have been at the forefront of developing user research methods.

[9.]
'Inclusive Design Toolkit'. 2007–2008 [online]. [Accessed 27th January 2009]. Available from World Wide Web: <www.inclusivedesigntoolkit.com>

[10.]
'Inclusive Design Education Resource'. [online]. [Accessed 27th January 2009]. Available from World Wide Web: <www.designcouncil.info/inclusivedesignresource>

Fig. 10 Sandbug electric sander by Matthew White manufactured by B&Q
Designed during a Helen Hamlyn Centre research associateship, the Gofer and the Sandbug addressed the needs of older users and those with reduced grip.

[11.]
Poynor, R. 2008. Video
Ethnography. 'Icon Magazine'.
May

[12.]
Norman, D. 1999. 'The Method
Lab'. Published by the Design
for Ageing Network (DAN),
London: Royal College of Art

[13.]
Gaver, W. 1999. 'The Method
Lab.' Published by the Design
for Ageing Network (DAN),
London: Royal College of Art

[14.]
Myerson, J. 2007. [Personal
communication]. 3 December

USER CONSULTATION

Looking broadly at the issue of user consultation, it is possible to imagine a spectrum of user involvement in the design process that stretches from:

a)   the designer not considering the user at all, through

b)   the awareness of needs and user research that characterise inclusive design, and continuing through

c)   models where the user is not only consulted by the designer, but is also physically engaged in configuring, making and eventually designing the product themselves. (Approaches under c) are covered on pages 182–185.)

In place of user insights, designers make design decisions based upon their own values, experiences and culture, according to the conditions of the project. User research methods, many of which borrow from ethnography (a type of field research used in anthropology, the study of human culture), attempt to suspend judgment of needs until observation of user behaviour has been undertaken. Design ethnography has emerged as a field in itself and some design consultancies now employ researchers to gather and sell packages of user research to clients. This aims to reveal evidence of consumer attitudes and activities that will shape the design brief. Aware that "research" can sound dry and statistical, the allure of "getting closer to the customer" is invoked. Video is commonly used to record research subjects as they go about their day-to-day activities. However, such methods have come under fire due to the hidden power relationship involved (11): despite commonly being undertaken for altruistic reasons (to tune products to users' needs), such research evidence can also be tapped to uncover new forms of persuasion that the corporate voyeur may then use to sell us particular goods and services.

Without access to user research data collected on their behalf, designers who choose to collect their own rarely have the luxury of time. As a consequence, they have to adapt scientific methods to fit their schedule. As cognitive scientist Donald Norman points out: "Methodologies in cognitive science, psychology, anthropology and sociology may be approximated so they can be used with speed by designers who do not need scientific precision. Answers can be approximate. They don't have to be precise. The benefit of many fast answers far outweighs any deficits." (12)

Before consulting users, design teams can undertake various activities that generate, pool and structure their predictions and insights into user behaviour. Discussing, sketching and storyboarding scenarios (featuring stories around the use of objects) can be taken further by role-playing. Props and sets can be built to help designers place themselves in the context of the users, while physical disabilities can be modelled with objects that intentionally make tasks harder, an example being frosted spectacles used to simulate visual impairment. These often quickly assembled, "ad hoc" creations help designers to empathise with users and draw out problems and solutions that may otherwise have remained invisible. Design consultancy IDEO, who pioneered many of the user research methods covered here, call this role-playing to generate ideas "bodystorming", and the use of

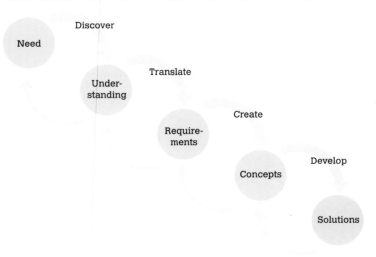

Fig. 11   Waterfall diagram of inclusive design process This diagram explaining the stages in the inclusive design process is part of the Inclusive Design Toolkit commissioned by British Telecommunications PLC as part of their Corporate Social Responsibility programme.

props and settings "experience prototyping". They have also used role play as performance to illustrate usability issues to their clients.

Within the realm of user research, techniques are many and varied. These differ in formality, depth and focus; some being aimed more towards collecting information on existing behaviour, while others are about testing new product concepts. Methods include individual interviews, short observations of tasks or shadowing over a longer period. User forums and focus groups are convened to discuss existing or forthcoming products and services, and prototypes are introduced to these sessions for feedback and user testing.

An experimental user research technique for application at the front-end of projects, called a "cultural probe", is also developing in popularity. Conceived for a project about increasing the presence of older people in their community, its designer William Gaver explains: "The cultural probes were packages of maps, postcards, cameras and other items given to elders in local test sites for their responses…we purposely left our requests vague, ambiguous and even absurd in order to evoke free and imaginative responses from the groups. The probes broke with scientific methodologies, instead pursuing a design approach seeking inspiration not information." (13)

Looking at various methods of user consultation in brief, as we are doing here, does not allow us to cover the guidelines of their use that may be vital to collecting the appropriate information. Like the market research techniques that came before them, it is important that consultations are carried out as neutrally as possible so as to avoid biasing the results. Those wishing to work with users in a structured rather than organic manner are recommended to study the techniques in more depth.

THE BOUNDARIES OF INCLUSIVE DESIGN

Although occasionally presented as such, the inclusive design process need not be linear and rigid. "'People-centred' is the touchstone for me", says Jeremy Myerson, Helen Hamlyn Centre Director: "there has to be some engagement with real people. Whether you have user groups, observations, you show them prototypes, you shadow them, give them diaries to fill in. As long as you have consulted users somewhere along the line…Hardcore inclusive design people think that you should talk to users and they should hold your hand all the way through the process. I'm of the view that there are periods when you need to rely upon your own creative autonomy. You need to speak and find your own voice as a designer." (14)

As Jeremy Myerson suggests, the process requires a balance between consultation and creation. While impossible literally to separate, the stylistic aspects of a design need not undergo the kinds of consultation discussed here for aspects of usability. In fact, most designers interviewed for this book believed that user consultation on matters of style ought not to be encouraged and represented manufacturers' desire for assurance of future sales rather than the search for genuine improvement. It was felt that focus groups concentrating upon appearance were essentially false environments because remarks would be prompted from participants on products that, if well designed, may not warrant comment in daily use.

As an area of design that attempts to redress social inequalities, inclusive design excites passionate support from those who practise it. Discovering it for the first

Fig. 13   **LTI TX1 London taxi** The TX range of vehicles developed by London Taxis International has been innovative in the field of accessible transport design. The current TX4 model includes features such as an integrated wheelchair ramp, highly visible grab handles and an improved driver intercom.

Fig. 14   **Electricwig Zoetropes for Billinghay** As part of a regeneration project that included redesigning public spaces and furniture, the designers installed a series of zoetropes (nineteenth-century optical toys consisting of a cylinder with a series of pictures on the inner surfaces that, when viewed through slits with the cylinder rotating, give an impression of continuous motion) depicting stories relating to the village. Signposts with intriguing names directed the public between them.

time, designers may be forgiven for mistaking this passion for a belief that the inclusive design process should be applied to all projects. But this is not the case. In sectors where style and identity come higher up consumers' priorities than use, designing for the old (or attempting an "inclusive style") is more than likely to at least alienate, if not exclude, the young.

Rather than being seen as an inseparable set of linear processes, the tools of inclusive design – the gathering of empirical evidence from users, working with them during development and satisfying the needs of as many abilities of people as possible – are to be added to the designer's traditional, intuitive, studio-based design practices. Each is there to be used as and when appropriate, governed by the context of individual projects.

DIRECTIONS FOR SOCIALLY RESPONSIBLE DESIGN

Despite the tools available and the various publications and conferences encouraging it, the inclusive design message can still be hard to sell to business clients. As a result, some designers have turned their attention to the public sector, where a socially minded outlook is intrinsic to clients' activities. As well as government-sponsored initiatives in schools, designers have found niches working with health service providers to ensure patient safety and on broadening access to transport (fig. 13, page 89). Others, such as design company Electricwig, have found work with local authorities, helping to regenerate public spaces by applying solid design thinking to seating, lighting and other designed elements. Their commission for Billinghay in Lincolnshire, UK, included public consultations that identified areas where people wanted to congregate.

This led to new installations of seating and the reclaiming of a public square previously cut off by roads. The designed elements include a series of zoetropes telling stories relating to the village, and fencing, which became a recognisable motif and upon which the public furniture was based (fig. 14, page 89). A more recent project, also by Electricwig in neighbouring Metheringham, began with a design workshop in which villagers explored how public furniture might enjoy a mutually beneficial relationship with plants (fig. 15, page 90).

Another method of ensuring an audience for socially responsible design is to focus attention on the developing world. By looking at the notion of inclusivity on a global scale, the most urgent challenge is to help those without access to the most basic standards of living. There is clearly a role for creative thinking in helping people to improve access to food, water, shelter, sanitation, healthcare, transportation etc but there is also a need for sensitivity. Encouraged by websites such as www.worldchanging.com and exhibitions such as Design for the Other 90% (fig. 16, page 90) at the Cooper Hewitt National Design Museum in New York, an increasing number of designers are turning their skills to helping those less fortunate than themselves. However, rushing in with product-based solutions can be hugely patronising. Developing world communities hardly lack creativity; it is everywhere in their improvised answers to everyday problems, realised with great economy of means. Even when product solutions help, the designer or entrepreneur needs to be aware of the social, economic and political fabric of the communities they aim to help or much

Fig. 15 Literature from workshop on Growing Furniture by Electricwig Public consultation merged with collaborative design when Electricwig conducted a workshop with the people of Metheringham on the subject of the coexistence of plants and furniture as the lead in to a public seating commission.

Fig. 16 Lifestraw designed and manufactured by the Vestergaard Frandsen Group Lifestraw is a portable water purifier that requires no external power and kills 99.999 per cent of waterborne bacteria. It was featured on the cover of the catalogue of the exhibition Design for the Other 90%.

development can be compromised. Pieter Hendrikse, designer of the much publicised Q Drum water roller (fig. 17, page 91), concedes that "it is still unaffordable to most people – those who need it cannot afford it and those who can, do not need it." (15)

Although many such products improve the lives of those living in poverty, they do so with charitable funding. Instead, affordable and empowering solutions are required.

The statistic that gave the name to the Cooper Hewitt exhibition is quoted in its catalogue by Dr Paul Polak: "Ninety-five percent of the world's designers focus all of their efforts on developing products and services exclusively for the richest ten percent of the world's consumers. Nothing less than a revolution in design is needed to reach the other ninety percent." (16) His conclusion as to why – designing for the rich is where the money is – overlooks the fact that the majority of designers who wish to help developing communities feel incapable of doing so. Although many of the projects within Design for the Other 90% come from an initial piece of lateral thinking (fig. 18, page 91), the real effort has come in financing, engineering and producing the products. These are all roles in which the designer – particularly one trained in the nuances of style – may be left wanting. If designers are to be useful in these conditions they must be all-rounders, prepared to step outside of their usual remit to play the part of social entrepreneur and project manager, as well as social and cultural anthropologist.

Prior to the spread of inclusive design thinking, many more product designers tended to generalise about people than do so today. Recognition of differences in ability has grown and has led to products that have genuinely improved people's lives. The language of inclusive design – as described in this section – tends to focus upon 'users'. While perhaps an improvement upon 'consumers', it is still a less-than-rounded descriptor for individual people who choose to buy products, and one that concentrates attention upon their physical abilities rather than their psychological needs and desires. The next phase of inclusion, if there is to be one, can address this by doing more to consider our complexities as freethinking individuals.

[15.] Hendrikse, P. 2007. 'Design for the Other 90%'. New York: Cooper Hewitt National Design Museum

[16.] Polak, Dr P. 2007. 'Design for the Other 90%'. New York: Cooper Hewitt National Design Museum

Fig. 17 Q Drum water roller by Pieter Hendrikse manufactured by Q Drum Ltd Although a highly ingenious solution to ease the physical burden of transporting water, the Q Drum cannot at present be manufactured cheaply enough to allow those who need it most to purchase it, making it an object of charity.

Fig. 18 PlayPump water systems by Trevor Field manufactured by PlayPumps International. Solutions such as this merry-go-round that harnesses the energy of play to pump water are imaginative, but nonetheless require the right context and backing to be truly effective.

MATERIALS AND PROCESSES

All designers necessarily have a relationship with materials – they think in materials when drawing, considering their properties in relation to the forms on the page. However, some make a particular effort to deepen this relationship. Through experimentation and testing of materials, designers discover their limits and enduring properties and become aware of suitable applications for them. New materials are often the catalysts that produce new technologies – the discovery of various substrates that could be written upon and played back created the opportunity for recording technologies (such as vinyl records, audio cassettes and compact discs). Yet when examining the motivation of designers, it is clear that there are different approaches to materials and technologies: those who pursue solutions through a deep understanding of existing materials and processes, and those who turn automatically to new technology. This section and the next look at why materials, processes and technologies are harnessed in particular ways by today's designers.

ASPIRATIONAL MATERIAL QUALITIES

The value we place on materials, properties and their manufacturing processes is determined not just by their intrinsic engineering, tactile and visual qualities but by the cultural associations they hold. Today it is not uncommon to find those who wistfully marvel at the signs of hand work in a thrown pot, but are unmoved by the precision of industrial ceramic powder pressing, a method by which inexpensive crockery is manufactured. Yet prior to the industrialisation that brought us such techniques, the traces of the maker's hand would have been commonplace. How that was manifested would have depended upon the kinds of objects we could afford.

Affluent "bourgeois" society, able to indulge in the collection of objects beyond the utilitarian, typically sets its aspirations of material qualities in contrast to those available to "the masses". When all goods were handmade, the bourgeoisie aspired to the skill of the finest makers who worked with precision and often embellished objects with decoration. Such detail distinguished their work from the "quick and dirty" efforts of volume makers, who had to balance speed and accuracy to produce sufficient quantities to earn their living. Ironically, the qualities once produced by these makers for the masses (such as the finger marks in the clay) are now among those sought after among today's aspirant society. This has come about because the mass production techniques that replaced the handmade as the way of making utilitarian objects reached a precision that matched the skill of some fine makers. While craft skill that displays machine-like precision is still sought and revered by those in the know and those who are prepared to pay for it, it has been devalued in the eyes of those who wish certain objects to show obvious differentiation from mass production. Hence, what was once considered crude becomes the bourgeois currency by which to show the ability to afford the craftsman's art.

The label "handmade" has become a strategic marketing tool, lending cachet to specific objects where handwork is considered superior. At the Bentley motorcar factory in Crewe, UK, an uncommon mix of the machine made and the handcrafted coexist in one product. The majority of the vehicle is made, like any

Fig. 1 "Proposta per la Lavorazione a Mano della Porcellana" Samos series (prog. 1122) by Enzo Mari, initially manufactured by Danese (1973), reissued by Alessi (1997) Rather than simply being about learning and illustrating material qualities, Samos encouraged reflection upon the nature of repetitive work, whether "craft" or "industry".

Fig. 2 Models from the project "Proposta per un" Autoprogettazione di Mobili' (prog. 1123) by Enzo Mari A series of configurations for furniture to be made by the public from standard sizes of rough-sawn timber and nails.

other, with the tools of mass production, yet specific interior components are "handcrafted". Leather is cut on a computer-controlled machine but is then handstitched by an army of seamstresses. Walnut veneers are bonded to aluminium sheet and placed in hydraulic presses to form dashboards, but where the veneers split, a team of artists painstakingly fill and repaint the wood grain. Components can be genuinely labelled "hand finished", but such activity begs the question: has all the effort genuinely produced a higher quality result than could be achieved with automation, or is handcraftsmanship being maintained simply to pander to out-dated cultural values?

MATERIAL AND PROCESS EXPLORATION

Observing the way that materials and processes have been used is an essential part of design education and over time creates an intuitive sense of what can effectively be applied in a given situation. Without needing to test them directly, designers know that certain materials, processed in certain ways, will have the necessary properties to do the job they are asking of them because they have seen them employed successfully in similar situations elsewhere. While teachable by rote, this material and process sensibility is best learned through hands-on experience. Hence, most three-dimensional design degree courses still follow the Bauhaus approach of investigating a range of materials to discover their advantages. This speculative, practical activity of playing and observing properties is a design method that can be honed to create products that make highly efficient and appropriate use of materials and production processes.

Beyond their formal education, many leading designers have undertaken such research, confining themselves to one material or process at a time to discover in detail the possibilities offered by each. Frenchman Jean Prouvé trained as a blacksmith before establishing a metal fabrication business that went on to produce furniture and prefabricated buildings. Prouvé's relentless experimentation led him to pioneer the use of aluminium in architecture. He argued that the root of creativity came from the application of theories and not academic knowledge alone, and was critical of architects who worked on unproven visions of the future. Italian Enzo Mari conducted a series of projects from the 1950s onwards, which focused upon using single materials and processes to make vessels. These included the use of welded steel sections from the construction industry, solid marble, porcelain and PVC tubing (fig. 1, page 93). In another project, Autoprogettazione (roughly translating as "self-design"), he used planks of timber in standard sizes available at hardware stores to construct items of furniture for the home, publishing plans of how to make them in a book (fig. 2, page 93).

This strategy of using materials in individual discrete units, like Lego, allows quick and intuitive investigation, but in order to explore a material fully, designers need to appreciate all of the possible ways in which it can be manipulated. In a press release for an exhibition in Milan in 2000, Ron Arad succinctly categorised these:

"In a slightly tongue-in-cheek press release for 'Not Made By Hand, Not Made In China' …I claimed that until recently there had been only four ways of making things. The process of making any object could be broken down into one or more of the following steps: Waste (chip, carve, turn, mill, chisel – the removal

Fig. 3 **Inflatable pendant lamp designed and manufactured by Inflate**
Inflate explored the process of high-frequency welding of PVC and subsequently manufactured a dizzying array of inflatable products.

[1.]
Arad, R. In: Fiell, C. and Fiell,
P. 2001. 'Designing the 21st
Century'. Colgne: Taschen

of excess material, for example), Mould (injection moulding, casting, rotation moulding, extruding – pouring liquid material to take the form of its vessel when hardened, for example); Form (bending, pressing, hammering, folding, vacuum forming – forcing sheet material into a shape, for example); Assemble (bolting, glueing, riveting, soldering, welding – joining parts together by any means, for example) and, I went on to claim, there is now a fifth way – Grow. An object can be grown in a tank, layer by layer, by computer-controlled laser beams [stereo-lithography]. Now I think all this can be reduced further – an object can be made by either adding or subtracting. Computers, with their zeros and ones, love it. With CNC (Computer Numeric Control), RP (Rapid Prototyping), GM materials and a little help from robotic friends, virtual can easily become actual; an image on screen rapidly transforms to a solid mass. Anything can be drawn, modelled and made." (1)

Although Arad used this description to illustrate how current technologies were changing the making process, his words powerfully rationalise the many processes available in a way that helps a structured investigation of each. Some such experimentation is done by designers simply to further their own knowledge, but in other cases it is undertaken as part of client projects to search for new directions for a particular material or process. After setting up the company Inflate, Nick Crosbie and his colleagues explored the possibilities of using the high-frequency welding of PVC sheet – the process used in making inflatables – for domestic products (fig. 3, page 94). Once they had exhausted this, they moved on to another process – dip moulding – whereby a steel tool is dipped into liquid PVC before being cured in an oven. By sticking to one process, Crosbie and his colleagues were able to master its idiosyncrasies and understand these as constraints. With dip moulding these included the fact that a small teat of material – the last undripped drip – formed on each product once dipped. Michael Marriott made use of this in his Dip Vase by push-fitting it into a hole in a piece of wood, forming the base of the vase, and providing an attractive contrast in materials (fig. 4, page 95).

Likewise, when Konstantin Grcic began working with glassware company Iittala, he took a tour of their factory before designing anything, and became fascinated by a particular piece of glass-pressing equipment. His resulting work for the Relations range innovatively used this machine to create durable and elegant stacking glassware (fig. 5, page 95) that solved the common problem of glasses wedging together and

Fig. 4 **Dip Vase by Michael Marriott manufactured by Inflate** Marriott's vase is made using a steel tool that develops a removable skin when dipped into liquid PVC and cured in an oven. The last drip is used as a means of fixing the vase to its wooden base.

Fig. 5 **Relations range of glassware by Konstantin Grcic manufactured by Iittala** On discovering a machine in Iittala's factory that could press glasses with changing wall thicknesses, Grcic used this as a feature of his Relations range, primarily using it to avoid the glasses wedging together.

cracking. Such an approach of identifying and being creative with the intrinsic properties of materials and processes already in use by client manufacturers shows a willingness to work in sympathetic partnership with industry, rather than imposing forms that require new technologies or machinery. To do so, designers must invest time and energy not only in their own experimentation, but also in learning from the technicians who work every day on the factory floor and who understand in detail what can be achieved. By posing sometimes naïve questions and responding to the answers, constraints emerge that guide the creative process.

Another approach taken to material-led projects is to begin with existing processes and subvert or re-work them in a new context. German design duo Vogt & Weizenegger brought selected European designers together with the workshops of the Institute for the Blind in Berlin to design new products that made use of their core skills of brush making and wicker work (fig. 6, page 96 and fig. 7, page 97). The resulting designs intentionally brought the material qualities of brushes and wicker to objects that would not normally contain them – brushes as egg cups, CD racks and ring boxes; wicker in coat hangers, radio casings and lampshades. Marrying another traditional method – macramé – with modern composite materials technology, Marcel Wanders created the Knotted Chair (fig. 8, page 98). A macramé surface is made from carbon fibre and aramid rope (a synthetic polymer), which is then hung on a frame and dipped in resin. As the rope becomes impregnated, it forms a strong composite material. Once dry, the rope is solid, forming a very light (although not especially comfortable) chair.

As an experiment in chair making, Wanders's design is intriguing, yet in production it is time-consuming and therefore expensive. Similarly, the Favela Chair by Fernando and Humberto Campana (fig. 9, page 98) presents an unusual and engaging aesthetic, its surface clad in off-cuts from the workshop floor. But once put into production, as it has been by manufacturer Edra, its concept is compromised when this cladding is no longer likely to be made from waste but rather cut specifically for the task. The validity of using each process is therefore related to the volume of products it is intended to serve.

The quality of particular materials has been the focus of many designs whose primary result has been to create spectacle. The approach of using familiar materials on a grand scale, such as Tokujin Yoshioka's installations of transparent straws (fig. 10, page 99), forming cloud-like walls, is an often-repeated strategy in window display, less common in product design. Reversing the method, other designers have applied strange and exotic materials to familiar forms. Tomáš Gabzdil Libertiny managed to produce his Honeycomb Vase by encouraging bees to make a hive within vase-shaped scaffolds (fig. 11, page 99).

Fig. 6 **Brushanger by Tim Parsons** One of the designs resulting from the project Die Imaginäre Manufaktur (The Imaginary Manufacture) organised by designers Oliver Vogt and Hermann Weizenegger for the Berlin Institute for the Blind.

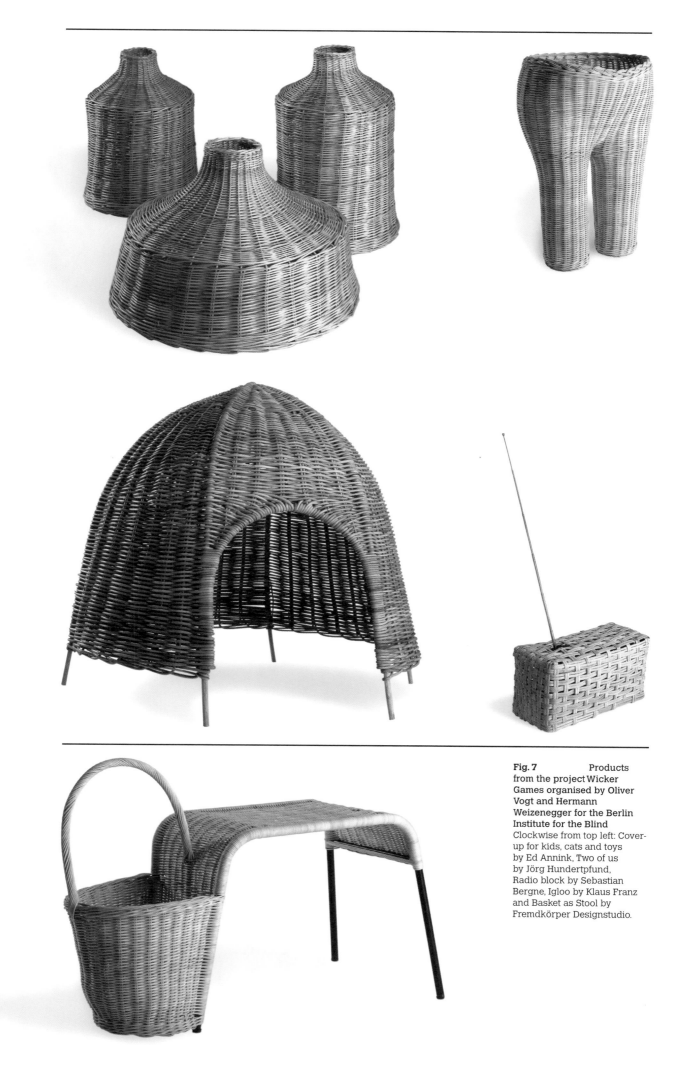

Fig. 7 Products from the project Wicker Games organised by Oliver Vogt and Hermann Weizenegger for the Berlin Institute for the Blind Clockwise from top left: Cover-up for kids, cats and toys by Ed Annink, Two of us by Jörg Hundertpfund, Radio block by Sebastian Bergne, Igloo by Klaus Franz and Basket as Stool by Fremdkörper Designstudio.

Fig. 8   Knotted
Chair by Marcel Wanders,
manufactured by Droog
Design Wanders allies high-
tech materials associated
with the aeronautics industry
with traditional macramé
weaving techniques to create
an entirely new way of
constructing a chair.

Fig. 9   Favela Chair
by Fernando and Humberto
Campana manufactured by
Edra The Campanas' Favela
chair uses unwanted off-cuts
of wood as an economical
decoration. Mass-producing
the chair presents the dilemma
of sourcing a large quantity of
off-cuts or compromising the
idea by cutting pieces afresh.

NEW MATERIALS

It is just as much the responsibility of designers to be aware of new developments in materials as it is for them to have knowledge of those commonly in use. Without this knowledge, they may overlook the most appropriate material for a particular task. Designers have often been called upon to promote new materials to show their potential. Associations who look after the interests of those who produce both new and well-established materials are in the business of engaging designers in promoting their use through competitions and showcase projects. Yet by attempting to espouse the virtues of any materials, it is tempting to be drawn into generalisations that are not always helpful. Carbon fibre may be incredibly rigid in relation to its weight but its appropriateness to a task requiring these properties will be determined by many other factors (such as cost, availability of production facilities and cultural associations of the material in relation to the object it is being used for). Such high-performance materials can even perform beyond required limits, an example being the lightness of the Light Light chair in carbon fibre by Alberto Meda (fig. 12, page 100).

We must guard against being seduced by the idea of new materials alone. In a field where media exposure can generate business, products designed in new materials create good copy. Instead, we must look critically at such projects to determine to what extent the new materials improve upon what was previously possible. What tangible progress do they offer or is credit being given only to their novelty?

In order clearly to see examples of genuine advancements through new materials and processes, it helps if we confine our research to one single object

type and examine changes to its standard design over many years. The cafe/public hall chair is a favoured typology upon which designers enjoy experimenting. It offers a tough challenge – as Mies van der Rohe apparently commented; it is perhaps harder than designing a building. Like type design for graphic designers, it comes with an enormous weight of historical precedent that both inspires and exhausts, through the realisation that so much has already been tried. New materials offer a fresh route: the challenge of marrying their specific properties to the complex and contradictory criteria the chair presents; strength with lightness, rigidity with comfort, durability with affordability.

Through a variety of texts and exhibitions, historians and designers have settled upon an accepted lineage of the most respected examples of advancement in chair design. 'Although we could start earlier, the first chair clearly to reassess traditional construction methods was Michael Thonet's work in steam-bent wood. Struck with the problem that curved wooden elements became weakened as they strayed from the straight grain (traditionally solved by cutting and glueing together small pieces so the grain followed the curve), Thonet experimented with laminating veneers and thin rods. However, the glue failed under high humidity. The solution was to use solid timber treated with steam to make the fibres temporarily pliable. Lengths could then be clamped into cast-iron moulds and once dried would hold their curved form, with the grain running around the curve. This innovation made fast, efficient production possible, removing time-consuming carving processes and enabled Thonet to become one of the first mass producers of wooden furniture. The most successful chair made using these techniques was Number 14 (fig. 13, page 100), made from just six

[2.]
von Vegesack, A. 1996. 'Thonet: Classic Furniture in Bent Wood and Tubular Steel'. London: Hazar Publishing Ltd

Fig. 10 **Installation of plastic straws by Tokujin Yoshioka at the Super Fiber Revolution exhibition** Tokujin Yoshioka has built a number of installations in which elements such as plastic straws are used in multiples of many hundreds of thousands. As such, they take on a new and intriguing form, in this case, being malleable as a new material with behaviour all of its own.

Fig. 11 **Honeycomb Vase by Tomáš Gabzdil Libertiny** Libertiny employs 40,000 bees to help create this vase, a home for flowers, created with the aid of flowers.

wooden components, 10 screws and two washers, 36 of which could be packed, disassembled, in one cubic metre (2).

While Thonet's chair was highly efficient structurally, in terms of comfort it hardly excelled. The next challenge was to find a means of contouring material to the form of the human body without resorting to padding or compromising the manufacturing rationality Thonet had established. A married couple working from Venice, Los Angeles, Charles and Ray Eames tackled this problem after developing experience moulding plywood for leg-splints for the US Navy during the Second World War. Thin plies were layered with glue and clamped in contoured moulds. By alternating the grain direction of the plies, components had strength both laterally and longitudinally. Once the glue set, the edges of the components were trimmed before lacquering. The process led to designs for lounge as well as dining chairs, with various leg configurations, their sculptural elegance and lightweight quality appealing to consumers (fig. 14, page 100).

However, the Eameses knew that for all its advantages over solid timber, plywood required a lot of processing and was unable to produce a body-hugging one-piece chair shell due to the limitations of forming the material in two planes. Plastics offered a possibility, but early compositions were brittle. On discovering fibreglass-reinforced polyester resin, the Eameses realised they had found a material that combined high strength, durability and tactile qualities with the desired mouldability to produce a one-piece shell. In 1950 their first mass-production plastic chair came on to the market and it remains one of the most comfortable examples to date (fig. 15, page 100).

Yet the story does not end here. Despite its many favourable characteristics, impregnating fibreglass matting with resin requires a number of operations: hand laying mat into moulds, pouring resin and after moulding, trimming excess material. In addition, both the matting and resin present health hazards and if badly mistreated the shells can crack. As plastics technology developed, it became possible to remove these operations by injection moulding a one-piece chair shell that was stronger and even more durable, yet flexible enough when sat on to "give". Robin Day

Fig. 12 Light Light chair by Alberto Meda, manufactured by Alias It is difficult to conceive of a context in which the extreme lightness of Alberto Meda's Light Light chair, made from carbon fibre, would be of genuine benefit when one considers the high cost of its manufacture in relation to plastics.

Fig. 13 Number 14 chair by Michael Thonet, manufactured by Gebrüder Thonet Thonet not only pioneered the technique of steam-bending wood but also industrialised it, his company becoming the first real mass producer of furniture.

Fig. 14 DCW Chair by Charles and Ray Eames, manufactured by Herman Miller and Vitra The bending Thonet had applied to lengths of timber was achieved across sheets when Charles and Ray Eames used layers of plywood in contoured moulds.

Fig. 15 Fibreglass Chair by Charles and Ray Eames manufactured by Herman Miller and Vitra The discovery of fibreglass enabled the Eameses to develop a one-piece shell, reducing the number of components and hence the cost of the chair.

pioneered the application of polypropylene in furniture with the Polyprop chair, which has been in continuous production since 1963 (fig. 16, page 101).

Since the Polyprop chair, there have been a number of admirable attempts to make plastic chairs that go beyond a one-piece seat and back, to produce a one-piece chair. Designers such as Joe Colombo, Verner Panton and Vico Magistretti all succeeded to some degree in exploring the limits of the technology. Yet one problem inherent in injection moulding held them back: the material requires an almost uniform wall thickness in order to cool evenly in the mould and not deform. This made it impossible for designers to make certain areas of the chair thicker where more strength was needed, and therefore to enhance the elegance of one-piece chairs. This uniform wall thickness and inelegance is most easily recognised in the ubiquitous white plastic garden chair (fig. 17, page 101), whose designer has expressed the desire to remain anonymous (3).

Jasper Morrison recognised a solution to this problem when presented with a sample of a new technique called gas injection moulding. It allows hollow cavities to be filled with plastic and air bubbles to be blown into them, pushing the plastic out to the walls where its strength is required. Other sections of the mould could be thinner where the plastic remains solid. A chair could be made with hollow legs, reducing weight, yet appearing solid, while seat and back could be thin, contoured panels. These advantages were both structural and aesthetic, and Morrison's design (the Air Chair for Magis, fig. 18, page 101) gave the one-piece plastic chair a grace it had not previously achieved. Since then, the technology has been used by a number of manufacturers, perhaps most successfully by Kartell who, together with designer Patrick Jouin, produced a transparent chair, Thalya, where the bubbles of air injected into the plastic can be seen (fig. 19, page 101).

At each stage of the development of the chair, these designers decided upon deficiencies in the then-current materials and processes being used and looked for opportunities to correct them. By establishing a critical position in relation to the object, they opened themselves up to spotting new materials and technologies that could be harnessed. It is this critical eye that designers need to nurture to provide the starting points for them to continue such chains of progress.

[3.]
Aldersey-Williams, H. 2000. "Common or Garden?" 'The Guardian Space Magazine.' July 20, p.9

Fig. 16   Polyprop **chair by Robin Day, manufactured by Hille** With his Polyprop chair, Robin Day replaced the hazardous and time consuming fibre-reinforced polyester resin with the durable, injection-mouldable plastic polypropylene.

Fig. 17   Generic **plastic garden chair** Injection moulding an entire chair usually presents the problem that the plastic must have a uniform wall thickness. Designers have struggled to produce elegant solutions using inexpensive plastics with such constraints.

Fig. 18   Air **Chair by Jasper Morrison, manufactured by Magis** The relatively new process of gas injection moulding used in the Air Chair allowed hollow cavities to be filled with plastic and air creating hollow sections. This changed the parameters of the possible form of a one-piece plastic chair.

Fig. 19   Thalya **Chair by Patrick Jouin** Jouin's chair does not improve upon Morrison's in terms of technological advance, but its use of transparent plastic displays its manufacturing process by making the injected bubbles of air visible.

DOMESTICATING THE INDUSTRIAL

It is rare for new materials to find their first use in the home, most being developed for industrial applications. Consequently, there are many examples of designers "domesticating" industrial material and details, finding an appropriate use for them among our everyday objects. Prior to the Eameses applying them within furniture, both plywood and plastic were uncommon materials in the home, whereas since then, they have become relatively common. Just as industry develops the high tech, it also searches out paths of least resistance and expense where the visual good manners of refined style are not required. Hence, products made cheaply for use within industry occasionally display signs of manufacturing efficiency that, while unsophisticated, can have an honest elegance. A number of designers have tried to smuggle such details into the domestic environment believing that, shown in the right light, we may come to appreciate them. An example is Michael Marriott's use of crush-bent steel tubing in his Courier shelving system for British manufacturer Established and Sons (fig. 20, page 102 and fig. 21, page 103). Square-section tubing of the kind Marriott used buckles when bent sharply, unless an articulated mandrel supports it internally. A cheaper method – crush bending – uses a bending tool that controls the collapse, bringing the top and bottom walls of the tube together but maintaining the flatness of the side walls. The resulting detail, commonly seen on school table legs, offers a voluptuous point of interest highlighted in Marriott's shelving.

THE QUALITY OF MATERIAL EXPERIENCE

The lack in modern plastics of attractive patina (the quality of surface that emerges from wear) has resulted in the degradation of the material quality of many everyday objects. While undoubtedly making very cheap products more widely available, where plastics have replaced metal, wood and leather, the property of ageing gracefully has often been replaced by shabbiness. This decline in actual physical quality has allowed craft to fill the gap, setting the array of sumptuous effects its processes allow in contrast with the cheapening of the industrially produced. For those who can afford them, craft objects allow their owners to revel in such qualities.

Although much of the value in certain craft objects emerges from the romance of the hand of the maker, some lies simply in the sensory experience of the materials themselves. The Splash Bowl (fig. 22, page 104) was made in a factory in Sheffield, UK, specialising in producing objects from pewter, the traditional metal used for making drinking tankards and hip flasks. Although it has an aesthetic associated with craft – it is irregular rather than precision-moulded – the dripping process by which it is made requires little time or skill and could easily be mechanised (fig. 23, page 104). By making it in this semi-controlled manner, each piece is slightly different, the pattern on its surface and the arrangement of solidified drips offering a record of the process of its creation. As it embodies very little skill in its making, its value emerges largely from its material qualities. This points to the notion that designers and industry could attempt to slow the diminishing material quality of our objects by searching for inexpensive techniques and formulations of material that give lasting value.

Fig. 20 Crush-bent table leg While it is possible to bend square-section metal tubing without it deforming, the process requires expensive tooling to support the tube from the inside. As a cheaper alternative, a crush-bending technique has been developed to allow the tube to uniformly deform.

Fig. 21 Courier shelving by Michael Marriott, manufactured by Established & Sons By using the crush-bending technique in the frame of his shelving for high-end manufacturer Established & Sons, Marriott encourages us to see it as an aesthetically pleasing detail, rather than an economic expediency.

Fig. 22   Splash bowl
by Tim Parsons, manufactured
by A.R.Wentworth The splash
bowl highlights a territory
between craft and mechanised
production where value is
neither based on making skill
nor precision manufacture, but
on an intrigue in uncommon
material qualities.

Fig. 23   Making
process for Splash bowl The
bowl is made by dripping
molten pewter on to a steel
tool. Although quick and
repeatable like an industrial
casting, every bowl has a
different arrangement of drips
and hence is unique, albeit
within controlled boundaries.

THE DURABLE AND THE SUSTAINABLE

It is worth considering the extent to which we should design objects to last as long as possible, while looking as good as possible. The durability and longevity of products is determined not only by the physical ability to do the job, but also by the strength of our emotional attachment to them. This is often far more fragile than the physicality of the object itself as it depends on our changing circumstances, whims and the peer pressures of fad and fashion. While there is an environmental argument for making long-lasting products and encouraging people to keep them for their usable life (the additional material and energy put into their production, spread over time, can amount to less than that needed to produce a number of less durable items that fail), the inexorable force of consumer culture drives the acquisition of the new forward at a rate that brings this approach into question. Is it the responsibility of the designer to play down fashion and promote the timeless?

[4.]
Aldersey Williams, H. 2008.
'Design and the Elastic Mind'.
New York: MOMA

Thinkers such as author and journalist Hugh Aldersey Williams have expounded the theory that to solve this dilemma design must mimic nature: "An organism dies once it ceases to have a use and ceases to have a use once it dies. A primary goal for designers now has to be to bring an object's material existence and practical utility into harmony." (4) But as the lifespan of many objects depends as much upon people's desire to keep them as it does upon their physical ability to last, it is impossible to predict a correct date of "death". Such a predicament suggests the deployment of materials that break down upon request – from durability to biodegradability – when we decide that the object is no longer needed.

Pragmatically, we must recognise that our predecessors did not have access to the knowledge of cause and effect related to using materials that we now have and that this presents us with responsibilities. While a few far-sighted commentators predicted the problems to come, based on the waste and pollution they could see, environmental concerns were simply not part of the psyche of mid-century designers. It was not until the space race delivered the first real images of the planet and the Club of Rome's report, 'Limits to Growth' (1972), expressed its fragility that sustainability began to enter public consciousness. Now, we are in a position to research product life cycles, cut out inefficiencies and avoid harmful and polluting processes. Lightness has become a recognised environmental virtue in products, providing fuel and material savings at various points in their life. Achieving high performance requires study. Now more than ever, designers and their clients need to build materials, research into their projects, setting their decisions into a sustainable framework of activity.

[1.]
Barnard, J. 2008. [Personal communication]. 14 May

[2.]
Gershenfeld, N. 2006. 'TED conference presentation, Monterey California' [online]. [Accessed 27th January 2009]. Available from World Wide Web: <www.ted.com/talks>

2.7

TECHNOLOGICAL INNOVATION

Technology can be described as any method of applying technical knowledge to a productive process. That knowledge may be of various kinds – of materials, of methods of production, of programming computers or other electronics, for example. With much coverage given to high and new technologies, it is easy to forget that even the simplest tasks within organised manufacturing constitute "technology", such as a jig to help drill a hole at the same point on multiple components. As new technologies emerge, designers are naturally interested in how these could be applied to new products. This section looks at a number of approaches that designers have taken to utilise technology and explores some of the products that have emerged.

HIGH-TECH MATERIALS

As discussed in the last chapter, particular new methods of doing things emerge from the discovery and application of new materials. Interest inevitably focuses upon those that attain the highest performance in relation to desired goals. Fusing lightness with strength has been one such common goal, fuelling developments principally in metals, plastics and composite materials (those made from two or more materials moulded together to give enhanced properties, such as bricks made with mud and straw, laminated plywood and fibre-reinforced plastics). The fetishising of carbon fibre-reinforced plastic to the extent that its visual appearance alone has become sought after is testament to it having achieved the pinnacle of this strength/lightness ratio. (Carbon-fibre effect sticky-backed vinyl – ironically adding neither

lightness nor strength – has become a staple for car customisers.) Yet with an expensive and time-consuming manufacturing process, its applications remain in those areas where performance is prioritised over affordability, an example being Formula 1. John Barnard pioneered its use in chassis design and also created an innovative suspension system using "flexures" – sections of the suspension's carbon fibre wishbones that literally flexed. As Barnard explains: "The suspension movement is gained by carefully balancing flexure length with width and thickness. When the balance is correct enough, movement can be obtained for an F1 suspension" [1]. Barnard went on to design aerodynamic carbon-fibre covers for the point at which the suspension attaches to the car body. These used a mixture of flexible- and rigid-setting resins with the carbon cloth to provide a pivot-point that allowed the suspension to move.

Areas of industry such as sport, aerospace and medicine produce a technological "pull" from their customers for the development of ever higher-performing materials that is far less evident among domestic consumer products. Consequently, when designers apply high-tech materials in the home, they must establish a genuine need for their use or their efforts can appear futile. While it is the luxury of the rich to afford superfluous performance, objects that provide it intentionally foster an obscene wastefulness. To avoid this trap, concerned designers are focusing their attention on the provenance of objects (how are they made, with what materials and under what conditions). By forging collaborations with material scientists they explore new formulations of materials that are no less useful but come from renewable

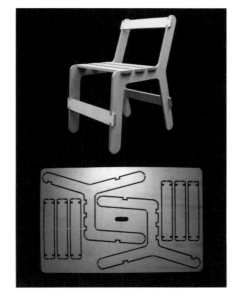

TAP WITH RUBBER MALLET

ENJOY!

CUT TABS

SAND TABS FLUSH

Fig. 1 **Chairfix by Ben Wilson** The availability of computer-controlled routing equipment allowed Ben Wilson to produce his Chairfix chair. Lines plotted on screen are translated into the movement of a cutting head with precision. The piece is cut accurately enough to be push-fitted together without screws.

sources, are recyclable or biodegradable. Potato starch, nutshells, bamboo and other forms of biomass are among many natural ingredients likely to find their way into our domestic products in the future.

CONTROL AND PRODUCTION

Developments in computing, the Internet and electronics have had an enormous impact on the design and manufacturing industries. From the presentation of ideas, drawings, model-making and prototyping, through to the control of manufacturing equipment, computers can be seen at every step of design development. But they have also had a profound effect upon concepts. Designers have grasped the idiosyncrasies of computers and electronics and made use of them to create designs never before possible. A number of these are discussed below.

Computers allow precision control of systems, which when applied to manufacture, allows precision automated production. This is broadly referred to as computer-aided design and computer-aided manufacture or CADCAM. Until recently the preserve of the factory, now almost every secondary school has some kind of computer-numerically-controlled (CNC) making equipment: routers, laser cutters, vinyl cutters, for example. The ready availability of this technology in local workshops has allowed designers to use it for quick prototyping or self-production projects. Inspired by Airfix model kits, where all the components came held within a plastic frame, Ben Wilson designed Chairfix (fig. 1, page 106). Using a computer-controlled milling machine, Wilson created a chair cut from sheet plywood but with its components held in place, ready to be pushed out and assembled at home. Perhaps the ultimate "flat-pack", Chairfix has no other screws or nails, requiring only a wooden mallet to construct it.

With these simple two-axis cutting machines becoming commonplace, the next wave of fully three-dimensional prototyping equipment is set to have even greater impact. In use in the product design industry for many years, technologies that enable computer files describing three-dimensional components to be transformed into solid models are being developed for the hobby and home markets. With home "3D printing" becoming a serious proposition, designers have gone from treating these rapid prototyping technologies as model-making tools to seeing them as manufacturing processes in themselves. Héctor Serrano's project Reduced Carbon Footprint Souvenirs (fig. 2, page 107), proposes a scenario in which the data to make miniature statues or buildings would be emailed to family or friends to be printed by them instead of being carried home. Extrapolating on such concepts, Massachusetts Institute of Technology's (MIT) Professor Neil Gershenfeld predicts a global manufacturing revolution sparked by these machines. By creating and touring fabrication laboratories or "Fab Labs", Gershenfeld discovered that, while affluent audiences created "products with a market of one" [2], developing world entrepreneurs used the labs to solve local problems, making tools, replacement components and unavailable products. By making almost anything manufacturable on site, the democratising of innovation – putting the production of their ideas in the hands of the people – becomes a genuine possibility.

Fig. 2   Reduced Carbon Footprint Souvenirs by Héctor Serrano This project proposed that instead of carrying souvenirs home, the data to make them could be emailed and new 3D printing technology used to print them in the place where they will be enjoyed. This should reduce the energy used in manufacturing, packaging and transporting them.

Fig. 3   The Basic Stamp Chip manufactured by Parallax Inc. The Stamp Chip is a microcontroller that can be connected to a home computer and programmed. It allows home users the ability to "craft" one-off electronic products more easily than ever before.

TECH-CRAFT AND PROGRAMMING

Gershenfeld's Fab Labs marry the power of material fabrication with tools to construct and programme electronic devices, an activity known as "physical computing". The Stamp Chip is one of a number of inventions that have brought physical computing to a "pro-am" audience (in this context, pro-ams are enthusiasts who, despite being amateur by dint of their having another occupation, nonetheless engage in their "hobby" with the seriousness of professionals). The Stamp Chip is a microcontroller that can be connected to a home computer and programmed using the language BASIC (fig. 3, page 107). Arduino boards are a newer development that augment the functionality of the Stamp and are easier to program. Such technology makes it possible to construct your own electronic products that in the past might have needed considerable investment.

As the ability to create electronic products escapes the corporate realm, so, too, the concepts that emerge no longer follow typical models. Hektor, by Jürg Lehni and Uli Franke (fig. 4 , page 108) and Pixelroller by rAndom International (fig. 5, page 108) are electronic products that enable large-scale murals to be printed or painted automatically. Hektor automates the use of a spray can, operating it via a system of wires and pulleys that enable it to reproduce screen graphics many times their original scale. Pixelroller mixes computer-print technology with the typology of a paint roller to allow a digital image to be rolled on to any surface. In both systems, the computer is aware of the location of the printing or painting device so it can ensure that the image is transferred accurately. Beguiling to watch, the large-scale freedom of expression both systems allow suggests they may never have emerged from a corporate product-planning meeting.

With technology becoming cheaper and knowledge of how to use it more readily available through the Internet, creative activists have started to find striking ways of making their presence felt. Members of New York-based Graffiti Research Labs (GRL), committed to "developing high-tech tools for the art underground" (3), glued an LED, a watch battery and a magnet together to create the first LED Throwie, a permanently illuminated miniature light source that, when thrown, attaches itself to any ferrous metal surface (fig. 6, page 109). GRL went on to produce thousands of Throwies, decorating metal-clad buildings, trams and public sculptures. By arranging them to form text on a board, sets of Throwies can be transferred simultaneously, creating removable illuminated graffiti. Co-opting higher technology, GRL pioneered projected graffiti by marrying a car battery with a suitable transformer to powerful LCD projection equipment.

While these tools show how technology can be a conduit for self-expression, other designers have investigated how objects can appear to express themselves. Andy Huntington and Louise Klinker's Tap Tap Box (fig. 7, page 109), as the designers explain, "is a construction toy capturing a fascination with rhythm and fidgeting. The system is built up of individual knock boxes. Each box has its own memory and is completely self-contained. As you tap on the top of a box, the box waits for a few seconds and then taps back what it has heard. At four seconds, the delay is just long enough to give the boxes a life of their own. Just long enough to wonder if they have forgotten." (4)

Applying similar skills on a large scale, Troika's Cloud at Heathrow Airport uses data to control over 4,000 mechanical flip-dots on its surface (fig. 8, page 110). As the dots flip back and forth from shiny to black

Fig. 4   Hektor by Jürg Lehni with Uli Franke
Hektor is the name of a system that translates on-screen graphics into painted murals via the automation of a spray can. The can is moved and operated from the computer by a series of motors, wires and pulleys.

Fig. 5   Pixelroller by rAndom International
By bringing together various technologies around the typology of a paint roller, rAndom International were able to create a device capable of painting digital images directly on to large surfaces.

and back, a wide variety of patterns flow over and animate the skin of the object. Other companies such as Luckybite have mixed the sense that the object itself is alive with the ability for the public to send information that will affect its appearance. Their Comment installation, a 26-metre-high wall of LED light tracks (fig. 9, page 110), sends visitors' comments on a visible journey, becoming legible as they pass through defined display "stations".

Like craftwork centred on material properties, techcraft offers the danger of becoming a self-conscious activity promoting only the skill of the maker, rather than a means of fulfilling broader goals. While proam enthusiasts are at liberty to indulge in designing primarily for themselves, designers for industry and the public sector are in the business of finding ways to apply technology that will have more widespread appeal.

[3.]
Graffiti Reseach Labs website' [online]. [Accessed 27th January 2009]. Available from World Wide Web: <www. graffitiresearchlab.com>

[4.]
Huntingdon, A. and Klinker, L. In: Cameron, A. 2004. 'IdN Special 04: The Art of Experimental Interaction Design'. Corte Madera, CA: Gingko Press

POETIC TECH OBJECTS

In an attempt to achieve this, some practitioners have tried to embody a poetic idea either in the method of production of their products or in the way they operate. Like a visual translation of the Tap Tap Box, the History Tablecloth memorises and displays the location of objects placed upon it (fig. 10, page 111). Developed at the Royal College of Art's Interaction Design Research Studio, the tablecloth uses electroluminescent material to create filigree "pixels" that give the impression of glowing lace. The cloth creates a halo around objects left on it, which fades away once they are removed. It is responsive, quietly and briefly recording the flow of objects it encounters.

Colliding computer animation with computer-controlled rapid prototyping, Ron Arad highlighted the sense in which a three-dimensional print-out of an object is but one "frame" in its evolution. For his Not Made by Hand, Not Made in China exhibition, he created and animated a vase-like form that bounced excitedly on screen before being frozen at various points in its cycle to be printed (fig. 11, page 111). The project took a postmodern approach to form – the designer could delegate its choice to the purchaser, allowing them to stop the animation at any point and print the result. Similarly, designers Reed Kram and Clemens Weishaar devolve the exact configuration of their Breeding Tables to a computer algorithm (fig. 12, page 112). Able to generate an infinite number of unique table bases to be folded from sheet steel, their software generates random forms within set parameters (such as foot position and table height). Drawings of the resulting forms are automatically generated and sent to lasercutting equipment (although their fabrication still takes place manually).

These projects raise questions about the role of the designer in the creation of form. By allowing aspects of a design to be left to chance, designers step down from their apparent position of controlling every detail. However, this generosity becomes an abdication of responsibility if the elements being made arbitrary would benefit from intelligent analysis. In Arad's vase, chance impacts most upon its aesthetics, but in Kram Weishaar's tables it has a greater influence upon material use. Not all of the tables can be as efficient as each other. If a computer can generate random versions of products, it can also be employed to help measure which one performs best outside of our subjective aesthetic judgements.

Fig. 6 **LED Throwies by Graffiti Research Lab** Created by glueing together an LED, a watch battery and a magnet, LED Throwies are permanently illuminated miniature light sources that will attach themselves to any ferrous metal surface and glow for the life of the battery.

Fig. 7 **Tap Tap Boxes by Andy Huntington with Louise W. Klinker** Tap Tap is a construction toy that, after a short delay, taps back any rhythm tapped on to it. Combinations of boxes can be made to tap on to each other creating complex rhythms.

Fig. 8   Cloud electronic sculpture by Troika for Heathrow Airport Terminal 5 Flip dots are mechanisms used in public transport information boards, flicking from black to white to hide and reveal parts of words. Design group Troika used the dots to cover their Cloud sculpture, enabling pre-programmed patterns to flow over its surface.

Fig. 9   Comment installation by Luckybite for The Science Museum Luckybite created an enormous, animated, visitor-feedback wall that enabled messages to be sent to it, becoming "trains" that travelled along LED light tracks.

Oscar Diaz, when developing a product for champagne company Veuve Clicquot, took advantage of the accurate calibration that computers can provide. In order to create a set of translucent glass vases that, when stacked together, revealed the client's signature orange, Diaz used the RGB values displayed in computer graphics packages to calculate the correct colours for each (fig. 13, page 113). By printing on to transparent acetate, overlays could be tested and given as samples to the glassmakers for matching.

While fascinating in itself, new technology can be a trap into which designers in awe of it fall, blinkered from the need to apply it effectively to progress our product-based culture. The objects that emerge from projects such as design group Front's Sketch Furniture appear to beg our forgiveness for their inadequacies as practical products on the grounds that their creation produced a spectacular performance (fig. 14, page 113) (Front used motion capture – an animation technique that tracks and records movement – combined with rapid prototyping to create furniture that looks to have been drawn in space). Yet if such projects are a genuine attempt to improve upon the development of chairs, tables and lamps, the technology used must be judged against all that have come before – and that could have been used instead. Tom Dixon's project Fresh Fat Plastic raises the same issue. The designer recognised that by removing the die from a plastic extrusion machine, it continually pumps out a toothpaste-like worm of hot, soft plastic, which can then be worked manually into a desired form (fig. 15, page 114). The material is attractive, having a glass-like lustre, and the process works effectively for small objects like bowls and lamps, but when applied to chairs it is difficult to work the material so as to avoid them being heavy and uncomfortable (fig. 16, page 114). Both examples point to the need for materials, processes and technologies to be chosen and used as appropriate to the objects they are making, regardless of how engaging they are to watch.

INTERACTION

Interaction design, an entire discipline unto itself, emerged from industrial design when those involved with designing electronic equipment, in particular computers, realised they were spending more time designing the way we interacted with them than on their physical form. In tandem, those involved in designing computer software faced the same problem: how can systems be designed around people rather than people having to change the way they think in order to use them? Without undertaking a history of interaction design – more than adequately covered by father of the discipline, Bill Moggridge, in his book 'Designing Interactions' (2007, Cambridge, MA: MIT Press) – it's worth noting its key achievements. It has been responsible for exploring and defining the layout of desktop, laptop and palmtop computers and mobile phones (still an unsettled typology with bar, clamshell, sliding and fanning varieties currently competing for market dominance). It has defined the input devices we have become familiar with, from remote controls, the computer mouse and numerous game controllers, to the touch-sensitive wheel of the iPod. And where would we be without the graphical user interface (GUI), with its desktop metaphor of files, folders and trashcans?

Fig. 10 **History Tablecloth by Interaction Design Research Department, Royal College of Art, developed with Rachel Wingfield** The History Tablecloth uses sensors and electro-luminescent material to leave glowing traces of objects left on it. These fade slowly once the objects have been removed.

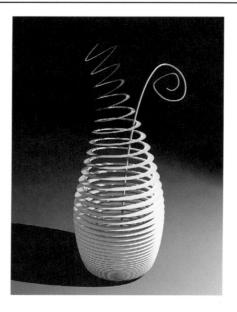

Fig. 11 **Bouncing Vase from the Not Made By Hand, Not Made in China collection by Ron Arad** Each vase-like form is a rapid prototype of one frame of an animation Arad made using computer software in his studio.

Fig. 12   Breeding Tables by Kram Weisshaar
A computer algorithm decides the exact form of Reed Kram and Clemens Weisshaar's Breeding Tables.

As well as incorporating technology into products to go on sale immediately, some designers are involved in speculating upon the types of products that might emerge in the future. A few large consumer electronics corporations, including Royal Philips Electronics in The Netherlands, regularly run projects that investigate the scenarios, functionality, interaction and appearance of the objects we might be using up to 20 years hence. Their Home of the Near Future project of 1999 examined social and technological trends and presented a vision of the smart home where objects became "assistants" or "companions" that would respond to our preferences. The Home Medical Box combines a video-conference portal and medical encyclopaedia with diagnostic tools to check heart rate and blood pressure and can send data, as well as images, to the doctor wirelessly. Part of the earlier Visions of the Future project, Hot Badges are dating aids that hold personal information about their wearer's likes and dislikes and flash when in the vicinity of another badge with matching attributes.

Perhaps ill-advisedly, such projects suggest that technology, packaged correctly, offers a utopian solution to our frenetic lifestyles. The time used to get to know someone or to visit the doctor is freed up, but to what end? And wouldn't we rather discover someone's interests for ourselves through talking to them rather than through a device? By generalising about desires and seeing technology as a cure for all ills, designers risk adding further unwanted layers of complexity to life. Possibly in response to such concerns, Royal Philips's recent SKIN Probes project instead used technology to reflect emotional states. Garments were produced that were "sensitive rather than intelligent" (5) and visualised emotional and physiological changes in the wearer's body on their surface (fig. 17, page 115).

[5.] -
Philips website. 2004–2009.
[Page no longer available].
<http://www.design.philips.
com/about/design/portfolio/
researchprojects/article-
14935.page>

[6.] -
Dunne, A. 2005. 'Hertzian
Tales'. Cambridge, MA:
MIT Press

[7.] -
Gaver, W. 2007. 'The Curious
Home.' London: Goldsmiths,
University of London
-

CRITICAL POSITIONS

Designers critical of the way technology has been applied to electronic products have emerged as strong voices within academia. Professor Anthony Dunne, leader of the Design Interactions course at the RCA and former colleague Professor William Gaver, now Head of the Interaction Research Studio at Goldsmiths, University of London, share distaste at the commoditisation of technologies into prescriptive objects that homogenise experience and behaviour. Both argue that technology as conventionally applied to common electronic object types has led to an optimum level of performance being achieved, reducing the designer's role to little more than that of packaging. These products, Dunne says, support a banal reality and condition us to act according to the rules of systems design pioneered by cognitive scientists. (6) Gaver contends that: 'Digital products – especially those for the home – do not have to reproduce our culture's preoccupation with work, consumption and entertainment. Instead, technology can encourage more exploratory engagements with life, providing evocative resources with which to discover new perspectives on ourselves and the world around us.' (7) His research associates have developed a number of projects (see 2.12 Design for debate) that propose alternative methodologies for the development of electronic products.

As well as meditations upon the electronic object, Anthony Dunne, with partner Fiona Raby and their RCA students, are investigating the future implications of bio- and nanotechnology. In contrast to the blindly utopian technological visions of the past, much of this work, rather than pushing commercial propositions, uses design as a tool for enquiry, exploring potential conclusions of current scientific 'advances'. These themes are also elaborated in 2.12 Design for debate.

Fig. 13 **RGB Vases by Oscar Diaz for Veuve Clicquot** Three nesting glass vases of different colours come together to create a volume displaying a particular hue of orange used by the client, Veuve Clicquot. Accurate colour matching was achieved using a computer.

Fig. 14 **Sketch Furniture by Front** Although bringing together a set of technologies never previously applied to product design, the objects resulting from Front's Sketch Furniture project are considerably less effective in their own right than the video performance showing them being made.

Developing from the Slow Food movement founded in Italy nearly 15 years ago, there is a growing network of designers who apply the same principles of reviving pleasure, quality and an awareness of nature and the environment given to eating, to the design, manufacture and use of products. In an on-demand world of 24/7 consumption, products that force us to slow down and take time to enjoy experiences can be seen as virtuous. Droog Design took the theme for their 2004 Milan exhibition, where "seniors" served customers a slow meal. The previous year, sometime Droog Design collaborator Dick van Hoff unveiled his Tyranny of the Plug range of kitchen machines – an entirely hand-powered set of appliances consisting of a food processor, blender, whisk and juicer (fig. 18, page 115). Arguments abound as to whether small gestures such as these have an impact upon energy usage. Yet rather than relying upon our guilt as an incentive, Van Hoff has done everything in his power to make his tools a pleasure to use, gearing them efficiently and constructing them from solid and beautiful materials. Consequently, they are far less likely to languish at the back of kitchen cupboards than their electrically-powered cousins.

Fig. 15 **Fresh Fat Plastic machine by Tom Dixon** By modifying a plastic extrusion machine, Tom Dixon created a tool for the free manipulation of hot plastic as a craft skill. A continuous worm of pliable hot plastic emerges from the machine that the operator must manually shape into a usable product.

Fig. 16 **Fresh Fat Plastic chair by Tom Dixon** The imprecise and spontaneous nature of the Fresh Fat Plastic process means that it is difficult to produce large objects that use material efficiently, this chair being a case in point.

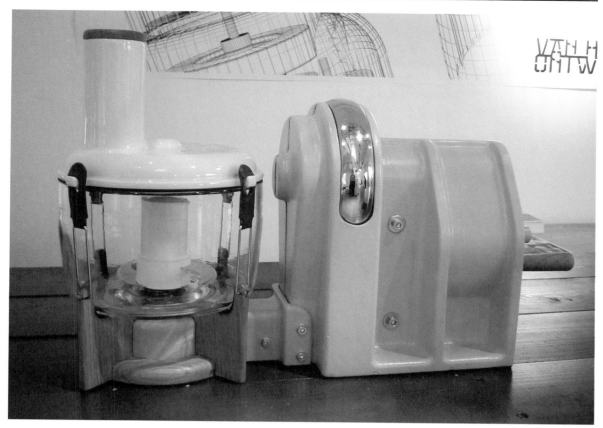

Fig. 17   **SKIN Probes**
project by Philips Philips's
SKIN Probes project used
soft, wearable technologies
to visualise emotional and
physiological changes in the
wearer's body on the surface
of their clothes.

Fig. 18   **Tyranny**
of the Plug human-powered
kitchen tools by Dick Van
Hoff Van Hoff's human-
powered kitchen tools make
use of precise gearing and
high-quality materials to
engage us more physically
in the act of food preparation
instead of relying upon
electrical appliances.

[1.]
Ali, T. "The Year That Changed the World". 2008. 'Sydney Morning Herald,' 5 January

[2.]
The exception to this is when the designer is working in-house for a manufacturing company. In such cases, they may inescapably find themselves in a hierarchy.

[3. 4.]
Bierut, M. 2007. '79 Short Essays on Design'. New York: Princeton Architectural Press

2.8

ETHICS

Ethics is the system of moral principles that helps us decide what we consider to be right or wrong. These moral principles, although shared by many people, are not absolutes but are personal and open to change. They guide our behaviour and, in relation to design, have an impact upon what designers choose to work on and how they go about doing it. This section does not propose a rigid set of ethical design principles – to do so would be to preach my own view. Instead, it points out the core dilemmas that product design sets up and discusses attitudes towards them.

DESIGN WITH A CLEAR CONSCIENCE

As societies become more civilised, greater levels of scrutiny and accountability are applied to human behaviour. Practices deemed acceptable in one period or in one culture become disgraceful in another. In the realm of object making, differences in where ethical lines are drawn are most marked when considering issues such as workers' rights, sources of materials, originality, the safety of objects in use and, more recently, energy usage, pollution and waste.

As different countries make advances in ethical controls at different rates, contrasts occur around the world that are easily exploited. The rise of Newly Industrialised Countries (NICs) in Asia, in particular China, has come about in no small part because the developed economies of the West discovered it as the cheapest and most enthusiastic source of manufacturing. "The Far East is now central to the future of capitalism", writes novelist and historian Tariq Ali. "China today, like Britain in the 19th century, is the workshop of the world. The impact of this on world politics has yet to be felt. The half-asleep giant might wake up one day with surprising consequences." (1)

Like nineteenth-century Britain, Chinese manufacturing leaves much to be desired by the ethical standards expected in developed countries today. With the majority of global production migrating to these Asian NICs, it is increasingly likely that designing a mass-produced product will mean having it manufactured there. The central ethical conundrum of product designers today, and one the vast majority choose to ignore, is how to be sure their work is manufactured under conditions that they deem acceptable. Yet such assurance is, to say the least, difficult to obtain.

Some designers have had the tendency to play down the importance of their ethical views in the work they do, not questioning the implications of their projects. In making an enquiry about the working conditions under which their product will be made, the designer may feel they are both challenging the authority of their client and overstepping the limits of their role. However, this is to assume two things, both questionable. The first is that the designer-client relationship is a hierarchy in which the designer is subservient, when in fact it should be an equal partnership. (2)(3) The second is that the designer's influence over the production of the object ends with the specification of materials, components and manufacturing methods. In truth, clients may welcome advice on where these could be carried out, by whom and under what conditions. To assume, without enquiring, that the client will necessarily put profit first before meeting their ethical responsibilities is to condemn them prematurely.

Raising such issues isn't easy. All the while, the nagging fear of losing future business eats away at one's resolve. "The spirit is willing. But the flesh, for the most part, remains weak" (4) as Michael Bierut puts

Fig. 1   'Icon'
magazine cover November 2006 'Icon' magazine's article 'Design is Evil' discussed the emergence of once taboo themes such as sex and death as inspiration for product designs.

it. He urges designers not to blame the client if they themselves are too weak to confront them – to flatten the hierarchy of the relationship and talk on equal terms. By nature of being in the relationship, designers are implicated in the actions that emerge from it. They may feel that they have limited power, but owe it to themselves and to those affected by the decisions made not to underestimate it, and to exercise it in line with their ethical convictions. If design is to serve society as it should, it must be done with a clear conscience. As Henry Dreyfuss said of the good industrial designer: "Occasionally he may lose a client, but he rarely loses a client's respect." (5)

THE ETHICS OF LABOUR

The first step for any designer when faced with difficult ethical decisions is to educate themselves on the facts beyond the headlines. Although by no means the only offending nation, the recent scrutiny of labour conditions there makes China an ideal case study for revealing ethical issues in the workplace. Writing on labour rights in China, Robert J. Rizoff, director of the China Working Group, an organisation of socially responsible businesses working in China, revealed widespread abuses but also suggested positive actions that companies can take to lessen their likelihood. In the magazine of the United States–China Business Council, a non-profit organisation of more than 250 American corporations that do business with China, Rizoff wrote that: "Labour rights violations are so widespread in China that violations can be presumed to exist in every factory until proven otherwise." (6) However, he immediately adds that factories owned by or having direct investment from foreign companies that stress the importance of good codes of conduct tend to have fewer violations.

China has what Rizoff describes as "adequate labour laws" (7), but claims that these are poorly enforced. Compliance with these laws costs money and critics say that with the government having a vested interest in the continued economic competitiveness of its manufacturing industry, it cannot be trusted to uphold them (8). Typical violations have included paying below the minimum wage, forcing staff to work beyond the 40 hour per week limit without paying overtime, denying them the minimum one day off per week, withholding and deducting wages without due cause, providing unsafe working conditions and engaging in physical abuse. Termination of employment upon illness or pregnancy and lack of compensation for work-related injuries and death have also been common (9). Crucially, although Chinese workers are allowed to form and join unions, these are not independent and must submit to governance by the All China Federation of Trades Unions (ACFTU). A report in the UK's 'The Guardian' newspaper described them thus: "Organised from the top down, they have little influence on personnel decisions and are often used by the government and management to placate employees." (10) As Rizoff's report states, this leaves workers "without representatives who can discuss violations with management. Workers who have tried to form independent unions or lead labour protests have been imprisoned." (11)

To safeguard their image at home, Western corporations have taken to implementing codes of conduct and policing these themselves or through professional monitoring companies. Sadly, these have been only moderately successful. The financial benefit of flouting the codes is tempting despite the risk of being caught, and the workers themselves are often unaware of the laws and guidelines in place to protect them, and hence do not necessarily protest.

[5.]
Dreyfuss, H. 1955. 'Designing for People'. New York: Simon and Schuster

[6. 7.]
Rizoff, R. J. 2004. "Beyond Codes of Conduct: Addressing Labor Rights Problems in China". 'China Business Review', March–April

[8.]
'China, like so many other industrialising developing countries, is genuinely afraid that enforcement of labour laws will reduce its so-called "competitive advantage" (cheap labour) and drive away foreign investment.' Chan, A. 'China and the International Labor Movement.' [Page no longer available]. <www.gbcc.org.uk/iss19_1.htm>

[9.]
'China Briefing'. 2000–2009. [online]. [Accessed 27th January 2009]. Available from World Wide Web: <www.china-briefing.com/news/2008/03/11/npc-official-china-labor-law-criticism-unfounded.html>

[10.]
Watts, J. "Wal-Mart backs down and allows Chinese workers to join union in Beijing". 2006. 'The Guardian'. 11 August

[11.]
Rizoff, R. J. 2004. "Beyond Codes of Conduct: Addressing Labor Rights Problems in China." 'China Business Review', March–April. For further reading: <www.uschina.org/public/documents/2006/11/labor-issues-corporate-responsibility.pdf>

[12.]   -
Pick, F. 1975. "The Meaning
and Purpose of Design". In:
Benton, C. (ed). 'Documents: A
collection of source material on
the Modern Movement'. Milton
Keynes: Open University Press

[13.]   -
Grcic, K. In: Fiell, C. and Fiell,
P. 2007. 'Design Now.' Cologne:
Taschen

Fig. 2   Lifelong
Bookcase by Kenneth Grange
After his mother's death
set him thinking about the
stagnant tradition of coffin-
making, Kenneth Grange
conceived one that would
serve another function – as a
bookcase – and bring a smile,
in his words, "at the end, just
as at the beginning, and have
a useful life in between".

Progressive foreign companies have begun to go further
by educating workers about rights and democratically
electing representatives among their Chinese
workforces. These actions produce pools of Western-
style employment practice that, while encouraging,
are in danger of being at odds with the methods of the
state-linked federation of unions. They nevertheless
offer recommendations that designers can take to their
clients that could have a real impact among the lives of
the workforce. In markets where not to manufacture in
countries like China would jeopardise competitiveness,
those benefiting financially need to do what they can
to ensure that the lives and livelihoods of those making
their products are protected.

A PROFESSION ADRIFT?

The ethical compromises around manufacturing are
a contributory factor in what could be described as a
wider malaise in which the product design profession
currently finds itself. Central to this is an identity crisis
that has strengthened over the past half-century,
resulting from its own success. Having helped to
achieve the goal of making Western society a relatively
comfortable place, abundant with affordable labour-
saving and entertaining devices, there is a sense in
some quarters that the hard work has been done – that
product design's traditional problem-solving role has
largely disappeared and that real problems are no
longer solved by designers but by policy-makers such
as politicians. Perverted by marketing, designers' skills
have been diverted into solving fictitious problems,
or into continually reworking perfectly satisfactory
products. As early as 1933, Frank Pick, the then head
of London Transport and a keen patron of design, said
in a public lecture: "I often think of the wretched
designer forced to improve on the best for the sake
of novelty. But it is the consumer's fault...if you would

not buy these products then they would not be made"
(12). After educating the public about the merits of
durability and honesty to materials, Pick encouraged
them to make demands of their shopkeepers who
would, in turn, pass these on to manufacturers and
their designers.

Regrettably, with the exception of a few small
organisations, consumers did not rise to the challenge
and the conceptual value and material substance of
designed products have continued to be diluted. In a
recent publication, designer Konstantin Grcic wrote:
"In the domains of services and facilities, design is
considered to be smart, producing intelligent solutions
to the specific demands of a situation. In comparison
to this, a lot of product design is seen to have lost its
integrity and original virtues to the marketing interests
of the large corporations. As the fundamentals of
social and ecological issues become ever more sensitive
to modern industry we need to rebuild a culture of
products that 'make sense'. The relevance a product
has to our life lies not only in its use, but also in how
it is made, what it is made of, and where it is made...
and finally who disposes of it and how?" (13)

DARK DESIGN

Rather than simply being complacent, many respected
commentators have suggested that designers have
begun intentionally embracing the amoral and even the
immoral. Unsurprisingly, as society has become more
liberal, tolerant and willing to push the boundaries
of taste and decency, so design has followed suit.
Designers are now tackling once-taboo themes such
as sex, death and war, albeit through one-offs, limited
editions and research projects rather than the mass-

mass-produced. In a cover feature article in 2006, entitled "Design is Evil" (fig. 1, page 116), 'Icon' magazine discussed the phenomenon showcasing designs including a set of bullets with their tips shaped into roses entitled, A last bunch of flowers for my girlfriend, (Michael Sans) and Traces of an Imaginary Affair, (Bjorn Franke) described as "a set of nine tools allowing you to inflict bite marks, carpet burns, love bites, scratches and bruises on yourself, giving the appearance that you are having an affair, to make your partner jealous". The text states that: "design's new willingness to address darker issues makes for dramatic imagery in a magazine, but will be viewed by some as further confirmation of the discipline's descent from a noble cause into shallow sensationalism." (14) It was right. In their latest book 'Design Now', distinguished writers Charlotte and Peter Fiell lambasted some of the work featured. Of the 'Icon' magazine piece they wrote: "In a recent design magazine article, dwarf figurines, Delft dildos and gun-shaped handbags were featured as the latest thing in design. Beyond asking, "What the hell is that all about?" we should reflect that if this is the state of contemporary practice then fundamental problems exist within certain areas of the design community." (15)

As the Fiells's quote suggests, some of the new work that deals with so-called darker issues does so in a trivial and sensationalist way. Imagery of guns, sex and death are simply applied to everyday objects in the vain hope of grabbing attention. When these images are used not to examine the profundity or seriousness of the issues to which they are inextricably linked, but simply to exploit the frissons of pleasure and guilt they may provide, the works become akin to pornography.

But just as the existence of pornography must not be used to censor valuable works of literature, film or art, dark design of a poor quality must not preclude others from being allowed to explore these subjects with greater depth and substance.

For example, death has provided the inspiration for a range of poetic, practical and thoughtful works of design in recent years including Kenneth Grange's bookcase that becomes your coffin (fig. 2, page 118), Nadine Jarvis' bird feeder (fig. 3, page 119) and Michele Gauler's project Digital Remains (fig. 4, page 119), in which access to a deceased person's computer data becomes a mediator in the grieving process. More controversially, Auger–Loizeau's Afterlife project (fig. 5, page 120) reveals the possibility of creating batteries using acids created by the body after death, during the process of decay. Although the project has raised the hackles of some critics, it is more than a technological stunt. The designers say that the batteries provide "an expression of life after death for those who are spiritually disconnected or demand tangible evidence". In contrast to the superficial application of imagery, each of these projects explores the relationship between death and the objects with which we live, examining how they may offer catharsis to those who own them.

Much of the consternation aroused by such work comes from a misreading of its context and of the designers' intentions (neither Michael Sans, Bjorn Franke's nor Auger–Loizeau's products were designed for use but to raise debate). Many commentators are yet to cast off the notion that a designer's products always represent an eventuality that he/she supports and is seeking to put in place. In fact, an increasing number of designers have rejected this role of the utopian visionary in favour of highlighting contemporary conditions and potential

[14.]   -
Bates, A. and James, L. 2006. "Design is Evil." 'Icon' magazine. November

[15.]   -
Fiell, C. and Fiell, P. 2007. 'Design Now.' Cologne: Taschen
                        -

Fig. 3   Bird feeder by Nadine Jarvis Moulded from a mixture of bird feed and human ash, Nadine Jarvis's Birdfeeder offers an alternative to scattering ashes by hand.

Fig. 4   Digital Remains by Michele Gauler This project explored the way that digital data belonging to the deceased could be accessed in a controlled way via personal access keys given to friends and family, to form part of the grieving process.

futures that they do not necessarily advocate. These cautionary tales are easily mistaken for the work of dangerous misanthropes if viewed in the traditional way. (16) The difference – not always discernable from images and sound-bites in magazines (or even the designers' own websites) – is the context of the work. While some pieces are intended to be manufactured and distributed, others have been designed specifically to generate debate around their implications and these tend to be shown in galleries or disseminated through publications. Whether it is these products, or simply the ideas they provoke that are intended for consumption, is likely to affect our ethical view of them. The discussion, representation, or even satirising of immoral acts and dark deeds is part and parcel of a free society, but the promotion and distribution of tools to aid them is more questionable.

The public understanding of design culture is slowly catching up with that of literature, film and other art forms where shocking images have become acceptable when part of an intelligent narrative expression. Like these art forms, designers will have to cope with the righteous indignation of self-appointed moral guardians, who, not prepared to look for deeper meaning in the work or engage in the debate it sparks, will dismiss it out of hand. However, far from being negative, this broadening of subject matter and the emerging context of design for debate provides a conduit for designers and their audience to reflect upon the state of society and the full spectrum of possibilities it holds – a role previously hampered by the expectation of presenting only positive imagery (see 2.12 Design for debate). With context playing such an important role in the ethical view of this work, designers may need to be more careful to communicate their intentions effectively.

Some, however, believe otherwise. A small number of designers have picked up on the benefits of being ambiguous about the planned outcome of their work with the express purpose of using any adverse reaction to fuel the debate (see 1.1 Design and politics). A big enough outcry may even stop others with fewer scruples trying genuinely to release similar products. Rather than eviscerate the work by declaring its hoax status, these objects and scenarios are presented neutrally – neither with a sales pitch nor a damning indictment. Faced with the question "Does the designer really think this is a good idea?", the viewer is encouraged to form his or her own opinion. Part of this process, explains Anthony Dunne, a leading exponent of design for debate, is to avoid the work being described as art. "If our work is categorised as art, it defuses it. We insist on it being design because people get uncomfortable with that. They say, 'How can that be design, it's not mass-produced'. Why does it have to be mass-produced? They say, 'But it isn't answering a need.' Well, why does it have to answer a need? You can raise all these questions by keeping it in that space…We borrow a lot from art but I see that as research." (17)

OBJECTS AS MORAL ACTANTS

To the high-minded designers and theorists of the last century, design had a social imperative. As founder of the discipline of design history, Nikolaus Pevsner put it: "To fight against the shoddy design of those goods by which most of our fellow men are surrounded becomes a moral duty." (18) Thanks to modern materials, especially plastics, the once elusive mixture of affordability and durability is commonplace (19) and the moral emphasis has shifted to ensuring products are conceptually as well as physically sound.

[16.]
Dunne, A. 2007. In: 'Design Interactions Yearbook 2007'. London: Royal College of Art

[17.]
Dunne, A. 2008. [Personal communication]. 15 January

[18.]
Pevsner, N. 1937. 'An Enquiry Into Industrial Art in England'. Basingtoke: Macmillan

[19.]
As discussed on p102, although plastics have brought durability at a low price, they suffer from an inability to age gracefully and their tactile qualities are often considered less satisfying than the materials they replaced. Hence the material substance of products can be said to have been diluted by plastics, despite their advantages.

Fig. 5   **Afterlife by Auger–Loizeau** The project explored uses for the latent chemical energy remaining within the body after death.

When considering concepts, designers are heavily guided by their own moral projection of what constitutes appropriate behaviour. Hence they must acknowledge the position of objects as moral actants (20) – that is, objects encourage and occasionally force us into certain behaviour deemed right or wrong. Designers, therefore, have the critical role of deciding to what extent their objects will direct our actions, and what they will direct us to do. Citing French sociologist Bruno Latour, Hans Achterhuis writes: "One of Latour's most famous examples is the safety-belt, that protests when it is not clasped on before starting to drive." (21) While the belt alone implies that we take our safety seriously by adding an alarm when not used, the design becomes fiercely paternalistic, forcing us to conform.

While many similar details are put in place for our safety (for example, power tools that won't start without their guards in place) the very concept of certain products is intended to shape us towards "being good". A case in point is Wattson, a home energy monitor (fig. 6, page 121). Although other monitors are available, Wattson is the only one that attempts to endear itself to us as an object of desire. Its slick black and white exterior, in the iPod vein, houses a red LED display on top (showing precise energy consumption in units) and coloured mood lights below (for a more general indication – blue for low usage, red for high). Its designers want us to place it prominently in the living room so that we may monitor our consumption regularly. Laudable though its purpose is, Wattson is a somewhat invasive and incessant reminder of our consumption and one that is likely to cause more than a little anxiety among users. Its designers must feel this is a small price to pay for the consequent reduction in energy use they hope it will achieve. However, the notion that designers should encourage self-imposed limits on what is still regarded as "normal" behaviour remains controversial.

Rather than forcing or shaming us into conforming, designers can look for ways in which products can help us be good while remaining sympathetic to our routines and habits. The Eco Kettle (fig. 7, page 122) tackles the problem of electricity being wasted by boiling a kettle-full of water when we need only a cupful (usually a result of our lazy desire to fill the kettle less often). By allowing us to fill it up completely and then transfer what we want to boil into a separate chamber, the product fits our existing pattern of use rather than forcing another upon us.

COPYING

The ethics of ownership is a naturally contentious subject in design. Every designer, knowingly or otherwise, will have reused elements from elsewhere. This book has advocated the borrowing of forms that are in the public domain as a strategy for attracting people to objects through familiarity (see 2.4 Collective memory and behaviour). Nevertheless, millions are spent each year to protect against copying, or to prosecute those who are caught doing it. The subject is made murkier by the fact that many areas of design are lead not by original thought but by trend, which can appear to advocate and justify direct appropriation.

While there is no value in producing new for the sake of new – the best of history must be built upon and improved – most designers recognise, as a matter of integrity, the need to differentiate their work from that of others. Where this threshold of differentiation begins – at what point he or she feels they have avoided encroaching upon the intellectual property (IP) of others – is personal and varies greatly among designers, manufacturers and across cultures. The

[20.]
Achterhuis, H. In: Van Hinte (ed). 2004. 'Eternally Yours: Time in Design: Product Value Sustenance'. Rotterdam: 010 Publishers

[21.]
Moore, Dr T. 2007. 'Whose design is it? How to protect your IP in China'. Report published by Sagentia

Fig. 6 **Wattson home energy monitor designed and manufactured by DIY Kyoto** Wattson is a home energy monitor intended to be left on show in the home. It indicates via mood lighting and an LED display the energy consumption of the household.

practice of producing counterfeit products, prevalent in parts of Asia, is seen as morally corrupt by Western standards, yet in some countries the notion that it is wrong has yet to develop fully. Dr Tim Moore of innovation consultants Sagentia points out that: "In mainland China, the years of communist rule since the 1940s engendered a culture where individuals could not own ideas; they were handed over and subsequently became the property of the state. Knowledge, it was considered, was better shared for the greater good of the country. It became natural for people to share ideas and the concept of IP as a valuable asset was unknown." (22) Moore continues to assert that although China has introduced legislation to protect IP, in his view "it will take much longer to change the culture than it did to change the law." (23)

Stories are told of parallel production lines for counterfeiting being set up by the same manufacturers commissioned to make the originals, thereby creating identical fakes. Customers are encouraged to split up their products and have various parts made in independent factories to cut down the likelihood of counterfeiting (24). On a recent visit to the China Import and Export Fair in Guangzhou, furniture designer Richard Shed saw copies of "Azumi LEM barstools, Arne Jacobsen Swan chairs and Ron Arad V&A chairs. They were like subtly mutated, interbred versions of the originals, all with oddly placed lumps and bumps and disproportionate limbs." (25)

There is an argument that says copies of design classics make them available on the mass market at affordable prices, expanding demand for the originals. One might even go so far as to suggest that such enterprises reflect the social ethos of bringing good design to the masses, that designers such as Charles and Ray Eames and Jean Prouvé applied to their work.

Would it not jar with their ideals to find the designs they had worked hard to rationalise for inexpensive mass production – now design classics – being sold at such comparatively exorbitant prices (the Standard chair by Jean Prouvé (fig. 8, page 122), originally designed for municipal buildings, currently costs around £470 from Vitra and auction estimates for originals reach as high as US$5,000)? Not that the Eameses or Prouvé would necessarily have condoned copying; aside from the lack of integrity, many copies compromise the quality of the official versions and royalties are not paid to the estates of the designers.

For practitioners educated to respect and pursue original thought, it is disturbing to see the way that copying and direct imitation, particularly in fields of design led by style and fashion, are accepted as the norm. A relatively successful young furniture designer recently boasted to a colleague that he just copied other people's designs and "changed them by 10 per cent". Sadly, the people who employ and publish the work of such "me-too" designers are often unaware that they are buying work of dubious integrity. However, some encourage it. Designer and client are likely to be able to make a successful living, the only drawback being the lack of critical acclaim from figures within the profession, who know that the work is derivative.

Even global giants such as IKEA – a company whose reputation has been built, in part, upon its "good design", have been caught selling direct translations of others' designs. Its Sture trestle, by ex-IKEA in-house designer Rutger Andersson, was banned from sale in Germany when courts there established it was a copy of a design called Taurus (fig. 9, page 123), by Jörg Sturm and Susanne Wartzeck, produced by German company Nils Holger Moormann (26). Such legal battles are tremendously costly and therefore represent great risk for small firms. Backers for Authentics, the company

[22. 23.]   -
Moore, Dr T. 2007. 'Whose design is it? How to protect your IP in China'. Report published by Sagentia

[24.]   -
Shed, R. 2008. "The China Chronicles." 'ID magazine.' June, p.42
                                    -
[25.]   -
Fairs, M. and Knutt, E. 2005. "Original Fakes." 'Icon' magazine. June
                                    -
[26. 27.]   -
Moormann, N. H. 2003. 'Moormann defeats Ikea in the battle against plagiarism'. [Page no longer available] <www.domusweb.it>
                                    -

Fig. 7   **Eco Kettle** **designed and manufactured** **by Product Creation Ltd.** The Eco Kettle allows control of how much of its capacity is to be boiled at any one time, allowing it to be filled fully but only one cupful boiled, if that is all that is required.

Fig. 8   **Standard** **chair by Jean Prouvé** **manufactured by Vitra** This chair was designed for municipal buildings and is an example of Prouvé's attention to rational mass production that reduces costs to a minimum while retaining durability.

who popularised well-designed domestic products using translucent polypropylene, were brought to the brink of bankruptcy by the costs of stopping their plagiarists in the US courts. (27)

With relatively superficial changes required to avoid prosecution and global budget brands that have the power to fight litigation openly selling barely legal translations of designs from others, originality is in danger of becoming a quality found only in high-end products. In-the-know consumers who wish to purchase products with integrity, designed and developed for the company who manufacture them, are increasingly having to pay for the privilege. By exploiting the fact that some consumers will not know the origins of a design, unscrupulous firms avoid paying for concept development, instead employing "designers" simply to draw up copies for manufacture.

In areas of design that are heavily influenced by fashion, it is sometimes hard to tell whether a product has been copied or the same form has been arrived at coincidentally. With certain forms and ideas becoming fashionable and many designers looking in the same places for inspiration, this is inevitable. Hence, many of the most innovative designers avoid fashion trends as inspiration, preferring to look elsewhere and chart their own unique path that others may choose to follow. Designer Robin Levien, who specialises in the industrial design of ceramics, takes care to source themes and formal influences from product genres other than the one being designed for. When working on tableware, cues may be gathered from other disciplines such as architecture, fashion design or jewellery. In doing so, Levien and his team arrive at proposals that are subtle aesthetic variations with a look "of their time", yet they are not copies of anything within the same field. They conform to Oscar Wilde's belief that the artist should provide "originality of treatment, not of subject." (28)

Thomas Jefferson, the third President of the United States saw both sides of the argument for protecting ideas as an inventor and was the administrator of the first US patents. He wrote: "Certainly an inventor ought to be allowed a right to the benefit of his invention for some certain time. Nobody wishes more than I do that ingenuity should receive liberal encouragement…In the arts, and especially in the mechanical arts, many ingenious improvements are made in consequence of the patent right giving exclusive use of them." (29) Although as Victor Papanek pointed out in 'Design for the Real World', when it came to his own inventions Jefferson never took out a patent, remarking of his hemp brake (a device for vastly speeding up the processing of hemp), "I shall probably describe it anonymously in the public papers in order to forestall the prevention of its use by some interloping patentee." (30) If copying of an invention could speed the spreading of its benefit and was therefore in the public interest, Jefferson saw that restricting its use to the owner and licensees of a patent could do more harm than good.

THE ETHICS OF MATERIAL USE

The ethics of material use can be considered to encompass our relations towards fellow humans, animals and to the planet as both a resource and an ecosystem. There is an ethical imperative to ensure humane behaviour in all aspects of the identification, extraction, processing, transformation into product and disposal of materials. While much of this falls neatly under the remit of sustainability (discussed in the next section), our attitude towards animals as materials stands out and hence deserves separate discussion.

[28.]
Wilde, O., Jackson, R., Small, I., Bristow, J. 2000. 'The Complete Works of Oscar Wilde'. Oxford: Oxford University Press

[29.]
Jefferson, T. In: Jefferson, T. and Foley, J.P. 1900. 'The Jeffersonian Cyclopedia: A comprehensive collection of the views of Thomas Jefferson'. New York: Funk & Wagnalls

[30.]
Jefferson, T. In: Papanek, V. 1974. 'Design for the Real World: Human Ecology and Social Change'. London: Granada Publishing Ltd

Fig. 9   Taurus Trestle by Jörg Sturm and Susanne Wartzeck for Nils Holger Moormann Nils Holger Moormann manufactures this ingenious design for a trestle that twists to ensure stability on uneven floors. It is made in solid beech and stainless steel. An almost identical version in plywood and painted mild steel produced by IKEA was banned from sale in Germany.

Fig. 10   Lasting Void by Julia Lohmann Lohmann's stool, made of fibreglass cast from a plaster mould of the ribcage of a calf that had died of natural causes, sparked much ethical debate when images of the process of its creation were printed in 'Icon' magazine.

There has long been debate surrounding the ethics of what materials are deemed appropriate for processing into products. The fur and ivory trades are the most obvious reminders of a colonial heritage of products containing materials now considered of dubious origin. Arguments still rage over the use of animal products in fashion, design and, of course, for food.

The designer Julia Lohmann set up an intriguing ethical debate with her stool entitled Lasting Void (fig. 10, page 123). Like a number of her projects, it encourages us to dwell upon our treatment of animals by presenting us with an uncanny form and revealing its source. The stool, made by casting inside the carcass of a dead calf and subsequently moulding this form in black fibreglass, is seductively organic and bears the unmistakable ribcage of its master. On seeing the piece, Alessandro Mendini (considered one of Italy's great design theorists and a respected designer in his own right) wrote an open letter to 'Icon' magazine and Gallery Kreo in Paris where the stool was being exhibited, describing it as "an extremely sad moment in the history of objects." He continued: "I can see no theoretical, aesthetic, methodological or anthropological reason which justifies the idea of immortalising a dead animal's last breath in order, sadistically, to propose it as an item for everyday use... The idea is cynical and pointless, it is simply turning the torture of a dead body into entertainment." (31)

In Lohmann's reply (printed in the same issue of 'Icon' magazine as Mendini's letter), she defends the piece on the grounds that the design did not cause the death of the calf – it died of natural causes – and was therefore considered unsuitable for consumption as meat. Far from being designed merely for entertainment, it is, she says, embedded with "ethical functionality" (32) – her neologism for the way the object prompts us to consider the ethical issues surrounding its production, and that of other related products i.e. those of the meat industry and the furniture made from its by-products.

From the tone of Mendini's criticism, it appears he believed the calf had been killed for the sole purpose of creating the stool, hence his ethical outrage. And why wouldn't he jump to such a conclusion if limited information had been given? Our view of Lasting Void's ethical status may well depend upon our knowing the circumstances of the calf's death and of the activities that led to its transformation into a stool. Once in possession of the facts, we can compare these to our own actions and views on the treatment of animals. The piece becomes an ethical barometer. As a reminder of the unseen materiality of factory farming, it may or may not be sobering to the committed carnivore. Yet those who literally believe that animals and humans are to be treated as equals may have difficulties condoning the interference with a dead body, no matter how it was obtained, and no matter how worthy the intended result.

Putting this specific case to one side, such work raises numerous questions. Do the boundaries of acceptable behaviour within the design of products and furniture differ from those of art? Should a piece of highly evocative work be allowed to traverse more ethical boundaries than something less affecting? Does the reproduction of a piece exacerbate any ethical transgression required to make it singly, or is volume beside the point in matters of right and wrong? As with the work dealing with dark subject matter discussed earlier, our ethical views may be coloured by our understanding of the context of a piece and the intentions of its designer.

Fig. 11   **The Natomo Family, Mali from the book 'Material World' by Peter Menzel** An astonishing achievement, Menzel's book captures the dwellings, possessions and members of statistically average families in 30 countries around the world. The contrasts speak for themselves.

[31.] -
Mendini, A. Open Letter to ICON and Gallery Kreo, 'Icon' magazine, November 2007.
-
[32.] -
Lohmann, J. Response to Alessandro Mendini, 'Icon Magazine', November 2007.
-
[33.] -
Huppatz D. J. 2007. 'Critical Cities Reflections on 21st Century Culture' [online]. [Accessed 27th January 2009]. Available from World Wide Web: <www.djhuppatz. blogspot.com/2007/06/design-for-other-90.html>
-
[34.] -
Grayling, A. C. In: Roberts, L. 2006. 'Good: An Introduction to Ethics in Graphic Design'. Lausanne: AVA Publishing SA
-

While design work can provoke debate about its own ethical status, some intends to elicit discussion around the ethics of the behaviour of others, in particular the conundrums surrounding new sciences. Many of these works concern the future making of objects, food and extensions to the functionality of the human body (see 2.12 Design for debate).

- -
ANOTHER WORLD

The astonishing disparity between the average wealth of families in countries across the world is starkly illustrated in Peter Menzel's book 'Material World – A Global Family Portrait' (Sierra Club Books, San Francisco, 1995), (fig. 11, page 124 and fig. 12, page 125). Sadly, as historian D. J. Huppatz's quote below suggests, many others have a tendency to consider "the world" as confined to the consumer society in which they live: "When a celebrity designer such as Karim Rashid, for example, states that he 'wants to change the world', the question we should be asking is, whose world? (See the book 'Karim Rashid, I Want to Change the World', New York: Universe, 2001.) Or, in response to his more recent challenge, 'Design Your Self: Rethinking the Way You Live, Love, Work, and Play' (New York: Regan Books, 2006), isn't it time we got beyond simply thinking about ourselves?" (33) However, as discussed in 2.5 Social inclusion, many designers may feel out of their depth working in the developing world when the common skills they use are not necessarily those most required. However, there are projects that industrial designers have become involved in that are set to have enormous effect there. An example is One Laptop Per Child (OLPC) (fig. 13, page 125), an education project instigated by MIT Professor Nicholas Negroponte. The project has developed a laptop that costs around US$175 and is now available, through government purchasing schemes, to children around the world. Its user interface was designed by Pentagram and the exterior by Yves Béhar.

Product design, as part of a wider manufacturing and distribution system, is a business of ethical compromise. The personal ethical decision that all designers face is that of how much compromise they are willing to accept when faced with the dilemmas their work raises. Philosopher A C Grayling sums up the predicament with these words: "Like everyone else, designers find themselves in a spider's web of duties – contractual duties, duties to clients, to stakeholders, to colleagues, to themselves and their work, and to society at large. It is sometimes difficult to serve everybody well, while at the same time fulfilling one's implicit duties to society. I think it legitimate for someone to say that they try their best, and to learn from failures." (34)

- -

Fig. 12   The Skeen Family, USA, from the book 'Material World' by Peter Menzel

Fig. 13   XO laptop computer by Pentagram and Yves Béyar manufactured by One Laptop Per Child
The One Laptop Per Child project aimed to dramatically reduce the purchase price of a laptop computer and make one specifically designed for children, available around the world, particularly in developing countries.

[1.]
William McDonough is an
internationally renowned
designer and the co-author
with Michael Braungart of
'Cradle to Cradle: Remaking the
Way We Make Things'. 2002.
New York: North Point Press

[2.]
Thackara, J. In: Bakker,
C. and van Hinte, E. 1999.
'Trespassers'. Rotterdam: 010
Publishers. Thackara's book
'In the Bubble: Designing
in a Complex World '(2005,
Cambridge, Mass: MIT Press)
also confronts the challenge
of sustainability.

2.9

SUSTAINABILITY

Sustainability – the goal of achieving equilibrium in the production and consumption of the planet's resources – is an ethical issue although its complexity and importance in product design warrants a section of its own. Its vastness as a subject makes it impossible to do justice to it in even one whole book; however, a number of the issues it encompasses are raised below.

OPPOSING SOLUTIONS

It is an ethical imperative that we should not leave the planet in a worse state than we found it. This statement applies to our built infrastructure and the products within it as well as to the natural environment. As campaigning designer William McDonough (1) and others have pointed out, with the information we now have about the damage caused by being unsustainable, it is profoundly unethical not to act positively or to simply do nothing.

With the exception of a few radicals, there is broad agreement about the difficulties we face in terms of reaching a sustainable ecosystem, yet there is huge disagreement about the methods and means to be used to achieve it. Although far more complex than this simple explanation suggests, one of the main disagreements is between imposing limits as opposed to allowing freedom to explore solutions. There is a pro-technology lobby that back far greater investment in research and development and the removal of top down regulation that, they say, impedes innovation. On the contrary, there are those who argue that our unquestioning deference to technology is what has led to our current predicament and that people-power

is the answer. Each side caricatures the other – it's the polluting, optimistic futurists against the hand-wringing, doom-laden nostalgics.

Innovation strategy expert John Thackara writes that "sustainability is hard to sell as a gruelling regime of limits – but not if we recast it as progress." (2) Traditional thinking on the subject is based around using less of what we currently use, but recycling and reusing as much of that as we can. Yet with economies based on growth, such an equation simply doesn't add up. We merely use up our precious resources at a slower rate. The result is our current anxiety around the consumption of products and energy and the consequent paternalism of governments and green lobbyists.

CRADLE-TO-CRADLE

But new thinking is emerging that challenges this model. Limits are imposed when our use of resources poses threats. Remove these threats and we will have unlimited resources. How can this be done? According to William McDonough, the answer is to change the way we think about materials. Along with Dr Michael Braungart, McDonough founded consultancy MBDC to promote and shape what they call the "Next Industrial Revolution". The firm's website states: "The industrial framework that dominates our lives now is fairly primitive. It is conceived around a one-way manufacturing flow – what is known as a 'cradle-to-grave' lifecycle. This cradle-to-grave flow relies on brute force (including fossil fuels and large amounts of powerful chemicals). It seeks universal design solutions ('one size fits all'), overwhelming and

[3.]
'MBDC website'. 2008. [online]. [Accessed 27th January 2009]. Available from the World Wide Web: <www.mbdc.com/c2c_home.htm>

[4.]
DuraBooks website. 2005. [online]. [Accessed 27th January 2009]. Available from World Wide Web: <www.durabooks.com>

[5.]
McDonough, W. and Braungart, M. 2002. 'Cradle to Cradle: Remaking the Way We Make Things'. New York: North Point Press

[6.]
Sprout Design website [online]. [Accessed 27th January 2009]. Available from World Wide Web: <www.sproutdesign.co.uk/lca.htm>

ignoring natural and cultural diversity. And it produces massive amounts of waste – something that in nature does not even exist... Instead of designing cradle-to-grave products, dumped in landfills at the end of their 'life', MBDC transforms industry by creating products for cradle-to-cradle cycles, whose materials are perpetually circulated in closed loops. Maintaining materials in closed loops maximizes material value without damaging ecosystems." (3)

Most recycling, McDonough and Braungart tell us, is actually "downcycling". That is, the resulting material is of a lower grade than the original, meaning the same product cannot always be made from it. However, this is not inevitable. They use their own book, 'Cradle to Cradle: Remaking the Way We Make Things', to demonstrate. It is made not from paper but from a waterproof, polymer recyclable to the same quality – an example of the closed loops to which the title refers. (4)

"Cradle to cradle" thinking is powerful because it appears to bring together the conflicting visions about sustainability. It promotes abundance, but through a symbiotic rather than an imposing approach to creation. It responds to our moral duties, but without setting us impossible limits. It embraces the need for technology, research and development, but applies these pointedly to the task of achieving equilibrium.

Such a model places great weight upon designers and their clients to rethink the current materials and processes they use. It challenges them to work with material scientists in order to find and implement these

closed loops. Such tasks can be read as limits, but they offer hope of a move towards the limitless. By embracing biodegradability (itself potentially part of a closed loop) and closed loop recycling within industry, McDonough and Braungart propose a model that is about being "100% good" rather than simply "less bad". (5)

LIFE-CYCLE ANALYSIS

Such a panacea is a big leap, especially as not all designers are the most scientifically minded of people. However, tools are available to help. For many years, eco-minded designers have used life cycle analysis to try to gauge the relative harm done in the processes from cradle to grave. Sprout Design, whose Binvention (fig. 1, page 127) helps with the separation of household waste, are an industrial design consultancy specialising in sustainable and inclusive solutions. Sprout say they "undertake a basic life cycle analysis at the start of every product design project. This allows us to identify the main aspects of the design that cause environmental damage and inspire creative new concepts to fulfil the brief while also reducing the impact." (6) During this process, they consider the resources (including energy) consumed by the ways in which:

raw materials are sourced

manufacturing is carried out

products are packaged and transported

products are used and disposed of.

Fig. 1 **Binvention recycling bin designed and manufactured by Sprout Design** Binvention is a product that allows easy separation of domestic refuse prior to recycling using conventional plastic bags.

Another rarely considered factor is the impact of marketing and promotion. By placing figures upon the impact of all these factors it is possible to achieve a kind of eco-quotient for a product. However, the complexity of such calculations can be vast and with contention over how it should be done, the figures are open to manipulation. There are various tools that help give ballpark figures <www.lcacalculator.com> and designers ought to attempt, as far as is realistic, to encourage their clients in the right direction. However, ultimately it may be the law that will have the biggest impact.

LEGISLATION

One of the greatest hindrances to recycling has been the lack of effective systems that facilitate collection of products before they are wrongly disposed of in landfill. While provision has been made for the likes of glass, cans, newspapers and some plastics, electrical goods often pose greater environmental threats. In response, the European Union recently launched the Waste Electrical and Electronic Equipment (WEEE) directive that makes producers and importers of electronic goods responsible for recycling their products. The directive ensures that businesses finance the cost of recovering and treating the types of products they import, re-brand or manufacture, and provide information on how

any new product might be reused or recycled (fig. 2, page 129). For designers and their clients, this means considering how an electrical product can be easily dismantled, enabling this reuse and recycling – a sensible consideration whether the product falls under the directive or not.

EMOTIONAL DURABILITY

Another way that manufacturers can be reconnected with consumers is through not selling them products, but by leasing them. Already popular with white goods such as washing machines, the notion that the manufacturer retains ownership of the object is a popular one for consumers because it puts the responsibility upon the manufacturer for repair and replacement of failed components as well as the WEEE obligations. In spite of this, extending this approach into products with which we tend to have a more personal relationship may prove difficult and may not necessarily be beneficial. Ownership can engender a greater sense of care and allows the personalisation of the object, through wear or planned customisation. This offers the opportunity for a strong bond to develop between user and object that can transcend fashion. Why is this useful for sustainability? Objects cherished in this way will be kept long after others are swapped for the latest model. Less desire for the new means less resource use manufacturing it, less energy recycling it or waste disposing of it. While making products physically durable sometimes clashes with what makes them recyclable, if lifespan is increased sufficiently this may be justifiable.

This is an approach advocated by Sam Hecht at Industrial Facility who tells us: "We try to ensure design is enduring, that people keep it around. If it's memorable and enduring, it treats design as a concept of quality; quality of craftsmanship, quality of thinking. That's a far greener, more sustainable product than one designed with sustainability in mind but without those values. What's the point of designing for recycling if it's a piece of crap, compared to designing something that's not designed specifically for recycling but that's going to be sticking around for a lot longer?" (7) Michael Marriott cites the Eames fibreglass dining chair as an example, recently re-released in polypropylene, its manufacturer Vitra says, for environmental reasons. "Fibreglass is nasty stuff to work with and you can't recycle it, but I don't think that matters when that chair has already lasted 40 years and will easily last another 40 or more. The new ones will need to be recycled, because they are so much less robust and will soon become grubby and rough-looking." (8)

Engendering this emotional as well as physical durability is the purpose of many of the approaches explored in this book, whether through qualities of form and materials, making poetic links, involving the user in the creative act or eliciting meaningful discussion.

Because no design work (or design book) is neutral, it will always be open to critique from at least one perspective. Hence, designers often shy away from promoting a particular piece of work as being especially ethical or sustainable in case this exposes it, or their other projects, to increased scrutiny. With such highly emotive issues and conflicting views on the right courses of action, there is a sense that anyone who puts their head above the parapet will be shot at. However, if progress is to be made and knowledge shared, designers and their clients need to be encouraged to declare their successes and face criticism of their shortcomings.

-            -

[7.]   -
Hecht, S. 2008. [Personal communication]. 24 January
-
[8.]   -
Marriott, M. In: Roberts, L. 2006. 'Good: An Introduction to Ethics in Graphic Design'. Lausanne: AVA Publishing SA
-

Fig. 2   WEEE directive symbol This symbol indicates that the product's manufacturer has duties under the Waste Electrical and Electronic Equipment directive and that the product should not be disposed of in landfill.

[1.]
Argan, G. C. In: Burkhardt, F., Capella, J., Picchi F. 1997. 'Why Write a Book on Enzo Mari?' Milan: Frederico Motta Editore (Argan was writing about Mari's Autoprogettazione project featured on page 93.)

[2. 3.]
Leadbeater, C. 2005. Speaking at conference Technology, Entertainment, Design (TED), Oxford, UK. Available from World Wide Web: <www.ted.com/talks>

2.10

PARTICIPATION

As discussed previously, one way of contributing to the reduction of waste is by designing in such a way as to provide a sense of quality that will make people less likely to dispose of products prematurely. Yet despite all of the form- and material-based attempts to encourage longevity, it can still feel something of a lottery as to whether objects endear themselves to people. The following section discusses design approaches that involve people in the creative process in the hope that personal connection will guarantee this long-term satisfaction. While being successfully applied to the design of objects, these participatory approaches have also become the tools of choice for a growing band of design consultancies looking to democratise their activities.

APPROACHES TO PARTICIPATION

There are two discernibly different strands to this work. The first, termed 'participatory' or 'co-design', is literally to design with the people who will be buying and using the products. These methods emerged from the user-centred approaches discussed in 2.5 Social inclusion. The second, which we will call "self-design" involves using people as active participants in configuring, building, completing or customising objects but differs from participatory and co-design in that it does not imply real-time collaboration with designers; rather, it indicates that the designers have intentionally allowed the purchasers/users to have a pre-defined role in some aspects of making the objects.

"Mari is right, everyone should design: after all, it is the best way to avoid being designed." (1)

This quotation about the sentiments of Italian designer Enzo Mari hints at one of the central theoretical reasons why anyone, not just designers, can benefit from involvement in designing what surrounds them. In the 1950s, the threat of totalitarian regimes was fresh in the memories of designers like Mari. Even a so-called free market did not necessarily offer sufficient opportunity for people to buy what was best for them. Despite the abundance of goods available to us now, many actually offer us quite narrow spectrums of choice. When industry's view of how we want our products to manifest themselves becomes out of sync with our actual desires, the more creative among us tend to take matters into our own hands. Design in this context becomes an expression of personal freedom and individuality beyond that available to us through consumption alone.

PRO-AMS

Many of those who express this individuality through making are not designers but "pro-ams" – professional amateurs who live their pastimes with singular commitment. As Charles Leadbeater, a writer and promoter of participatory models of design and innovation reminds us, some of the key commercial product genres of our time, such as the mountain bike, emerged from grass roots innovation by users rather than the lone genius inventor or the R&D departments of bicycle manufacturers. (2) As Leadbeater recounts, users in Northern California, frustrated with racing bikes and traditional "sit up and beg" road bicycles, combined gears from the former with frames from

Fig. 1   Readymade Magazine Readymade Magazine continues a long tradition of the sharing of creative and expedient tips for home décor and self-made objects.

Fig. 2   Creative Commons Licence logos Creative Commons licences allow creators to assign different ways in which others can use their work.

the latter and brakes from motorcycles to create the first mountain bikes or "clunkers". Small companies grew to service this group of users and kept growing. It took 10–15 years before the mainstream bicycle manufacturers took notice and now, 30 years later, 65 per cent of all bicycle sales are of mountain bikes (3). All of which resulted from the self-interested diligence of a group of enthusiasts.

OPEN-SOURCE

Collaborative innovation is of course not new – it is simply a buzz phrase for an activity that has happened since communities were formed and people began sharing knowledge. These practices are still very much in evidence despite the very notion of community, particularly in cities, shifting from one defined by locality to one formed by shared interests. Magazines such as 'Practical Farm Ideas', 'Readymade' (fig. 1, page 130) and websites such as <www.Instructables.com> continue a tradition of publications based upon people sending in "how to" articles. California-based O'Reilly Media has been a key exponent of knowledge sharing, not least through its magazine, 'Make'. Subtitled "technology on your time", it contains instructions for useful and whimsical products, usually containing simple mechanics or electronics. Many also included software hacks reflecting O'Reilly's roots in the collaborative software movement that became known as open-source.

It is worth briefly exploring the background to the open-source movement in order to see how the lessons learned are being applied to product design.

THE CATHEDRAL AND THE BAZAAR

In the early days of the computer industry, just as in any society, the essential structures were being built and it made sense for software developers (hackers – before it became a dirty word) to share source code and modify it for their own needs, adding improvements as they went. But as the industry grew and software became a competitively saleable commodity, companies became inclined to protect their code and build in safeguards against unsolicited use. This change so outraged some of the early protagonists that they committed themselves to foiling secrecy within corporations by wilfully making public new code for others to use, causing the emergence of a strong open-source community.

One of these early pioneers, Eric Raymond, coined the phrase "the cathedral and the bazaar" (3) to represent these two opposing models of behaviour. The corporate software developers build the cathedrals – Microsoft being the most potent example – where they employ thousands of developers working secretively to improve their programmes for periodic release every few years. Conversely, the bazaar refers to the community of programmers and software engineers who share code and help build systems in an open and collaborative way, uploading them to the net for continual use and improvement by others.

It is easy to assume that such decentralised structures would fail to produce anything coherent. However, the most prominent example – the Linux operating system and products emerging from it (such as the popular Firefox web browser) – have become genuine rivals of the wares of the major cathedral-based developers.

One of the central reasons for the success of the open-source model was that it allowed the developer-users to personalise the software for their own needs, rather than relying upon the cathedral-based producers to predict them.

Fig. 3   **Freitag F-Cut web tool by Severin Klaus**
Thanks to Klaus's tool, visitors to Freitag's website can see the lorry tarpaulins the company uses to make bags and select which portion they would like theirs to be made from.

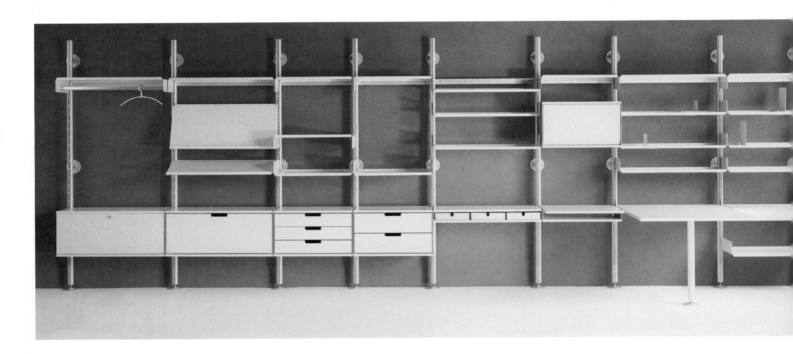

Fig. 4   606 Shelving
System by Dieter Rams,
manufactured by Vitsoe The
flexibility designed into Rams's
shelving system means it can
be easily reconfigured to fit
new spaces should its owners
move. Designed in 1960, it is
still in production today.

Fig. 5   Do Scratch
lamp by Marti Guixé,
manufactured by Droog
Design Essentially a painted
light box, this lamp requires
its user to scratch at its black
painted surface for light to be
able to shine through.

The open-source model has become the core principle behind websites that rely on user-generated content such as Wikipedia. Like software programs, written content can be edited, improved upon and uploaded, gradually improving quality. Yet as a model that relies upon a critical mass of user involvement, quality starts out low and remains patchy, improving greatest where there is most "traffic". By accepting these early stages of development as usable, critics have accused mass collaboration projects of lowering our expectations of quality. (4)

While enterprises run by and for its customers will happily let them define its direction, businesses with shareholders may feel differently. The counter-argument against the collaborative process is that it inherently lacks singular vision. The customer as developer may have short-term goals that are easily fulfilled, but can they effectively contribute to the long-term direction of a business? Companies, like politicians, need to gauge the opinions of the people, but for success and respect they also need to display their own convictions and employ those with suitable experience. Such people may or may not be discovered using an open-source model. As collaborative processes are embraced by product design, there is much discussion about what is delegated and how.

CO-DESIGN AND PARTICIPATORY DESIGN

Product design is an inherently collaborative process. Except for a select band of designer-makers, at some point in the design process discussions occur about the best way of doing something. Even the most hermit-like designer will discuss the brief with the client, present their work and liaise with production managers. What these new collaborative models are proposing is that "the design bit" becomes a more open activity, based less on the intuition of the designer and more on needs made evident through discussion with those the design affects.

While the term "participatory design" implies that a designer is participating with other stakeholders (such as users, purchasers, manufacturers, retailers) to improve the end result, co-design suggests an even flatter hierarchy where no single stakeholder is considered to be "in charge". Instead, all of the parties involved input ideas, expertise and energy to bring new products to the market.

While some consultancies are applying this model face to face, it is on the Internet that it becomes most powerful, with websites becoming forums for developers to communicate. One example is CrowdSpirit, an online community that proposes, designs, invests in and organises the manufacture of new electronic products. The website enables the process to happen by managing various stages, including allowing the community to vote for which ideas ought to be developed and to define product specifications. It is an example of what has become known as "crowdsourcing".

Importantly, CrowdSpirit's community allows different amounts of involvement. You can become part of the community and simply observe developments, or you can become a more active participant in various stages, depending upon your expertise or finances. It caters for those who do not want to be designers or developers but want to have a say in the kind of products that might be developed – a feeling that is absent from our dealings with large corporations.

[4.]
Richmond, S. 2007. "Critical Mass". 'RSA Journal.' December.

Fig. 6 **Do Add chair by Jurgen Bey** Bey's chair has one leg shorter than the other three, requiring the user to find something, such as a pile of magazines, with which to prop it up.

Fig. 7   Hat Lamp by Curro Claret Wall and table versions of this lamp have been made. Both consist of a light fitting with a wire frame upon which the user is intended to place a hat, thereby making a shade.

Fig. 8   Bracket Shelves by Curro Claret Claret's shelving system consists of folded metal brackets, which the user positions, fixes to the wall and on which they then sit found boxes and crates.

Such enterprises pose the question of who owns the intellectual property that they generate. To protect the interests of open-source producers, a new set of licences has been introduced called Creative Commons <http://creativecommons.org>, to allow creators greater control over how their work can be used (fig. 2, page 130). Rather than work being either protected or not, CC licence symbols refer to different ways in which the work can be used by others.

AN ENDANGERED SPECIES?

It is highly likely that over the next 5–10 years, three-dimensional printing equipment (see 2.7 Technological innovation) will become available for the home market. Marrying this technology with online crowdsourced design opens up the possibility of downloading and printing products at home, just as we are able to do with documents today. Three-dimensional scanners, already available, allow designers to scan and upload objects for others to download and print. With more and more tools empowering the public to become designers and manufacturers, will designers themselves become an endangered species? At a recent conference, CEO of global design consultancy IDEO Tim Brown advised: "I believe that letting go as designers, and engaging in a collaborative process, is the biggest challenge from a conceptual point of view for us as designers... If we don't embrace it, it'll happen anyway." (5)

But to what extent will designers be left behind by this shift? Crowdsourced innovation bypasses the traditional corporate infrastructure of which some designers are part. Yet, crowdsourcing without design input is likely to produce products that lack the refinement that designers traditionally bring. As Tim Brown suggests, designers may have to fit into this new model – it may even force them to objectify still

further what it is that they offer – but they will have a place nonetheless (6). The notion that non-designers will either want to, or be able to, define effectively in detail the physical aspects of a product, is doubtful. Just as home printing gave people the opportunity to be typographers, few did so to a high standard, thereby highlighting the skills within the profession. While there are some interesting examples of the public being given the opportunity to define certain visual aspects of objects (discussed below), these commonly amount to them simply being offered options predefined by designers rather than any broader freedom. For the sake of both the designer and non-designer, a balance between valued input and necessary expertise must be struck. While collaboration may ensure the design fits all, at some point we must acknowledge the primacy of the designer as having heightened visual and/or technical acuity, and allow him to do his work.

SELF-DESIGN

As was proposed in 2.5 Social inclusion, it is possible to describe a spectrum of user involvement in the design process that ranges from 0 per cent (the designer not involving or considering the user at all) to 100 per cent (the user designing the entire product). The lower end of the scale can be said to represent traditional industrial design practice. As their involvement increases, the user is first empathised with, then actually consulted by, the designer. Beyond this point, they begin to get physically involved in defining the object. This territory can be defined as "self-design".

Under this umbrella, there are many distinct approaches that require differing levels of expertise and commitment on the part of the user.

[5. 6.]
Brown, T. 2007. Speaking at Intersections conference. 25 October

Fig. 9   Candloop by Sebastian Bergne manufactured by Details Bergne's design turns the usually ostentatious candelabra into a modest and minimal object, borrowing a used wine bottle for its base.

Fig. 10   Techno Tapas by Marti Guixé While many people follow, adapt or make up recipes, few other than professional chefs pay much regard to form. Guixé reconfigured the ingredients of typical tapas dishes making them less messy to eat, publishing the results in a book.

The first – open products – allows the user to configure or customise them. An obvious example is the desktop of any computer that can be personalised with our own choice of image. Similarly, Freitag, a company that makes accessories from recycled lorry tarpaulins, has a website that allows customers to personalise new bags. Using a cookie-cutter-like tool, they can select which area of the tarpaulin their bag will be made from (fig. 3, page 131). Open products may also be modular systems or kits of parts that we put together to suit our own needs. Vitsœ's 606 shelving by Dieter Rams offers just such an opportunity (fig. 4, page 132).

The next category is unfinished products, where the user must complete them before use. This may involve assembly, decoration or the addition of an object of their own (if this is considered as a design approach primarily intended to create an enjoyable experience, it stands in contrast to that of flat-pack furniture whereby the purchaser is made to assemble their product for the sake of economy). As a protest against bland uniformity, Dutch advertising agency KesselsKramer created Do, a brand to encourage participation and personalisation. Curators Droog Design recruited designers to come up with Do products and the results were shown at the Milan Furniture Fair in 2000. Two examples from the range are Marti Guixé's Do Scratch lamp – a black painted acrylic light-box that requires the user to scratch off the paint to let the light through (fig. 5, page 132) and Jurgen Bey's Do Add chair which has one shorter leg, requiring it to be propped up with books or magazines (fig. 6, page 133). The underlying benefit to this approach is that

the designer has intentionally left something out in order for the consumer to find pleasure in supplying it. Whereas one can imagine a certain enjoyment in scratching the paint from Guixé's lamp, Bey's chair looks like a dangerous liability. Should its short leg slip from its supporting pile of literature, the sitter will be unceremoniously catapulted onto the floor – hardly a recipe for endearment?

Successful unfinished products allow the owner to give a personal contribution without needing to show a high degree of skill. Curro Claret's lamps require hats to act as their shades (fig. 7, page 134), while his wall storage brackets invite us to use found boxes to create a striking and unique system (fig. 8, page 134). Selling something incomplete is a challenge to conventional wisdom and hence such products tend to be marginalised into more avant-garde retail outlets. One that has found a more mainstream audience is Sebastian Bergne's Candloop candelabra (fig. 9, page 135) that simply requires an old wine bottle to act as its base.

The final category of self-design before the user literally becomes the designer is the recipe. Just as with cooking, instructions are provided along with a list of ingredients (materials). The product becomes weightless – consisting only of the transmission of an idea. User becomes manufacturer. Marti Guixé's Techno Tapas project literally brings together cooking and product design, re-working tapas dishes to make them cleaner and more enjoyable to eat (fig. 10, page 135).

Yet even more so than with unfinished products, building a product from scratch is a leap of faith the uninitiated may find daunting. The designer must do

Fig. 11 Ecolo by Enzo Mari, limited edition manufactured by Alessi
This set of four vases in a presentation box has been made by cutting new forms into used plastic detergent bottles (see page 16).

all they can to simplify and clarify the process via the instruction material. The project becomes as much about information design as product design. Examples include Enzo Mari's Autoprogettazione (which means literally self-design) featured on page 93. This book of designs for domestic furniture was not, as many people mistakenly thought, about doing away with industry in favour of the homemade. Mari's thinking held that if we all had experience of making furniture ourselves, this would give us a more discerning eye towards the quality of what we found in stores. An uncannily similar project was undertaken in the 1990s by Tord Boontje entitled Rough and Ready Furniture, although rather than printing scale drawings, Boontje gave away 1:1 scale drawings on to which the components could be laid as they were being assembled.

A slightly different approach was taken by Mari in a later project, Ecolo. Instead of building with raw materials, he proposed that people modify used plastic bottles into vases. Again, an instruction booklet was provided offering suggested designs, and an

accompanying sticker that "certified" the creation. Like Autoprogettazione, Mari had an ulterior motive. Ecolo could be obtained in three ways: buying the label and instructions to do-it-yourself; buying one already cut and labelled; and buying one cut, numbered and signed by Mari (Alessi later produced a box set of four as a limited edition (fig. 11, page 136)). As well as encouraging appreciation of the value of the disposable bottles, the project became a meditation upon the value of labour, presentation and provenance.

Similarly, Daniel Charny's Pigdogs (fig. 12, page 137) are cut from two-pint plastic milk bottles. Designed as "votive objects" – symbols of our desire to recycle more, and to help alleviate our guilt that we do not – Charny and his team conducted a workshop showing the public how to make their own. Special gold-metallised versions were on sale and instructions could be taken away.

-          -

Fig. 12   Pigdog
by Daniel Charny Turning the everyday into the extraordinary, Charny designed a way to turn a plastic milk bottle into a pig with a few cuts of the scissors. A metalising process then gives each pig a lustrous coating, creating an object of contemplation around the subject of recycling.

[1.]
Brown, T. 2007. Speaking at
Intersections conference,
Gateshead, UK. 25 October

STRATEGIES AND SERVICES

This section is about a shift that has been taking place in product design from designers dealing with the physical task of designing products to their involvement in strategy. The notion that designers used to stick to designing objects is an oversimplification. Company directors occasionally formed close relationships with designers, who would advise, usually informally, upon directions that may be taken. What has changed is that designers are now formalising this process, offering services to clients that are about shaping their future business models and organisational structures. By framing what they do differently and forging new interdisciplinary collaborations, designers have discovered clients and projects that take them outside of the traditional confines of the profession. One of these new areas of business, discussed below, is the design of services.

GOING UPSTREAM

From an early stage in their history, product design consultancies recognised that once they had gained the trust of the client then they were in a good position to sell them other kinds of work. This was not entirely cynical – by offering corporate identity, packaging, point-of-sale design and so on alongside designing the product, they could ensure all elements worked harmoniously.

Hence, the role played by larger design consultancies shifted from providing product-specific knowledge and skills to directing a company's image. This required an overview of their activities and future strategy. Consultancies, as well as selling the physical results of design, began to sell knowledge and advice about how organisations conceived of their offerings and their brands. This process of designers becoming advisors on the strategic direction of company policies is referred to in the profession as "going upstream".

The first step in this process, and one which many designers have long been battling for, is to become part of the process of defining the brief rather than only being involved in implementing it. Beyond this lies the notion that no actual product design brief will be answered, but that the focus will be upon broader themes. This, Tim Brown from IDEO admits, is "an insurance policy" (1). In times of recession, companies may cut back on product design services as they spend less on developing new products. However, if designers are selling thinking that helps define the appropriate direction for companies, this can be sold at any time and is, if anything, more crucial during recession. It allows designers to be involved where there may not be a product to be designed, opening up their client base to include service providers, charities, government departments and other organisations.

This movement "upstream" can also be seen as a way for designers to confront their usual sense of impotence – the feeling that they are small cogs in a machine over which they have no control. By placing themselves within a sphere of greater influence, they have the opportunity to advise clients on the big issues as opposed to only being able to make small changes to products "downstream".

Yet going upstream does not always mean losing touch with the task of designing the object; rather it can be about framing it in the right way. Its advocates would claim it is about working through big and messy problems methodically, with the appropriate people, to arrive at tangible solutions. An example is the work of the Design Against Crime Research Centre, based at London's Central Saint Martins School of Art and Design. The centre aims to promote awareness of the ways in which design can reduce crime by undertaking exemplar projects resulting in new products, services and environments. The ambition is broad but the results are still object based.

DESIGN THINKING

Central to this move upstream is the notion that the thinking used during the design process is usefully transferable to a broad range of disciplines. Splitting up and analysing the processes they use has enabled designers to identify tools and methods they are able to pass on to non-traditional clients. Encapsulated in the phrase "design thinking", these include learning how to observe and empathise effectively with people, ideas generation techniques including building prototypes, presenting ideas in the form of stories, scenarios and experiences and managing interdisciplinary teams of experts. (2) While the intuitive form-based and craft-based skills are sometimes still used, they are downplayed so that design can be seen as a general problem-solving activity, rather than being specifically object-centric.

Tim Brown explains that "describing this process of design thinking was a way of demystifying some of the pieces of the design process that anyone who is not a designer has often found mysterious. It was useful firstly because it gave people reassurance that there was something behind what we did, that it wasn't just serendipitous, and secondly it allowed us to look at those methods and say: 'well, why wouldn't you apply them to designing for a social system, a service, or outside the traditional business sphere?' and all of those things we wanted to work on." (3)

Based on this principle, Stanford University in the United States opened its D-School to teach design skills to students from different departments including business, science and engineering. Head of the D-School David Kelley has stated that: "We decided that designers are going to be the people who integrate the technology and the process and are the glue that holds these experts together." (4) Similar aspirations can be seen in Design London, a venture combining the design expertise of the Royal College of Art, the technological knowledge of Imperial College's Faculty of Engineering and the business acumen of Imperial's Tanaka Business School.

Tim Brown is passionate about extending the D-School idea back further so that everyone can have a level of design knowledge as well as written literacy: "Just imagine if everyone who came out of secondary school had reasonable skills in visual problem solving." (5)

SERVICE DESIGN

Interaction design (see 2.7 Technological innovation), in stepping outside of the confines of the form of the object and embracing behaviour and computer interfaces, was a sign of the flexibility of design

[2.]
Brown, T. 2006. Speaking in lecture Innovation Through Design Thinking, MIT, USA. 16 March. Available from World Wide Web: <http://mitworld. mit.edu/>

[3.]
Brown, T. 2007. [Personal communication]. 11 December

[4.]
Kelley, D. In: Moggridge, B. 2007. 'Designing Interactions'. Cambridge, MA: MIT Press

[5.]
Brown, T. 2007. [Personal communication]. 11 December

[6.]
Downs, C. 2007. Speaking at
Intersections conference,
Gateshead, UK. 25 October.

[7.]
Downs, C. In: Moggridge, B.
2007. 'Designing Interactions'.
Cambridge, MA: MIT Press

thinking. It established a new colony that grew into a distinct discipline. Since then, a new colony has emerged from this – that of service design.

Service design began to form when the experience-based thinking previously applied to designing "tech-products" was considered in relation to whole services. It can be seen as an extension of the remit of interaction design in that some of the interfaces and equipment that interaction design dealt with became components within services. (Cash points, ticket machines, mobile telephones and websites have all benefited from the expertise of interaction designers, and all enable access to services such as banks, public transport, telecommunications.) However, whereas interaction design tended to deal specifically with chip-based technologies, a service may be designed without necessarily including these. Consequently the technology-based skill-sets of interaction designers became only one of many that service designers might call upon.

Chris Downs of service design consultancy Live/Work explains that "Service design is a multidisciplinary practice that applies design thinking as the umbrella process / practice that brings all of these people [interaction designers, communication designers, management consultants, operations experts etc.] together in a slightly different way than had previously been considered." (6) "Services are run and operated throughout the world, but they're not often designed. They're not crafted to the same level of expertise that products, interactions, and interfaces are." (7)

DESIGNING EXPERIENCES

By its nature, service design is not object-centric. Although we occasionally interact with services through objects – using what service designers call "touchpoints" – the objects are a means to an end, not an end in themselves. As opposed to many of the products we buy, where, besides functioning, we invest in the status they confer, many services leave no visible trace that we have used them. As a result, the emphasis in designing them shifts away from desirability and status towards clarity, simplicity and efficiency in use. That is not to say that the touchpoints of a service must be bland and uninspiring – rather, to endear themselves to us, they must first of all work, and work well.

Using various methods, Chris Downs and his team at Live/Work test the effectiveness of their clients' services, map the relationships between all those involved, prototype improvements and produce a blueprint to help ensure that quality is maintained (fig. 1, page 141). As part of this process, they transfer knowledge and empower their clients to improve their services themselves. One example is a co-design workshop undertaken with the staff of the Baltic Centre, an art gallery in Gateshead, England.

According to Downs: "Visitors to the Baltic don't like the big £3 donation sign as they find it confusing when it is actually free entry. The staff don't like it either. It makes them feel uncomfortable and they often feel the need to explain it to customers. But they've never had the tools or known how to make changes to their working environment. So [at the workshop] they just got a big piece of paper, blanked out the 'pay us £3' and on the back wrote 'Did you love us? If you loved your experience with us, how about a donation?' It was a really quick service prototype that transformed the mood of the staff and the visitors."

[8.] -
Downs, C. In: Moggridge, B. 2007. 'Designing Interactions'. Cambridge, MA: MIT Press
-

- - -
FROM PRODUCT ENVY TO SERVICE ENVY?

Leading commentators and practitioners in the field, including Live/Work, have argued that a shift towards providing more services is one way of getting us to consume less 'stuff'. They propose that if the value within products we buy could instead be delivered through services, these could be made more sustainable by design. The problem is that one of the main reasons why we consume so voraciously is that owned products express our individuality in ways that services currently do not. Consequently, Live/Work say there is a need to design into services the visible signs that have been used in order to provoke in others a sense of "service envy" (8).

The danger is that, to appeal to a wide market, envy will be generated in generic ways that can be avoided through ownership. For example, while, if funds allow, we have the option to buy a new car every few years, alternatively, we can decide to keep it, look after it, perhaps personalise it with accessories and develop a long-term relationship with it. After a few years, the car loses the generic "enviability" of being a new car and its value becomes more personal. If a car is provided as part of a service, it is highly likely that "service envy" would be engendered by ensuring all of the cars remained new, therefore stopping the possibility of this personal connection developing. Services need to find ways of allowing people to express their values in highly personal ways, which may have less to do with conspicuous consumption and more to do with responsible and emotional desires.

- -

Fig. 1 Workshop by Live/Work at The Baltic Centre for Contemporary Art, Gateshead The team at Live/Work conducted a design workshop with staff at the Baltic on how they could improve the experience of visiting the gallery.

DESIGN FOR DEBATE

This section examines the ways in which designers use their work to question conventions of design practice and other societal norms. While the desire for designers to differentiate their work from that of others can imply a critique of what has gone before, what materialises are often small modifications that challenge little. However, there is a growing understanding that rather than simply questioning the form and function of an object within a framework of production and consumption, design can further be used as a means of questioning those systems. Having grasped design's ability to manifest fictional spaces and props, practitioners are using these to present scenarios about design, technology and human nature.

[1.]
Barthes, R. and Heath, S. (trans) 1978. 'Image, Music, Text'. New York: Hill and Wang

[2.]
Ambasz, E. 1972. 'Italy: The New Domestic Landscape'. New York: MOMA

OPPOSITION AND CRITIQUE

Once mainstream thoughts and actions become established, critiques are ripe to emerge. "To criticise," wrote Roland Bathes, "is to put into crisis…something which is not possible without evaluating the conditions of the crisis" (1). Designers who use their medium to engage in effective critique must therefore first understand the nature of what they are criticising, before proposing alternatives. This suggests that they ought to have an overview of the structures and motivations that often go unquestioned in mainstream design practice.

At the beginning of this chapter, three ways of considering the ideological positions of designers were discussed. Curator Emilio Ambasz defined these as: conforming to, wishing to reform, or utterly contesting the systems that have shaped society (and hence design) thus far (2). By recognising the state of society and establishing what they think about it, designers can position themselves within Ambasz's model, learning from the techniques of others who define themselves similarly.

Design history, dating back to the Arts and Crafts movement, can be seen as a series of oppositional stances (Arts and Crafts movement versus mass-produced Victoriana, modernism versus decorative styles and hand-work, postmodernism and Pop Design versus modernism, for example) each attempting to establish a new orthodoxy to replace the last. According to Ambasz's model, many of the prime movers of each era would have been "reformists", changing the system through participation. Those he described as "in contest" have more radical views. Rather than take part in a system they fundamentally oppose (even in order to reform it), factions within this group withdraw from designing objects for production and distribution. Instead, they used their design skills to give expression to their critical positions and to communicate alternative possibilities. It is here that we find a territory where design is used primarily to provoke debate.

Although there is a long history of critique about the nature of manmade artefacts, the 1970s Italy that Ambasz was writing about, and the decade thereafter, was perhaps its richest period in design. In the hands of a close-knit band of trained architects, products and furniture became critical essays against what was seen as the blandness of European modernism. Studio Alchymia, Superstudio, Archizoom and Memphis were among the most prominent avant-garde groups, engaging in exhibitions, performances and the sale of one-off or small-batch works. Although Memphis was

Fig. 1 Robot 4 by **Dunne and Raby** According to its designers, this robot is very needy and cannot move around on its own. It performs very difficult calculations but we are not party to these, our role being to serve its quietly voiced desires instead.

Fig. 2 Robot 3 by **Dunne and Raby** This robot uses retinal-scanning technology to decide who has access to what data. The user must stare intently into it in order to be recognised.

[3.]   -
          Similar
theoretical positions have been
termed variously: "anti-design"
(by the more extreme groups
within Italy's avant-garde of
the 1970s), and "interrogative
design" (by conceptual artist
Krzysztof Wodiczko, director
of the center of Art, Culture
and Technology at MIT).
Spaniard Marti Guixé has also
contributed to the language of
design criticism by describing
himself as an "ex-designer"
while still working in the field.
          -
[4. 5. 6.]   -
Dunne, A. 2008 [Personal
communication]. 15 January
          -

by far the most publicised of these, it was also the most commercially orientated and to some degree eclipsed the more critical positions of its forebears. After its demise, fewer dissenting voices were heard, although the prime movers from this period, such as Alessandro Mendini, Andrea Branzi and Ettore Sottsass, became highly respected figures within Italian culture.

With the appearance and success of Dutch group Droog Design in the early to mid-1990s, a new awareness of conceptual design opened up around furniture and home accessories. Starting as curators of a collection shown through themed exhibitions, Droog is not, as is often mistakenly assumed, a collective of designers. Formed by designer Gijs Bakker and design-historian Renny Ramakers, Droog initially brought together products from Dutch designers that expressed the "dryness" of their name (droog is Dutch for "dry"). Their first outings expressed a dual critique of the excesses of 1980s design culture and the anti-intellectualism of mass marketing. Through these exhibitions, numerous publications and acquisition of parts of the collection by high-profile museums, Droog became a unique cultural force despite not being manufacturing-focused. However, as their exhibitions have become more pluralist and their spartan playfulness has become a signature of Dutch design, there is a sense that Droog have lost their critical edge. Like earlier radical design groups, the arguments that their products embody often fall on deaf ears as their forms are subsumed into the mainstream as easily consumable trends.

-          -

CRITICAL DESIGN

Professor Anthony Dunne and Fiona Raby coined the term "critical design" in the late 1990s during their time as researchers in the Computer Related Design Research Studio at the Royal College of Art in London. While they don't claim to have invented a new category, it has become a popular label for design that elicits debate (3). Dunne explains: "For us, it's simply the idea of design as critique. It's happened in the past...and will continue into the future. Critical design was just a useful way to articulate what we were doing at that time in a particular context...It's more a set of loose affinities and shared aims." (3)

According to Dunne, the primary purpose is "to make people think...For us, the interesting thing is to explore an issue, to figure out how to turn it into a project, how to turn the project into some design ideas, how to materialise those design ideas as prototypes, and finally, how to disseminate them through exhibitions or publications. We're not interested in trying to find a manufacturer to put them into production...We hope the work will inspire people and encourage them to see things differently and open up new spaces for discussion."(4)

This reticence towards manufacture reflects the fact that the work is aimed at provoking thought among the general public, rather than persuading industry to refocus its activities. In his first book 'Hertzian Tales: Electronic Objects, Aesthetic Experience and Critical Design', Dunne quotes from Raymond Geuss's 'The Idea of a Critical Theory' in which he explains that "Critical theories aim at emancipation and enlightenment, at making agents [i.e. the public] aware of hidden coercion, thereby freeing them...and putting them in a position to determine where their true interests lie." (5) In this light, Dunne sees critical design as a necessary addition to, rather than a replacement for, mainstream business: "I can't see any deep social or

Fig. 3   Local Barometer by Interaction Research Studio, Goldsmiths University of London The Local Barometer brings information from classified advertisements into the home via a series of boxes with screens. The user cannot control the content; where the advertisements come from is decided by the current wind direction, determined by a weathervane placed outside the property.

cultural value in what comes out of big businesses. Cultural risks are avoided at all costs. Their perception of people has to be extraordinarily narrow and shallow otherwise they can't sell products on a mass scale. They have to ignore everything that might make people different like culture, education or taste and deal with the lowest common denominator. That's fine, that's business. It's the world we live in...But the problem is that so many of our experiences today are mediated by these mass-produced products and services, that the idea of 'humanness' embodied in them – because they are mass produced – is so impoverished that the more we interact with them, the more we become subtly conditioned to this very low level of being. I think if designers can come up with alternatives that respond to our complexity and put them into even batch production, that's fantastic. The work Fiona and I do explores the more theoretical aspects of this." (6)

CRITIQUING THE ELECTRONIC OBJECT

Electronic products do not have an established critical tradition of the kind that has developed for furniture. In 'Hertzian Tales', Dunne takes the position that "design research should explore a new role for the electronic object, one that facilitates more poetic modes of habitation: a form of social research to integrate aesthetic experience with everyday life through 'conceptual products.'" (7)

A former colleague of Dunne, William Gaver, now Head of the Interaction Research Studio at Goldsmiths University of London, shares this view, stating that: "Though digital technologies often seem the epitome of science and engineering, the methods we use in designing them need not be governed by such traditions.

[7.]
Dunne, A. 2005. 'Hertzian Tales: Electronic Objects, Aesthetic Experience and Critical Design'. Cambridge, MA: MIT Press

[8. 9. 10.]
Gaver, W. 2007. 'The Curious Home'. London: Goldsmiths, University of London

Interaction design can be a more subjective affair, with designers working in opinionated uncertainty and their products serving as tools for enquiry". (8)

In the work that has emerged from the research studios headed by Dunne and Gaver, and Dunne's own practice with partner Fiona Raby, there is a sense of wilful contrariness towards the methods and values of the commercial industrial designer. In particular, there is a shift away from objects that provide us with prescribed results "on-demand", to those which have more passive or ambiguous roles. For example, their project Technological Dreams Series: No.1. Robots, questions the notion that robots will necessarily be subservient, humanoid "companions". Like people, their robots have personality traits and skills that do not have a clear purpose, but that we may learn to live with in time (figs 1 and 2, page 143). A similar lack of prescribed intent is behind the examples below. They formed part of William Gaver and his team's contribution to Equator, a six-year interdisciplinary project "investigating new ways of interweaving the physical and the digital in everyday life" (9).

The Local Barometer (fig. 3, page 144) is a series of multicoloured boxes to be placed around the home, with screens upon which information from classified advertisements is displayed. However, rather than being controllable, the current wind strength and direction determines which adverts are shown. "Ads are selected from areas that are upwind of the home, and the harder the wind blows, the greater the distance becomes from which the ads 'travel'," Gaver explains (10). The devices puncture the daily routine with information we may otherwise filter out, prompting unusual thoughts and free associations.

Fig. 4 **Plane Tracker by Interaction Research Studio, Goldsmiths University of London** The Plane Tracker plays out the likely flight paths of passing aircraft after receiving data that determines their destination. It turns what might otherwise be the annoying sound of aircraft overhead into a participatory event.

Fig. 5 **Drift Table by Interaction Research Studio, Goldsmiths University of London** Through the small, round window in the Drift Table, an aerial photograph of the United Kingdom slowly scrolls in the direction of the heaviest object on the table.

[11. 12.] -
Gaver, W. 2007. 'The Curious
Home.' London: Goldsmiths,
University of London

[13.] -
Flusser, V. 1999. 'The Shape of
Things: A Philosophy of Design'.
London: Reaktion Books
-

Looking like a collision between the Jetsons' television and an Eames chaise, the Plane Tracker (fig. 4, page 145) collects data from passing aircraft. It then takes the viewer on the journeys of their likely flight paths using a modified version of Google Earth. It is, its designers say, "intended to give people a feeling of connection with distant parts of the world via the planes that physically pass by overhead." (11) However, they add that "like the Local Barometer, the system does not dictate how it is used. People may find their imaginations stirred in ways that have little to do with geography." (12)

Finally, the Drift Table (fig. 5, page 145) shows moving, digitised, aerial photographs of Britain through a circular window in a coffee table. Unlike the two previous projects, the Drift Table has an element of controllability, in that the image scrolls in the direction of the heaviest weight placed on the surface of the table. The effect, like that of being in a hot air balloon, encourages the consideration of details of topography as it moves across the landscape at slow pace. Although it can be reset and coordinates entered, this is intentionally difficult, encouraging its users to "travel" in their chosen direction at the device's own speed.

These products do not pretend to serve an essential need. Instead, they add a layer of intrigue, sitting alongside our existing devices, their functions (if not their styling) offering a quiet, non-confrontational presence. Their ambiguities of purpose enable us to engage in speculation, sparking our imagination rather than simply feeding us an implicit message.

As discussed previously, James Auger and Jimmy Loizeau's projects tend to take a more confrontational position, hoping to engage the public and the media in a discussion of ethically sensitive proposals. Developed for military use, Telepresence is a system by which it

is possible to remove the visual and aural senses from the body's actual location, replacing them with real-time input from recording equipment located elsewhere. Auger–Loizeau's project investigates the social narratives that such a system might present, such as a "rent-a-body" service where the client can "visit" unethical places or "attend" meetings or events without physically being there. (fig. 6, page 146).

CRITIQUING SCIENCE

While Anthony Dunne's PhD thesis, which led to his book 'Hertzian Tales', and the work of William Gaver's Interaction Research Studio offer critiques of the narrow scope of mass-produced electronic objects, critical design now encompasses many other subjects. Within their teaching roles on the MA in Design Interactions at the Royal College of Art in London, Dunne and Raby have encouraged their students to explore the future implications of emerging bio- and nanotechnologies – the manipulation of particles and organisms on a microscopic scale.

As it becomes clear that important aspects of our futures will be influenced by research undertaken in the concealed world of the laboratory, and much of what occasionally slips out may be characterised as monstrous (the famous mouse wearing a human ear being an example), a role opens for designers to become facilitators of a measured engagement between science and the public.

Whereas scientists may claim to be involved in value-free research (13), its ethical implications can be highly emotive, particularly when certain applications are proposed. In the case of genetically modified

Fig. 6   Social Telepresence by Auger–Loizeau James Auger and Jimmy Loizeau's project investigates the implications of bringing the military technology of telepresence – the ability to experience another place through real time recorded images and sound – into the social realm. Here a viewer at home uses the service to "visit" a location they may not feel comfortable attending in person.

(GM) organisms used in farming, food containing GM ingredients began to be rolled out and used before any consensus had been reached regarding their safety. Rather than simply reflecting the positive benefits of these technologies, designers can visualise a range of potential outcomes. By extrapolating the possibilities in tangible ways (for example, through models, images and films), the public can get a handle on the subject matter more directly than through dry, text-based documents. While such a role may seem fanciful, researchers interested in nanotechnology applying for government funding are now being asked to say how they would work with the public to address the ethical and social issues their research brings up. (14)

The Material Beliefs research group, also based at Goldsmiths University of London, has been set up with just this purpose in mind. The group's website proposes that "successful collaborative design projects [between design researchers, scientists and the public] can operate as cultural litmus paper, gauging public perception, imagining potential issues and generating awareness before radical new technologies arrive in the public domain changing irrevocably the fabric of our lives." (15)

Although some designers working in this territory have to simulate organisms using traditional model-making techniques, the SymbioticA Lab at the University of Western Australia actively encourages creative practitioners to take part in "wet biology" practices in a biological science department (16). In the UK, prior to setting up Material Beliefs, Tobie Kerridge undertook a project where a couple's donated bone cells were cultured in a laboratory at Guy's Hospital,

before being combined with precious metals to create rings. The couple were able to own and wear rings ("Biojewellery") made from the bone tissue of their partner (fig. 7, page 147). Included in the remit of the project was a live public debate where the process and outcomes were presented and reactions to it were recorded.

The Biojewellery and work from SymbioticA featured in critical design's most high-profile outing, the 2008 Museum of Modern Art, New York exhibition, Design and the Elastic Mind. The show, which contained applications of technology by designers, engineers and scientists for frivolous as well as serious ends, was described by the 'New York Times' as: "As revolutionary in its own way as MoMA's Machine Art exhibition of 1934". (17) However, the director of the Design Museum in London, Deyan Sudjic, contends that: "The Machine Art link could be seen as being quite two-edged because Design and the Elastic Mind is presented as being about how design is interpreting and understanding contemporary views of science. But, of course, the Machine Art show was really about how designers made objects that looked as if they were machine-produced but were actually laboriously made by hand and hence, it was actually based on wishful thinking about mechanisation. One could see this current show in very much the same speculative light." (18)

Whether such designs for debate will have any genuine effect depends on how well they tackle subjects of widespread public concern in measured ways and make these meaningful for both the public and those who will be implementing them.

[14.] -
Corbyn, Z. "Special Deliveries Get Smaller". 2008. 'Times Higher Education.' 19 June
-
[15.] -
'Material Beliefs website'. 2008 [online]. [Accessed 27th January 2009]. Available from World Wide Web: <www.materialbeliefs.com/diary>

[16.] -
'SymbioticA website'. 2008 [online]. [Accessed 27th January 2009]. Available from World Wide Web: <www.symbiotica.uwa.edu.au>
-
[17.] -
Sudjic, D. 2008. [Personal communication]. 4 April

[18.] -
Ouroussoff, N. "The Soul in the New Machines". 2008. 'The New York Times.' 4 April
-

Fig. 7   **Biojewellery by Tobie Kerridge with Ian Thompson and Nikki Stott** The structure of these rings was created using lab-cultured bone tissue donated by the couple that the rings were being made for.

03 Process

THE ELUSIVE DESIGN PROCESS

Writing in MIT's journal, 'Design Issues', David Ryan wrote of the design process: "It is the lifeblood of design and the key to creativity for the designer. At its basis, it is a methodical and even understandable process, but it is always mysteriously mutated by the designer…it is a formula and beyond formulas, it is at once accessible and mysterious, it is the essence of design, it is the struggle and the discovery." (1)

What is it that makes this process so difficult to grasp? A huge number of designers and theorists have tried to describe it, define what it should be and teach this to others, but there is still no consensus as to what constitutes a definitive design process. This chapter discusses this conundrum, looking to philosophy for assistance and going on to examine the use of tools that most designers would agree to be useful.

[1.]
Ryan, D. 1997. "Enzo Mari and the Process of Design". 'Design Issues'. Volume 13 Number 3, Autumn

[2.]
Heskett, J. 2002. 'Design: A Very Short Introduction'. Oxford: Oxford University Press

[3.]
Fletcher, A. 2001. 'The Art of Looking Sideways'. London: Phaidon

[4.]
Watson, L. In: Fletcher, A. 2001. 'The Art of Looking Sideways'. London: Phaidon

[5.]
Fletcher, A. 2001. 'The Art of Looking Sideways'. London: Phaidon

A GUIDE TO PERPLEXITY

The first reason that the design process is hard to define lies with language: "Design" is both noun and verb. Writer and educator John Heskett usefully pins down the many correct applications of the word in English with a "seemingly nonsensical sentence: 'Design is to design a design to produce a design'". (2) He explains that every use of the word "design" in the sentence is grammatically correct: the first denotes the field, profession or discipline; the second is the process or action; the third is the expression of that process in the form of a plan, concept or proposal; and the final usage is reserved for the end product.

If that were not enough, the application of the word "design" has become so broad that it no longer necessarily maps on to these descriptors. As well as becoming associated with meretricious goods ("designer jeans", for example) it has become common in the description of processes where creativity is at best peripheral and often non-existent. An example would be "kitchen design" which, instead of denoting the conceptualising of the room and its individual elements, is the service of helping a customer choose and position a set of ready-made items. Some would say many contemporary design consultancies have been complicit, if not influential, in allowing the meaning of design to change, by moving their "offer" from an open, partially intuitive process guided by client discussions, to a set of selectable packages from which the client can pick and mix.

It is worth reminding ourselves here of the real meaning of creativity — itself a word in need of more selective use. In his startlingly abundant collection of almost everything connected with the subject, 'The Art of Looking Sideways', designer Alan Fletcher wrote: "Creativity is a compulsive human urge which demands more than ritual actions or routine responses, and is only valid when one is trading beyond experience." (3) Fletcher quotes biologist Lyall Watson, who proposes that creativity is "that moment of insight [which] becomes the creative act as a joining of two previously incompatible ideas." (4) "Insight," Fletcher contends, "is unreasoning." (5)

Hence, creativity requires us to get out of our depth, and, in responding to the situation, suspend our disbelief in order to consider the bringing together of ideas, concepts, forms and so on, never before thought possible or appropriate.

When seen in this light, we are able to recognise that much of what purports to be design is not in the least bit creative. The definition and execution of a staged process does not automatically involve creativity. It will lead to outcomes, but these may be nothing more than an amalgamation of existing thoughts used in a similar form. "Design is about enjoying risk", says Sam Hecht. "Give me a design that involves no risk and you give me a copy." (6) It is a rare designer indeed who has never conducted a lazy project, falling back upon existing strategies, signature styles and personal preoccupations, yet it is something to be aware of and to guard against. If we never feel challenged, uneasy, in need of a bolt from the blue, or to go in search of new knowledge during a project, we need to ask ourselves: "Are we really being creative?"

It is possible, and in fact common, for designers to undertake projects (and entire careers) without being particularly creative. This is because, in order to reduce the risk of failure, experience is invoked by repeating past methods and forms instead of being used to help navigate forays into the unknown. Experienced educators Harold Nelson and Erik Stolterman discuss this problem in relation to design education: "Design learning," they tell us, "is different from most other traditional forms of education based on academic disciplines or professional areas of expertise. Designers are educated with the understanding that they are expected to produce unexpected outcomes." (7)

Sadly, despite this clear difference, much design education consists of learning a standard set of activities and being taught to practice them in a linear way, similar to how most trades and professions are taught. However, we will see below that far from being about developing a rigid, standardised method, the design process itself needs to be reactive to the needs of the project.

Even when trying to adhere to the notion of a fixed design process, examples to follow can look very different. The star designer sketches on a napkin and hands it to his assistant. The design department of a large corporation undertakes a year's worth of research, prototyping and testing. On the one hand, design is seen as flamboyance and intuition, and on the other, as an apparently logical, almost scientific endeavour.

Yet is the quest for logic not at odds with the way the design process plays out in our minds? Attempts to let logic rule appear to be undermined when chance or unexplained intuition butt in and appear to make a valuable contribution. Good ideas do not present themselves in an orderly way as a result of a carefully chosen string of processes. They can be difficult to come by one minute, flow in a flurry the next. They often appear to emerge from our subconscious mind as we engage in "unthinking" activities such as train travel or having a shower.

The obsession with arranging thought is, according to designers and academics Ralph Ball and Maxine Naylor, being offered as a replacement for genuine creative acts. They observe that: "There is, in the

[6.]
Hecht, S. In: Fiell, C. and Fiell, P. 2007. 'Design Now'. Cologne: Taschen

[7.]
Nelson, H. and Stolterman, E. 2009. 'Advanced Design institute website' [online]. [Accessed 27th Janury 2009]. Available from World Wide Web: <http://www.advanceddesign.org/publications>

background, a latent imperative that the design process should be orderly, tidy, and rational when the world plainly does not work like this. Yet a cultural nagging, ambient and constant, prevails; if only we could get all of our systems in place then everything will work and everything will be fine. Time spent managing the process has overtaken the creative activity of actually generating something. Filing is now more important than forming. This in turn reflects a culture that lacks autonomous self-confidence and a willingness to trust in risk… Organising is a preparatory and retrospective process, not a generative one. It is useful when consolidating that which, in general, has already been proved to work, but it does not function well as a device for the generation of new ideas." (8)

The design process requires intuition because it requires predictive action – we must have a go in order to see and test the result, and in having a go we may as well try to make the right choice rather than a random one. Research helps us to make appropriate choices but it can only assess what already exists. Hence, designing only through researching existing forms and not "intuiting" new ones (albeit in response to research) will lead to a repetition of those forms. Intuition, Ball and Naylor contend, is "a sense of the rightness of something ahead of the proof or verification." (9) Research is useful before – to identify the best of the past and improve upon it – and afterwards, to test the effectiveness of your design, but in between, intuition must take its rightful place.

[8. 9.]   -
Ball, R. and Naylor, M. 2005.
'Form Follows Idea'. London:
Black Dog Publishing

[10.]   -
White, S. 2008. [Personal
communication]. 23 June
             -

-                    -
A PHILOSOPHICAL MODEL

In order to better understand the design process, we need a model that describes what is happening in the mind. For this we need a philosophical perspective.

Stefan White is an architect, designer and academic who has studied the relationship between the design process and contemporary philosophy. He offers the following insights into the way we perceive objects and how they come into existence through design: (10)

"Traditional philosophies have explained our relationships with objects through a notion of 'determination', and this is true of philosophers from Aristotle through to Kant. Determination works by classifying and naming what we do, think, make etc. by resemblance (or not) to other things; for example the traditional divisions of beings and objects into genus and species. A thing gets its identity by the principle of how it's determined in relation to other things. A dog is not a cat. 'Hi there! – no I mean him not you…' Contemporary critical philosophers call this kind of thinking 'representation'.

Representation starts with comparisons or analogies. It asks, 'Do I recognise it'. It is based on the past, because you have to already have an identity with which to compare it – so it doesn't deal very well with the new – something you've never seen before. What do you call that? If you're trying to create things, this model implies you will always be trying to relate them to something you have seen before."

White continues: "Gilles Deleuze is principal among a number of contemporary philosophers who have offered alternative explanations as to how objects become determined, and it seems to concord with the designers' experiences I've come across. Deleuze doesn't start with comparisons or analogies; he instead proposes that life is a process of differentiation, a process of 'splitting'. This means that all living beings

– including designers – are working in non-reversible time by a process of selection and distinction. We are constantly choosing and branching, and, with every choice we make, we change what reality is.

In Deleuze's logic of sense, each one of these 'splittings' is an event within a series, but is not necessarily instantaneous. There might be a whole load happening at once or just one after the other over a period of time. However, it's a movement towards an exploration. It's an unknowable goal. And that's the key point. In a representational view, in a way, things are pre-determined. You're not creating anything truly new – you are simply discovering something that's already there. Deleuze argues the opposite: that ideas don't come from somewhere else. They are immanent rather than transcendent. We are not simply referencing objects that at the beginning of the design process are somehow there, but beyond reach, but instead truly creating experimental positions, 'events' which we then 'check' against our expectations by choosing to select them or ignore them."

-          -

DISCOVERY OR CREATION?

Designers occasionally make reference to the representational model when they describe the end of the design process as a discovery of something rather than the creation of it. It often feels like that, and with good reason. The constraints guiding the project will set up boundaries that many of our ideas will fall outside. When one does manage to tick all the boxes, especially if the solution seems quite simple, the notion that no one has ever come to the same conclusion can seem far-fetched. The sense that someone else must have the same idea plants the thought that we have

discovered, rather than created it. However, the sense of rightness of an idea, concept or design is nonetheless in our heads and defined by our own notion of what has guided the project. When we see this sense of rightness in the designs of others, it is because we can also see the reasons behind their choices.

White explains: "Deleuze isn't saying representations and representational thought do not exist and are not useful. He is instead clear that it's just one of the modes of thought but there is another one. Traditional semiotics (which emerged from the representational model) imagines an already existing world where sense is possible (see 1.3 Reading form). Deleuze says, 'you can see the world like that – yes it does tend to appear to operate like that – but how did we get there?' How did all these signs and symbols get to the point of coherence where they can be understood, and isn't that what's really happing all the time? Language is becoming sense, as we make sense from it. We got there by trying to make sense of experience. Representational thought is a short cut that we practice instead of thought, instead of making new sense."

"According to Deleuze", White tells us, "the object is only ever more or less "determined". There's only the continued branching towards a more determined object. So even when you get towards the end of the design process (you've decided exactly what chair you want, how you want it to look, what materials you want etc.) you still have to go and get it made. And as you well know, when you do, another whole series of diverging selections and choices comes into effect, because this process of determination of the indeterminate happens at every stage. It is, for Deleuze, the very process by which all objects are "given" to us – how we are able to make sense of the world as consisting of objects we interact with. In design, the process is the same, but our role is more active, mediated and conscious. Design is the guided process of determining objects. In this process, there will always be more or less important decisions, but all of the selections will have a role in making the object singular. For example, a less or more important decision might be about how difficult, time-consuming or energy-wasting it is to return to an earlier decision point or 'splitting'".

"In relation to design then", White proposes, "Deleuze's position would be extremely pragmatic. As a designer, you would simply be asking [of your work] what does it do? What affect (11) does it deliver?" Deleuze suggests that instead of attempting to categorise things, we should make a "chart of affects" – a kind of diagram of the real impacts they will, can and do have on the other things around them, and that we place them in relation to.

By being aware of these models of thought, designers can consider to what extent they are concentrating on what will be representational, as opposed to what will be most affecting. For example, when designing a chair, are they asking themselves, "What type of chair do people want?", "How do people want to sit?" or "How do people want to be affected?"

TOOLS OF EXPRESSION

White contends that, to get the most out of them, we should see tools of design, such as drawing and model-making, in terms of their affect rather than simply as devices for representing thoughts: "[In the design process] we're using a series of tools that allow us to tentatively order our thoughts ahead of a final, yet still experimental, decision. These processes of thought are not separate design ideas – they are embodied in the process of selection. For example, there is no such thing as a blank page, because you've got all of your memories, all your life experiences that you're bringing to the point where you're making that choice as to what line to draw. At the same time, that line is utterly experimental because you don't know everything that you can draw. At the moment before drawing the line, your potential for expression is limitless (which is what the fear of the blank page is all about – not that it's empty, but that it's actually so full, and what is drawn out might be a disappointment). It's unknowable because you've never been in that precise situation. Even if you try your hardest to repeat what you've drawn before [or exactly what you are thinking], it always comes out slightly differently."

White cites Robin Evans, in his book 'Translations from Drawing to Building and Other Essays' (1997), who proposes that the power of the drawing lies precisely in this fact; that it doesn't look like what you wanted it to look like. "There is no deterministic relation between what is represented, and the representation in the mind of the person attempting to draw what they think. The power of the drawing to be creative is that it will always be different from the representation you try and make it conform to."

"The root of this", White explains, "lies in the fact that design tools such as drawing are 'expressions', like words, but that, taken literally, these differ from what is actually 'expressed'. For example if a designer (the 'expresser') draws a chair (the 'expression') the

[11.]
Not to be confused with effect, meaning change or consequence, affect is a technical term in psychology and philosphy meaning a desire or emotion that influences behaviour.

sense we make of that drawing (what is 'expressed') will be to picture a complete chair, even though what we are literally seeing is just some lines on a page. Importantly, the sense we make of the expression is filtered through our own interpretation, governed by our life experiences. This explains how one expression can be understood to mean many different things by different people. The chair I picture in my mind when looking at the drawing will be different from the one you picture. While we might think that the more detailed ('determined') the drawing is, the more alike our interpretations will be, even this is not guaranteed. For example, many members of the general public cannot understand orthographic projections (12) but the indeterminate chaos which the drawing attempts to 'control' into a single interpretation is what is special about it. The drawing enables determination, it is determinable, it is not complete chaos, and at the same time it is never totally determined or decided."

White continues: "If your being is engaged in the design process you're expressing your intuition about that design process and it's only through expressing these expressions that you get to look at them retrospectively. As a designer you don't see the expression [the lines on the paper], you see what it expresses — what kind of chair is it, was it the kind of chair I wanted? The point of a drawing or model is that it creates an expression of our intuition of the sense created by sets of relations. By creating an expression of these relations, it enables us to manipulate and interrogate what these relations might be, and what affect they might have. Without the expression, we are unable to attempt to discover what it expresses. Some very clever people might be able to do all of this inside their own heads, but it is very doubtful that they would do anything other than repeat their own presumptions.

[12.] -
Orthographic or orthogonal projections are views used within technical drawing that illustrate objects, plans and buildings from one angle, without perspective. The lines are drawn at right angles to the plane of projection (the view point of the drawing) and hence can be accurately dimensioned.
-

This process of thought is what enables us to look beyond our own experience, and test and challenge our habits of thought — to create the new. Deleuze refers to this testing mode of thinking, and all the external expressions made which attempt to interrogate beyond our direct experience, as 'diagrammatic'. He does not mean a particular type of drawing, but all potential ways of thinking (non-representationally). To Deleuze this is intuition, and he puts it as the highest level of thought. Intuition is not just emotions or feelings — that is the pejorative understanding it from representation. Intuition, in what we have discussed here, is affect — it is the logic of sense — it is the process by which we come to be able to manifest 'the rational'."

- -
DESIGN IS EXPERIENTIAL

Deleuze's thinking, when applied to the design process, reveals why chance encounters and intuition make a contribution. If the design process is experiential rather than logical — that is, it is a journey upon which our whole being embarks and anything that happens to us on that journey and has happened to us in the past affects the choices we make — then the way we are affected will in turn influence how we shape what we are designing. This will be mediated by all the kinds of expressions we can make, including the rational. As much as we can try to plan a logical design process using tools to help us understand, iterate and improve the set of relations within the project, any number of other influences (some of which may not be conscious) may interject. Rather than devaluing a planned process, this awareness allows us to consciously set out to have a number of experiences (reading texts, seeing exhibitions, having discussions etc.) that can complement typical design tools. However, what it must also do is to allow any useful (affective) insights, wherever they come from, to change the direction of both the design and the pre-planned process.

In their drive to package and sell design as a formula, many consultancies have put in place a linear design process into which clients can easily buy. The activities within each stage become highly familiar and, as creative tools, no doubt occasionally yield creative outputs. Yet the standardised nature of this approach does not allow for the individual character of the project to shape the way it is tackled. What happens when an insight early on in the project suggests a direction other than what has been proposed, quoted for and sold? Furthermore, if a process has been undertaken successfully on one occasion, there's no guarantee that it will be successful again. This is because what led to a successful design was not necessarily the planned ingredients, but may have been a random insight that happened to arise during the process. That is not to say thinking tools are useless. For example, brainstorming is an acknowledged way of trying to force insights to occur, often with a degree of success.

-           -

TAKING DECISIONS

With all of these factors influencing us, it is worth reflecting upon how we go about making decisions. Again, philosophy can offer guidance, starting with why the journey begins. Stefan White informs us that: "Deleuze talks about there being an 'inducement to act'. [In design, these are the reasons we are undertaking the design process. This book has discussed many subject-related ones but others may be more basic, such as earning money to survive, or altruistic, such as improving society.] These inducements are felt repeatedly and are described differently by various philosophers. For example, in Freud, it is the 'pleasure drive' and 'death drive'. Deleuze argues that, whatever the reason, we tend to want to put ourselves in to composition with things that agree with us rather than disagree with us, and our desire to repeat agreeable actions induces us to pursue particular paths. This can become very complex as we gain more experience – we have to work much harder in order to select amongst the possible inducements."

"[According to Deleuze's interpretation of Spinoza] inducement", White continues, "is about capacity. Being sad is having a reduced capacity to act and joy increases that capacity. This is what drives us on through the stages of a process – an attempt to increase our capacity to act." If we are to do this – to advance the design process – White contends that we must find a way of expressing our intuitions in some form, so they can be useful to us.

"If we start to try and express intuition using a rational language (for example, if we start trying to express the object according to what it is and what it isn't), what our intuition was grasping escapes. Rather than being pinned down for examination, it is destroyed. Like butterflies in glass cases, to become purely aesthetic compositions, they had to be killed. We are not being frivolous or wilful, therefore, to insist on the value of intuition; it is the only way we can create the new."

We might therefore consider that a sense of indifference or uncertainty in the design process means one of two things. The set of relations we are considering (the "current design") is not increasing our capacity to act. It is not allowing us to take the project to the next stage and therefore must be changed. Alternatively, the method of expression we have chosen to use (sketch/drawing/model) is not increasing our capacity to act, in that it has not adequately revealed the benefits of this "current design". A more effective form of expression must therefore be used. When faced with this sense of uncertainty, we must therefore consider if it is the design, or the way it is being expressed, that is at fault.

Finally, the philosophical modes discussed here offer insight into the way experience is invoked. As White describes, there are two possible methods, one beneficial and one counter-productive: "You can't not use your experiences, but you can use them in two ways: in a representational way, to copy what has gone before, and if you do this they will be restraining you from producing the new. Alternatively, you can use your experiences to lead you to make good choices.

There's no reason why you can't obtain knowledge of the (likely) outcomes of your choices. The more times you undertake the process, the more you get a logic of sense of the process – that that kind of decision is a crucial one, or that one isn't going to make much difference. There is a subtle but vitally important difference between this tacit knowledge and the belief that it establishes a pre-conceived formula."

Thinking about design, and indeed life, through Deleuze's model ought to be inspiring because it suggests that the more we throw ourselves into experiencing it and being affected by it, the more resources we are able to call upon to help guide us in our decisions. It encourages us to judge objects on their individual merits in terms of how we are influenced by them, rather than upon their relationship to existing archetypes. It advocates originality with purpose, not new for the sake of new (or indeed old for the sake of old). It recognises that familiarity has a place in creating emotional responses, but that we should beware of applying it by default. Finally, it breaks us free from the tyranny of an imposed methodology and embraces generative and responsive action.

-           -

[1. 2. 3.]
Bürdek, B. 2005. 'Design :
History, Theory and Practice
of Product Design'. Basel:
Birkhäuser

3.2

DESIGN METHODOLOGY

If we buy into Deleuze's observations regarding the value of being guided by insights and intuition – that unproven hypotheses and not the application of cold logic are what lead us to the new – this implies that we should take attempts to apply systematic logic to the process of design with a pinch of salt. However, we must recognise a distinction between the act of creation and the framework within which it sits. A design methodology is an organisational structure within which creative acts occur. It is a means of visualising the process, categorising the sets of relations within the project, and of suggesting an order in which they may be tackled. Rational thinking is therefore useful in order to avoid us getting lost in what, in a complex project, could appear to be a tangled web of conflicting and interrelating factors. That said, rationality should not be invoked in order to suggest an entirely rigid process, or one that must be repeated verbatim for each project; to do so would be to repeat the well-meaning mistakes of many designers and design theoreticians. What is required is an understanding that the nature of the project will influence the choice of methods that are appropriate at any given time.

DESIGN AS SCIENTIFIC METHOD

Design methodology evolved in response to the rationalisation of industry. Bernhard Bürdek, who has written extensively on the subject, tells us that once industry had begun rationalising construction and production methods, "It was not possible to continue practising the subjective and emotional methods of design...It was thus an obvious step for designers to try to integrate scientific methods into the design process so that they could be accepted as serious partners in the sphere of industry." (1) However, this presupposes that the subjective and emotional methods of design were indefensible to industrialists. Rather than communicate the value of intuition as a necessary ingredient, designers chose to hide it behind, among other things, the apparent logic of geometric forms. Designers attempted to build and follow methodologies that would allow them to demonstrate to their clients that creation itself could be scientific, rather than just the organisational structure in which it operated.

This was seductive because the design process as a whole benefits from a sense of structure, and in explaining a project, a choice could be made to emphasise this over any intuitive creative acts that, in themselves, defy logic. In addition, designers are apt to "post rationalise" their intuitive decisions, overlaying them with a sense of logic identified after their creation. The success of the axiom "form follows function", debunked by David Pye (discussed on page 23), can be seen in the light of this attempt to show design as an objective method in which the designer is simply guided by predefined signals.

It is worth noting that some of the most successful design that emerged from post-war Italy came from designers who, while demonstrating a structured process, were able to "intuit" creative responses to the problem of overhauling the country's architecture and design. They did this through establishing trusting relationships with industrialists, rather than convincing them of their scientific methodologies.

FROM DETERMINISM TO EMPIRICISM

Bürdek explains that three branches of the humanities have influenced design methodology: semiotics (the study of how meaning is constructed through our understanding of signs); phenomenology (the study of experience in terms of phenomena, from a first-person perspective, for example); and hermeneutics (the study of theories and methods of the interpretation of texts and systems of meaning). (2)

For semiotics to be useful, we must be able to interpret everything as a sign. To do so we have to have discovered the meaning of the sign previously. Hence, semiotics ignores experiences that cannot be "read", (yet, as has been discussed, it is precisely these that may be seen as the essence of the new). It is these direct experiences that phenomenology recognises. Hermeneutics has a more over-arching aim, not just to explain the nature of ideas, but also to propose how those ideas came about. It is clear to see how this maps on to the notion of a design methodology; if we can understand how our good ideas have been arrived at, we may define a method to enable us to have more. However, as Bürdek tells us: "Hermeneutics [like design methodology] is not a mechanical procedure but an art" and was "criticised for its universal urge to generate uniform interpretations." (3)

By combining hermeneutics with empiricism (deriving knowledge from experience and observation rather than theory), we arrive at the basis for much modern design methodology. This finds designers attempting to understand and react to sociocultural conditions,

and testing their designs in situ to check their effectiveness. What is more contentious is that it also tends to embrace market research as an instrument for determining the content of products prior to their design and the use of focus groups after it.

The move from hermeneutic-led singular interpretations of good design to empirical market-oriented thinking is also expressible through the contrast between modernism and postmodernism – a move from "top down" theories espoused by an intellectual elite to the "bottom up" embracing of popular taste.

While many designers have shunned the restrictive purism of modernist thought, there is unease at the notion of letting the pendulum swing too far back in the direction of the market. "The quest for quality", explains Achille Castiglioni, "never grows out of some market survey. Market surveys mainly reflect established images and will never produce an innovative project." (4) After all, it is designers who, while able to acknowledge the desires of the market, are also the ones who have actionable access to new technologies, materials, methods of manufacturing and strategies of thought that offer them the ability to create something the market didn't know it wanted.

When applied as market research, empirical methods are primarily about reassuring big business that its investment will produce a return. Turning to the market for advice often throws up conservative propositions, not because that is what will necessarily be bought, but because it is not in its nature to collectively propose innovative alternatives. Companies infer that the consumer is unwilling to step too far outside of their existing experience and this justifies the production of

[4.]
Castiglioni, A. In: Polano,
S. 2001. 'Achille Castiglioni
Complete Works'. Milan: Electa

[5.]
Bürdek, B. 2005. 'Design: History, Theory and Practice of Product Design'. Basel: Birkhäuser

bland goods. Yet this apparently risk-averse method could, in itself, be seen as a risk. In applying such methods, companies miss the opportunity to introduce major innovations that could lead the market. If their competitors get there first, the risk-averse will be left behind.

VISUALISING THE PROCESS

The father of design methodology, Christopher Alexander, in his book 'Notes on the Synthesis of Form' (1964), explains his theory of how complex design problems can be broken down into sets of requirements, visualised as trees. These trees, which hold individual requirements on their branches, allow each requirement to be identified and analysed individually. Requirements may themselves branch into subsets containing further requirements. As the project is thought through, requirements are gradually replaced with proposed solutions until the whole tree is covered.

While this method allows for the visualisation of complexity, it does not necessarily bring to light situations where, in meeting two individual requirements, a separate problem is generated.

In his later work, 'A Pattern Language Which Generates Multi-Service Centers' (with Sara Ishikawa and Murray Silverstein, 1968) Alexander describes the infinite scalability of the concept that all designed elements consist of a pattern of design language and that each patterned element is connected to others in the same context. For example, the pattern language of a building connects to and offers the context for its rooms, which in turn have a pattern of their own which is linked to the language of the objects within them and so on. Alexander explains the concept as part of a methodology to empower individuals to plan and create architecture from the scale of entire regions down to individual rooms. By emphasising the co-relatedness of all forms, Alexander champions the idea that a broad understanding of context should be the fundamental driver of product form.

As Bürdek explains, this view has taken time to gain currency in product design: "Up until the 1980s, context was generally understood to mean only those practical demands (such as ergonomic conditions, construction specifications and manufacturing options) that designers had to take into consideration in their designs. In reality, however, the design is often dominated by an entirely different set of conditions...it has become increasingly important to design contexts...or provide contexts as models of interpretation for design. The question today is not 'How are these things made?' but 'What do these things mean for us?'" (5)

TYPICAL MODELS OF THE DESIGN PROCESS

Typical models of the design process describe it as a linear set of steps where each must be completed successfully in order to continue to the next. This linearity is broken only by failures that lead the designer back to earlier steps to rectify whatever had caused the problem. Relying too heavily upon such diagrams can be problematic for a number of reasons. As generic descriptions, they assume a level of complexity in a project, which may be entirely different to the actual one being undertaken. As mentioned earlier, they also enforce a rigidity that does not allow for insight to suggest alternative courses of action or models of development. A typical design process chain contains:

Defining broad aims (brief)

Understanding constraints/context etc.

Defining specific requirements

Exploring design solutions

Testing and analysing solutions

Communicating/realising chosen solution (completion)

This order is upset in a variety of circumstances. Specific requirements may appear to be incorrect (misdirected or unambitious, for example) upon exploration of possible solutions as unforeseen possibilities arise. A playful process of research and design that is unimpeded by over-specific sets of criteria can lead to discoveries that meet the broad aims effectively, but may conflict with specific aims if these are set prematurely. In addition, testing and analysis occasionally throw up such fundamental problems that a rethink of the specific requirements is the only option. A degree of fluidity is needed to ensure that the completion of a tidy process is not placed above arriving at the best possible product. While interjecting with additional stages or returning to previous ones may be costly, designers must be prepared to argue a case for when they are necessary.

-            -

THINKING TOOLS

The remainder of this chapter is concerned with a number of tools designers use to develop ideas. These are introduced briefly below. As we have learned, insights can develop as a result of all manner of uncontrollable factors and the impact of these should be considered alongside those that develop from more traditionally recognised sources. However, for most designers, the well-established methods of observation, drawing and model-making still lie at the heart of their development of ideas. While appearing in many other walks of life – we may observe then draw a still life, or assemble a model from instructions – in design, none of these methods is an end in itself. Each enables a particular set of cognitive processes to occur that prompt decision making. Their power lies in their use as thinking tools.

In observation, we deconstruct what we perceive, consider its parts, the forces acting upon them, and how they join and support each other. We take in material properties and qualities and consider from all of these, how we might apply this knowledge elsewhere. Inga Sempé shows a clear example in her Lunatique Table for Ligne Roset (fig. 1, page 163). Sempé used the foldability of a ring-handle from her mother's bedside table as part of a discrete height-adjusting mechanism for an occasional table (fig. 2, page 163).

In drawing, we generate a representation of our thoughts that we are subsequently able to interrogate. A cycle of expression, consideration and further expression drives the process onwards. In model-making, we are finally able to grasp our design literally, to assess how it interacts with its context and to test it empirically. Like drawing, the very process of making models is a form of expression, which prompts new ideas – not just the assessment of its results.

Besides these "artistic" methods, design and the business community have developed their own thinking tools. Based upon the understanding that insight requires the short-circuiting of accepted methods and ritual actions, tools such as brainstorming are specifically designed to encourage irrational thinking and the juxtaposition of unlikely pairings. By forcing the expression of unreason, we are able to reassess its potential as "the new reason".

Fig. 1   Lunatique
table by Inga Sempé
manufactured by Ligne
Roset The ring handles in
her mother's bedside table
provided the spark for the
adjustment in Inga Sempé's
Lunatique table. She then
designed a mechanism that
allowed the height of the table
to lock when the ring sat flush
with the tabletop.

Fig. 2   Ring handle

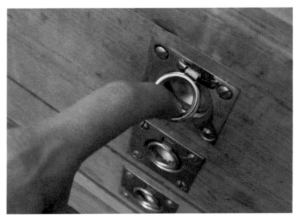

OBSERVATION

"It is something of an effort to look at things around us with our minds as well as our eyes. We so soon accept them unthinkingly." (1)

Frank Pick, the patron of design who commissioned the famous Underground map while head of London Transport, highlights the overlooked nature of the everyday. Surrounded by the familiar, we are inclined to "switch off" and are only prompted when difference breaks our routine. Transplanted to another place – in particular, another culture – our observational ability is stirred and we begin to notice even the smallest of details. As designer Alan Fletcher aptly puts it: "Blinkered by habit, we glance around rather than look with acuity. In effect, the eye sleeps until the mind wakes it with a question." (2)

This selective absorption is necessary to avoid information overload, but if we can short-circuit this system we may develop the advantage of seeing what others miss. In other words, we may teach ourselves to see. Fletcher continues: "We forget that we learn to see. We are not given the world but make it through experience, categorization and memory." (3)

OBSERVATION AS DESIGN EDUCATION

Renowned architect and designer Aldo Rossi once noted that: "Perhaps the observation of things has remained my most important formal education, for observation later becomes transformed into memory. Now I seem to see all the things I have observed arranged like tools in a neat row; they are aligned as in a botanical chart or a catalogue, or a dictionary. But this catalogue, lying somewhere between imagination and memory, is not neutral; it always reappears in several objects and constitutes their deformation, and in some way, their evolution." (4)

Rossi's sentiments are mirrored by Jasper Morrison who advises us that: "The practice of seeing is a designer's most vital education. Everything seen and assessed will have an influence on the way he designs" (5). Not only is observing from the overlooked minutiae of our surroundings something from which we can learn, it is an ability that designers and other visual artists should try to hone. Just as a good musician can deconstruct a song by hearing it, define the key and timing and talk with authority about the nuances of its composition, good designers can develop the equivalent skills in relation to objects. The senses become attuned to properties such as visual weight, proportion, poise, and patina (the way materials develop traces of use and wear). Experience of the use and abuse of objects combines with this visual observation and informs us of the likelihood of an observed component to be fit for its purpose. To a degree, this knowledge is able to save us the task of testing every material when observation has shown them working (albeit at particular dimensions and under specific conditions).

But beyond amassing an encyclopaedia of tools for design practice, learning to see offers an opportunity for liberation. It enables us to form our own narrative around the use and effect of objects to accompany the stories fed to us by our commodity culture; to see where things actually end up and what they really mean to people.

[1.]
Pick, F. In: Benton, C. (ed).
1975. 'Documents: A collection of source material on the Modern Movement'. Milton Keynes: Open University Press

[2. 3.]
Fletcher, A. 2001. 'The Art of Looking Sideways'. London: Phaidon

[4.]
Rossi, A. 1984. 'A Scientific Autobiography'. Cambridge, MA: MIT Press

[5.]
Morrison, J. 1990. 'Jasper Morrison – Designs, Projects and Drawings 1981–1989'. London: Architecture, Design and Technology Press

Fig. 1 Bicycles of **Japan** Seeing many images of the same object type reveals a language of details. A small collection of pictures of bicycles seen on the streets of Japan shows a propensity towards small wheels and folding frames rather than the Western emphasis on racing or mountain bikes.

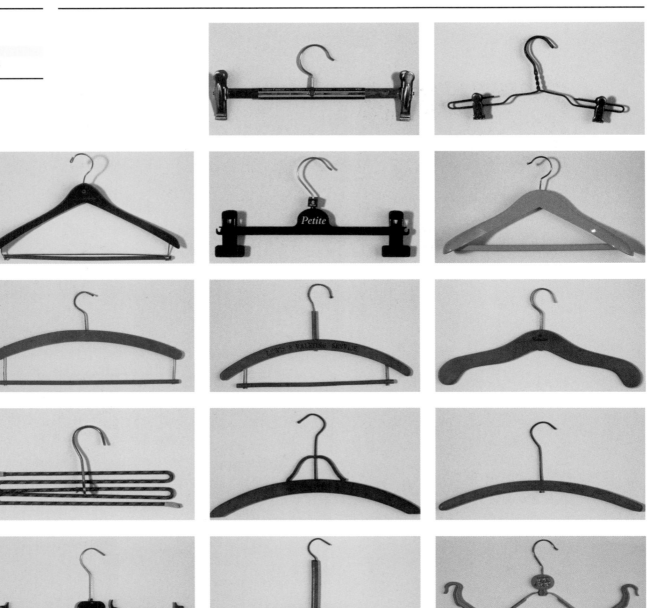

Fig. 2 Images from '50 Hangers', a picture book by **Tim Parsons** Part of a collection of 50 coat hangers donated by friends, these images enable us to see how different designers tackled the task of designing the humble coat hanger and to identify subtle differences in their character. Responses range from the commonplace through to the kitsch.

Fig. 3 Sample collection by Tim Parsons Many of these objects have little or no financial value but are kept because they demonstrate something – material properties, a forming of fixing method, a structure. They offer both inspiration and valuable reference.

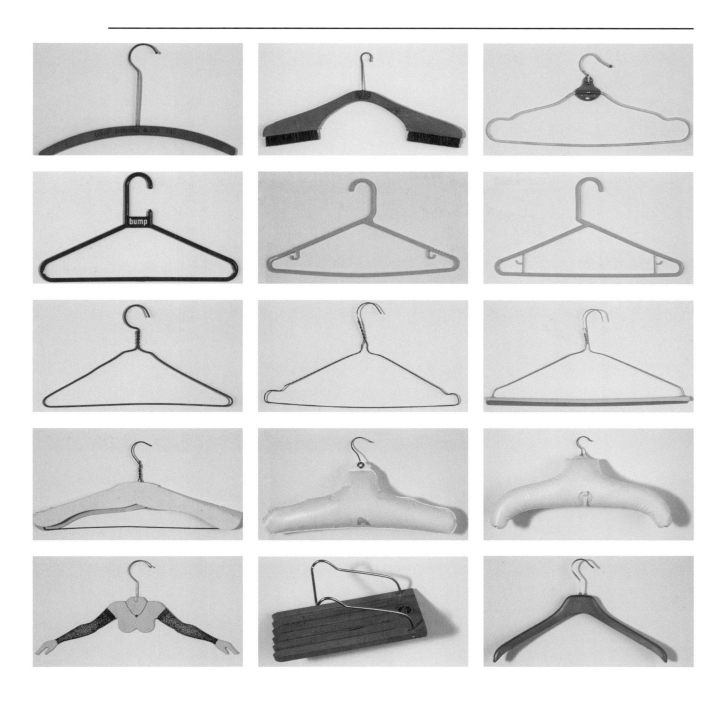

Fig. 6   Bird-boxes
at Boisbuchet, France The
multiplication creates a
spectacle and a sense of
a "bird community".

Fig. 7   Documenting
a manufacturing process
Bristles are fed between
wires, twisted by machine
and "shaved" to make
bottlebrushes.

The photographs of Richard Wentworth and the work of Neil Cummings and Marysia Lewandowska, specifically the book 'Reading Things' (1993), encourage us in this direction. It is also intrinsic to the French concept of the "flâneur" – an outsider figure who walks the city, taking in its every nuance. An entirely different animal to the tourist, the "flâneur" values experience over the tick-boxing of attractions. Design consultancy IDEO has attempted to instil the spirit of the "flâneur" into the modern traveller via a series of guidebooks entitled 'Eyes Open' that shun the tourist trail in favour of the more obscure charms of our major cities. (6)

In design practice, observation has the paradoxical role of providing education by suggesting methods that might be adopted, while simultaneously offering the opportunity for conscious differentiation. While there is a limit to what we are reasonably able to investigate, it is the lazy and misguided student who wilfully shuns research in the belief that this will allow him uninhibited access to new ideas. Through awareness, we are able to avoid repeating history, take account of it and, if we choose, build upon it.

Observations of objects or processes often elicit in the designer (or indeed in anyone) a sense of inspiration that can manifest itself in a variety of ways. Upon hearing that an American critic had recreated his piece, Equivalent VIII (known colloquially as "The Bricks") by buying and arranging bricks from a local builders' yard, the minimalist sculptor Carl André was moved to write and thank the critic for helping him to understand the difference between an artist and a layperson. "When the layperson sees something that inspires them, they are moved to recreate it", he says, "When the artist sees something that inspires them, they create something else."

Rather than distinguishing the creative from the uncreative, it is perhaps more useful to consider the urge to copy what we see, as the base level of creative maturity that we all must pass through and leave behind in order to find our own voice. A stage above might be described as one of being able to extract and transpose form, method or strategy from what is being observed and apply it effectively in a new context. This ability can be very effective for designers creating new work (see 2.4 Collective memory and behaviour).

This combination of different interdisciplinary ways of doing things is well established as a tool for innovation and is obviously one that has observation at its core. Described recently by Frans Johansson as The Medici Effect in his book of the same name (2004), the author named the phenomenon after the Medici family of Florence who were credited with helping to kick-start the Renaissance by bringing together an enormously varied group of individuals from different disciplines and cultures.

Accurate observation and its use to prompt analogies, is of particular value in the definition of the essence and stylistic emphasis of an object not yet designed. The Mood Board (a collection of images that convey a particular sense of style and character), despite reaching the status of high cliché, is a useful tool in the communication of nuanced concepts of form, if used with care and rigour. By observing successful products in certain market sectors, an awareness of trends and preferences can be built up for the purposes of following them or preferably to enable differentiation.

[6.]
'IDEO website'. 2009. [online]. [Accessed 27th January 2009]. Available from World Wide Web: <www.ideoeyesopen.com>

Fig. 8 Display as installation The mass of variations is displayed proudly by the retailer and prompts us to look at the detail differences.

Fig. 9 "Family tricycle" This homemade "family tricycle" illustrates its owner's ability to create a practical item not available in the marketplace. It represents ingenuity and a non-conformist outlook.

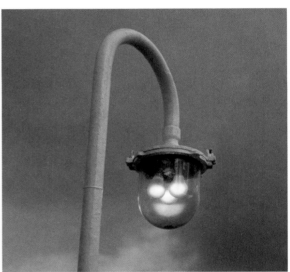

Figs 10–13 Character-isation We are prone to see faces in products and designers have been known to play upon this. These pilons appear to be an army of robots rampaging across the Belgian countryside. The stapler has been given character by the positioning of a fixing, giving it an eye. The viewer appears to be a conscious piece of "friendly" styling, whereas the ship's lamp has developed a face by a trick of the light.

Fig. 14 Customisation The friendly appearance of the Renault Twingo (also a product with a distinctive face) has prompted this owner to add his or her own touch. This suggests the notion of designing products that explicitly encourage users to customise them.

Fig. 15 Acknow-ledging behaviour An architect wittily predicts the use his arched doorway will have and populates it with stone pigeons. Behavioural observations can lead to designs in tune with our unconscious actions.

Noting typical specifications, such as layouts, features, finish and materials, gives a picture of the apparently immutable elements of a typology and hence the opportunity to rethink it. We are able to ask: Which elements are of real value and which have been appropriated out of conceit?

COLLECTIONS

The usefulness of observed detail has a habit of planting in designers the bug of the collector. Collections hold a particular professional intrigue for designers, which can set them apart from those who collect for pleasure or financial gain. In collecting one typology of object, the designer builds a picture of the many possible ways by which such an object can be determined. The collection creates a three-dimensional mind-map of designs for that object, which becomes especially useful should the designer then turn his hand to the task of designing that kind of object himself. This also explains the popularity among designers of books concerned with single typologies, such as Daniel Rozensztroch's taxonomies of coat hangers ('Cintres', 2002) and brushes ('Brush' (with Shiri Slavin, 2005)). Similar books that have been compiled by designers themselves include Jasper Morrison's 'A Book of Spoons' (1997) and Alexandra Martini's 'Litter Only: A Book About Dustbins' (2000). The camera and the medium of print, of course, enable the space-saving capture and storage of these collections and it may be that you find yourself embarking upon such activities yourself (fig. 1, page 165 and fig. 2, page 166–167). It is here that the designer becomes something of a part-time anthropologist. An acute example is Sam Hecht of Industrial Facility who, instead of focusing upon an individual typology, has for the past 15 years been amassing a collection of objects from around the world that cost less than five pounds each. Brought together in the exhibition and publication 'Under a Fiver' the items display everything from kitsch to functionalism, each offering its own peculiar insight into aspects of contemporary culture.

SAMPLES

Perhaps even more common among designers is the behaviour of collecting material, product and process samples. Just as interior designers are known to collect colour swatches, product designers are apt to hoard items that demonstrate characteristics (including colour) they enjoy and may subsequently find useful (fig. 3, page 166). Having such samples to hand can be invaluable when working on a project. The ability to hold, feel, sense the weight, strength, flexibility or otherwise of a material, to feel its texture or see how light plays off its surface; these sensory experiences are vital aids in the decision-making process, helping us grasp the tangibility of concepts before the final modelling begins.

The previous pages show a photo essay of design inspiration. Each image was taken because it demonstrated a technique, arrangement, example or strategy that was striking and could inform a future design project. All designers do this, either with a camera or sketchbook, or if they are fortunate enough, a photographic memory. You might consider starting a similar collection and categorising the pictures to provide easy future reference (figs 4–18, pages 167–171).

Figs 16–18   **Reuse**
Examples of objects reused in a new context. Ammunition fashioned into a toy helicopter, bottle tops as a café tabletop and a bollard made from a car wheel.

IDEAS GENERATION

Although ideas can be triggered any time and in particular through the processes of observation, drawing and model-making covered in this chapter, designers, management consultants and theorists have identified methods that specifically encourage the generation of apparently fresh thinking. In addition, they have developed tools that facilitate the organisation of thoughts that help focus decision-making. These methods and tools are discussed below.

STARTING WITH WORDS

As has been proposed, a mix of logical structuring, irrational intuition and experienced judgement goes into an effective design process. It requires a degree of flexibility, but one thing is fixed; we all must start at the point of recognising, or defining, the scope and aims of the project. Discussions with clients or colleagues will usually guide this and hence it is, most commonly, through words that we arrive at a notion of what we want to achieve. Matching the verbal intention with an agreed physical solution is of course the challenge. Words have the habit of forming different images in the mind's eye and hence are best augmented with visuals, material samples, or other "props" where possible to avoid diverging notions of where the project is heading. However, there is another stage in which words can be more useful. That is in helping us understand, iterate and improve the set of relations within the project, before the visual work begins. Once broad aims have been defined, avenues of research and key themes the project might deal with can be identified. It is here that tools such as mind-mapping and brainstorming become useful, firstly to simply pin down and bundle

disparate thoughts and subsequently to allow focussed investigation of categories and sub-categories, eventually resulting in verbal design ideas.

Once a number of ideas that all seem equally viable and fit the brief have been proposed, a decision is needed as to which to take further. There are various design management tools that try to rate concepts logically, based on charting their likely success against chosen criteria. These pseudo-scientific methods offer no guarantees and it could be argued that it is at such a point that logic should be abandoned and intuition and experience brought to bear. When the "real" design work of transforming words into objects starts, the potential or otherwise of these verbal or written ideas will become apparent.

MIND-MAPPING

A mind-map is a simple diagram that enables all the possible directions a project may take, and the sub-categories and ideas within them, to be put down on paper as they come to mind. As thoughts are laid down they are grouped, prompting us to ask ourselves if each new thought is part of an existing group or requires a new one to be started.

Mind-maps commonly have a radial structure intended to evolve from the centre out, hence why they are occasionally called spider diagrams – the analogies of the spider's body with legs radiating out in all directions, and the building of its web, can both be seen as appropriate. A pyramid or family tree layout is also occasionally used, but this provides a more limited and defined amount of space on the page for ideas to be added and reinforces the sense of hierarchy.

Figure 1 shows a typical mind-map from a short design project about clocks. The subject of the brief or overarching theme is placed centrally. Around this

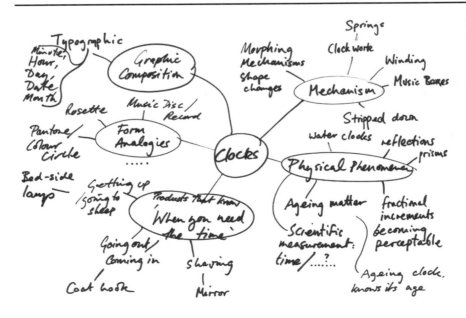

Fig. 1   **Mind-map**
A simple mind-map from a short project about clocks. The central theme branches off into sub-themes that in turn yield individual product concepts.

[1.]
Miller, G. A. 1956. "The Magical Number Seven, Plus or Minus Two: Some Limits on our Capacity for Processing Information." 'Psychological Review', 63.

are islands of themes that clock design could explore. Branching off from the themes are sub-themes that form the basis of design ideas. For example, the theme that examines "when you need to know the time" produced the response "shaving" which led to the idea for a clock set into a shaving mirror (fig. 1, page 172). Cross links may be made when ideas appear to be appropriate to more than one theme; for example, the idea of a water clock could have emerged from the theme "physical phenomena" or "mechanism".

Mind-maps prove useful because they allow us to focus attention on one theme at a time and suggest ideas or sub-categories that relate to it. Their ease of use aligns with the findings of cognitive psychologists who have discovered that the human brain has the capacity to deal with a limited number of "chunks" of information at any one time (1). By splitting the design problem down, we are able to make best use of our imperfect mental resources.

The radial, branching form of a mind-map implies that we arrive at all of our ideas through this gradual narrowing down from core subject through any number of themes and sub-themes until we reach defined product ideas. Yet anyone who has completed a mind-map will know that the experience tends to include random product ideas popping up for which we then feel we must create a theme and link back into the core subject – post-rationalising it as part of our logical thought process. Although slightly perverse, this has its advantages by allowing us to then build upon the themes and categories that these chance thoughts suggest. However, by not always developing logically from the centre, mind-maps can take on somewhat chaotic layouts, which critics argue is nothing more than a visual expression of the confusion in the mind. They also do not necessarily facilitate choices, but simply map out the enormity of the possible range of ideas from which one might choose.

Mind-mapping can be done individually or in a team with a chosen facilitator to draw the map from the members' suggestions. Software is also available from various companies to enable the easy construction of mind-maps on the computer.

BRAINSTORMING

The structure of a mind-map implies that only ideas considered appropriate to the context of the project and its related themes are worth recording. We are inclined to think in terms of "what fits", which can reinforce existing models and practices. Brainstorming attempts to turn this on its head and jolt us out of routine thinking.

Brainstorming is a collaborative process and therefore requires a group of people. At its core lie the concepts that one idea triggers another and that the combination of ideas can lead to innovative solutions. While this may seem possible individually, it becomes exponentially more effective when many trains of thought are allowed to intersect. As the process involves the collective sharing, mixing and development of ideas, individuals must be prepared to give up ownership of their ideas for the benefit of the project. Protecting "your idea" from being mutated by others is counter-productive to the process. Ideas in all their stages of development should be noted down for evaluation at a later stage, hence participants ought not to be concerned that an idea will be eclipsed and lost in the process.

Through its evolution and use (which spreads far beyond design), various rules have become recognised for ensuring effective brainstorming (2). Yet as a process concerned with breaking rules, it must be recognised that most of these have a flip-side and are open to interpretation. Therefore, rather than provide separate lists of dos and don'ts, the following headings try to encapsulate the theories behind various aspects of the process.

FACILITATION

Brainstorming requires a facilitator – someone whose job it is to keep the ideas flowing. They may also be the person noting down ideas as they emerge, although it is beneficial if a separate scribe can be appointed. A key principle of brainstorming is to flatten hierarchy. The boss's ideas are of equal importance to those of the tea-boy. Hence, the facilitator does not direct the session from a position of authority, but allows it to ensue by lubricating points of friction or inertia. They must encourage those who have an idea to speak rather than putting people on the spot. They can throw in their own suggestions as a participant, but must not prioritise these. At quiet points, the facilitator should try to prompt the group by asking questions differently or by giving an example and asking for others. A calm, optimistic and informal demeanour is likely to help alleviate any feelings of pressure amongst the participants. Finally, the facilitator must be aware of and be prepared to enforce certain rules, in particular, the need to have only one person speak at a time, and to stop the critiquing of ideas.

[2.]
These sections are built upon rules identified by global design group IDEO: <www.ideo.com/about/methods>

SUBJECT FOCUS

The session needs to begin with a statement of the problem. The terms in which this is couched are essential to prompting a positive response. If it is too vague, participants struggle to find where to start; too specific and they can go into immediately detailed, prescriptive solutions. Imagining a brainstorm for the clock project mentioned above, the brief asked for

design ideas for X type of clock for X market at X price point to be made by X supplier, but rather than using this, it is likely to be more effective to start discussions around how we perceive and use clocks that will build into a general sense of what the object means to us. We might ask seemingly obvious questions such as "What is a clock?" and "What do clocks enable us to do?" in order to draw analogies with other things that do the same. This will also help us to tie our solutions in to genuine needs and desires and avoid irrelevant novelties. Instead of thinking about improvements only in terms of the object in question, it can be useful to list ways that other objects give benefit (efficiency, comfort, convenience, education and so on) and then map these back on to the object you are working on. This creates the non-linear thought process we are looking for. For example, what might an "educational clock" look like?

CRITIQUING

The perspective that a bad idea can trigger a good one justifies the "no criticism" rule that should be applied in all brainstorms. If bad ideas are suppressed, fewer good ones will emerge. In fact, the very concept of discussing good and bad ideas should be actively set aside at the beginning of the brainstorm; the goal is ideas, and lots of them. If the group focuses on judging and rating ideas, they are diverted from the task of simply responding to them by thinking up more. While it is impossible to completely suppress our judgement, brainstorming asks that we channel any critical thoughts into expressing a preferable idea (no "buts", only "ands"). This notion that value-judgements are to be suppressed causes some people to dismiss brainstorming as worthless. But this is to ignore the fact that value-judgements are welcome afterwards. However, during brainstroming, facilitators are encouraged to allow what may appear to be wildly

Fig. 2 IDEO Method Cards Global design consultancy IDEO has been generous in their desire to share their working methods. These cards help designers during brainstorms or as prompters when considering the future direction of a project.

off-target ideas in order to act both as triggers and to provide the necessary suspension of disbelief that enables innovation to occur. They therefore need to strike a careful balance between this and allowing the session to spiral away from the chosen subject. Deviation within limits may provide the essential ingredient to spark a good idea.

EXPERTISE

It is tempting to think that including experts in brainstorming sessions would be counter-productive; after all, the point is to break with convention and avoid any sense of intimidation or deferment to those with greater knowledge. However, by bringing together experts from different fields and ensuring that they follow the same protocols as other team members, the cross-fertilisation of their expertise may prove highly effective. The key is to ensure that the focus remains on breadth of ideas from everyone and not depth of detail.

NOTATION

A brainstorm is a process of ideas generation rather than ideas selection; therefore the end result is not one great idea but, hopefully, a large number of ideas that subsequently need analysing. For this reason, it is essential that every idea, no matter how apparently insignificant, is written down or sketched. Whatever the means of recording used, participants, the facilitator or the appointed scribe must do it quickly so as to avoid interrupting the flow of thoughts that is emerging. Hence, longhand descriptions covering several lines must be avoided in favour of quick keywords or at most, single sentences. Sketching is to be encouraged and the need for skill and accuracy played down (even a misunderstood sketch in the brainstorming environment can trigger another contribution). Again, due to this

triggering effect, notation must be highly visible to all participants and should be allowed to spread around the walls as the brainstorm unfolds. Ideas hidden in the back of a flip chart are unable to inform the current thinking and lose the chance of forming part of an important connection. The use of marker pens on large, easily pasted-up sheets or, if possible, large-sized Post-It notes can help keep all the material readable.

By allowing the thought that "anything goes" and nothing is beyond the scope of change, brainstorming opens up new possibilities. Such methods come under fire from pragmatists because they lead to many unusable suggestions and as such can seem to represent a desperate, unstructured search as opposed to a rational plan of action. However, it is precisely such plans that tend to revert to known methodologies and produce staid ideas. The inappropriate thoughts that appear during ideas generation are perhaps best considered as necessary waste in a process of elimination, like the many discarded sketches before a design is perfected.

BRAINSTORMING METHODS

Various designers and design companies have produced sets of cards that aid brainstorming and individual ideas generation, and have marketed them to designers, architects and business people. These include IDEO's Method Cards (fig. 2, page 174): "IDEO Method Cards show 51 of the methods we use to inspire great design and keep people at the center of our design process. Each card describes one method and includes a brief story about how and when to use it. The cards are divided into four categories, Learn, Look, Ask and Try…It's a design tool meant to help you explore new approaches and develop your own." (3)

[3.]
'IDEO website'. 2009. [online]. [Accessed 27th January 2009]. Available from World Wide Web: <www.ideo.com/methodcards>

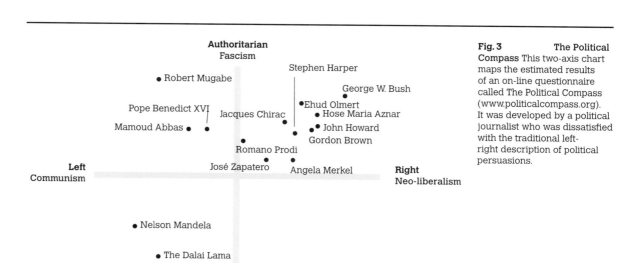

Fig. 3   The Political Compass This two-axis chart maps the estimated results of an on-line questionnaire called The Political Compass (www.politicalcompass.org). It was developed by a political journalist who was dissatisfied with the traditional left-right description of political persuasions.

[4.]
'We Make'. [online]. [Accessed 27th January 2009]. Available from World Wide Web: <www.flowmaker.org>

[5.]
'Domus' magazine. 2006. September

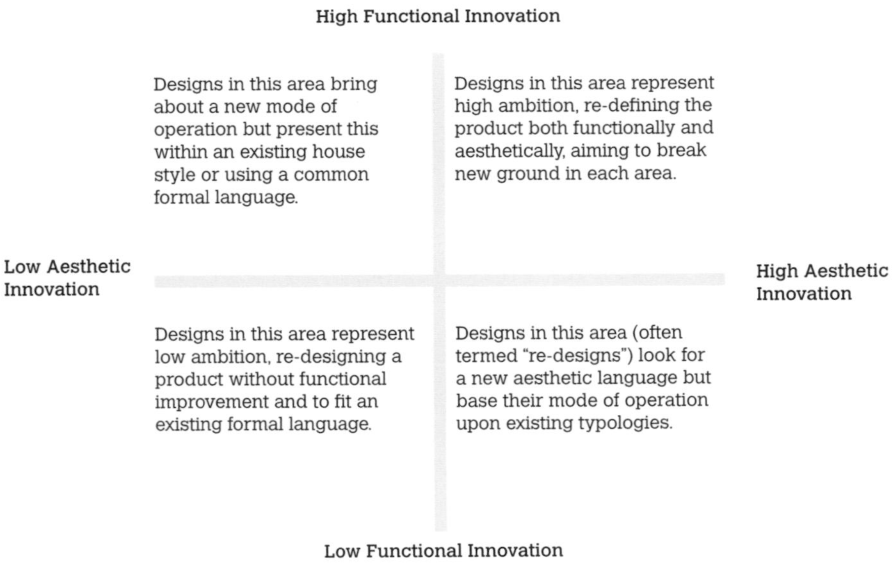

FLOWMAKER

Sarah Johnson and Jason Allcorn, partners in design company We Make and sustainability group [Re]Design, developed Flowmaker, a set of 54 cards with five colour-coded suits consisting of instinct, personality, ageing, play and potential. Like IDEO's Method Cards, there are no fixed rules for use, the intention being to generate non-linear thinking. Its designers suggest approaches such as dealing one from each suit to imply a brief, or using single suits to evaluate concepts and analyse existing products (4).

LIVING

Italian designer Enzo Mari worked with Paolo Gallerani in the 1970s to produce a set of cards entitled "Living", which were printed and sold by product manufacturer Danese. Reprinted in the September 2006 edition of 'Domus' magazine, the cards contain descriptions of professions, types of home, places, neighbours, flatmates and belongings. By dealing a selection, a random but nonetheless feasible picture of a person's life situation is created. The intention is to lead to the consideration of scenarios that encourage the designer to consider life beyond their own narrow frame of reference and away from dangerous generalisations about people, lifestyle and culture.

'Domus' wrote: "Enzo Mari's card game seems to tell us that our cities do not accommodate "types" of living, but infinite combinations of practices and feelings, each different to the other and all absolutely logical if we bother to understand them. It shows us that our classifications are only feasible if we know how to dismantle and reassemble them all the time, without ever treating them as real substitutes for life itself. Enzo Mari seems to be saying that to discover the unpredictable combinations of daily life and its spaces, we need the systematic rigour of an outlook, which, by accepting chance, can dig out the unforeseeable. But that is the point: to get closer to the infinite variety of the world outside we need rigour, a method, and precise rules. Like those of a card game." (5)

Taken to its (il)logical conclusion, if the cards are simply a trigger for thoughts, they could contain anything at all, even random shapes and patterns. In the context of thinking about a design problem, revealing a card will prompt an attempt to associate whatever is on it with the task in hand. Such attempts to bounce the mind around in a non-linear way have become linked with the term "lateral thinking" after the book "The Uses of Lateral Thinking", published in 1967 by Edward de Bono.

CHARTING INFORMATION

As we have seen, the way that ideas are arranged and juxtaposed can have an effect upon our ability to make connections between them and hit upon new discoveries. It is therefore no surprise to discover that those in the fields of design and business consulting, who sell "innovation services", make use of a wide range of methods to manipulate and visualise data. These include, among others, creating grids of attributes, using two-axis charts and Venn diagrams. These are explained in more detail below.

ATTRIBUTE LISTING

Attribute listing is a method of generating alternative product specifications by comparing and contrasting different mixes of attributes that a product could be designed to possess. Each attribute of a product is listed (for this book we would list size, shape, weight, paper thickness, type of binding, number of pages, number of colours used in printing, for example).

High Functional Innovation

Designs in this area bring about a new mode of operation but present this within an existing house style or using a common formal language.

Designs in this area represent high ambition, re-defining the product both functionally and aesthetically, aiming to break new ground in each area.

Low Aesthetic Innovation

High Aesthetic Innovation

Designs in this area represent low ambition, re-designing a product without functional improvement and to fit an existing formal language.

Designs in this area (often termed "re-designs") look for a new aesthetic language but base their mode of operation upon existing typologies.

Low Functional Innovation

Fig. 4   Map of the ambitions of a design project Although reverting to stereotypes, this map helps us to define the ambition of a design project in terms of functional or aesthetic innovation or conformity.

Then, as many variations of each attribute would be listed; for example, under weight we would list various stages from light to heavy, and under binding, we would list perfect, spiral, sewn and so on. A grid of possible attributes emerges and by reading across these, products with a huge range of different specifications are revealed. Compared to other methods of generating ideas, attribute listing is among the most tedious and tends to throw up nonsensical results (such as a round, spiral-bound book), but may on occasion enable us to hit upon combinations we had not previously considered.

[6.]
'Political Compass'. 2001–2002. [online]. [Accessed 27th January 2009]. Available from World Wide Web: <www.politicalcompass.org>

TWO-AXIS CHARTS

Simple L-shaped, two-axis bar and line graphs compare two kinds of data, for example product sales against time. However, using a cross-axis creates four fields where X and Y values can be used to map two sets of opposites. For example, a chart (fig. 3, page 175) called The Political Compass (6) maps people's political persuasions by juxtaposing the traditional left and right wing continuum (the X axis) and an authoritarian versus libertarian continuum (the Y axis). Where a person is placed is determined by their answers to a set of questions that produces data resulting in an X, Y coordinate.

The same system can be used to map the ambitions of a design project (fig. 4, page 176) by, for example, creating axes for low to high aesthetic innovation (X axis) against low to high functional innovation (Y axis). Although this specific subject reinforces a troublesome form/function divide, the resulting chart nonetheless shows four recognisable approaches in each corner:

> Top right (high functional and aesthetic innovation) is the most ambitious project, redefining the product both functionally and aesthetically and breaking new ground in each area.

Bottom right (high aesthetic but low functional innovation) denotes a redesign that looks for a new aesthetic language, but bases it upon an existing, unchanging, functional typology.

Top left (low aesthetic and high functional innovation) would represent a product that brings about a new mode of operation but presents this within an existing house style, or using a common formal language.

Bottom left (low aesthetic and functional innovation) is an unambitious project that redesigns a product without functional improvement and to fit an existing formal language.

Axes may be exchanged to explore other opposites, such as high-low cultural appeal or small-large market take-up etc. Charts such as these are used to define the position of competitors' products and to visualise where new products might be situated.

VENN DIAGRAMS

Named after their inventor, mathematician John Venn (1834–1923), Venn diagrams consist of overlapping areas, commonly circles, and are used to visualise all the possible relationships between sets or groups. They are useful for ideas generation because they visualise the intersection of fields; the area of overlap denoting a potentially creative combination. Fields could represent many things including disciplines, markets and subjects. The diagram by Charles Eames (fig. 5, page 177) overlays the interests of the designer, the client and society to define the territory in which, in his words, "… the designer can work with conviction and enthusiasm".

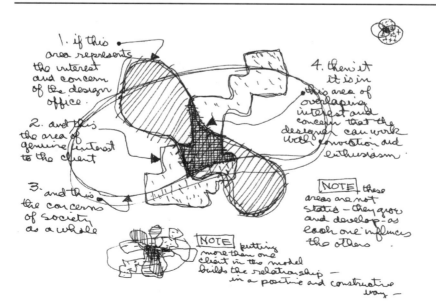

Fig. 5   Diagram by Charles Eames An example of a Venn diagram, Eames describes the interests of various parties (client, designer, society) as two-dimensional shapes that overlap each other. The area where all three coincide represents the most fruitful area for collaboration.

[1.]
Pipes, A. 2007. 'Drawing for
Designers'. London: Lawrence
King

3.6

DRAWING

This section is not about how to draw but is rather about theories of drawing. Why do we do it, what are its applications and how does it help us in the design process? Drawing is almost unquestioningly promoted as being beneficial in design schools around the world yet how many of us really understand what it does for us? As with many of the subjects touched on in this book, a full study is not possible here, but a number of concepts are expounded that will hopefully prompt deeper investigation.

WHY DRAW?

In his book 'Drawing for Designers', Alan Pipes tells us that: "A designer's drawing has three main functions: it is a means of externalizing and analysing thoughts and simplifying multi-faceted problems to make them more understandable. It is a medium of persuasion that sells ideas to clients and reassures them that their brief is being satisfied. It is a method for communicating complete and unambiguous information to those responsible for the product's manufacture, assembly and marketing." (1)

As Pipes explains, drawing is done for different reasons and hence, the first task for a designer is to know why he is drawing. Is it a sketch (fig. 1, page 178), a drawing (fig. 2, page 179) or a rendering (fig. 3, page 180, fig. 4, page 181, fig. 5, page 181)? The problem with these terms is that they do not sufficiently imply one of drawing's three functions (which we may boil down from Pipes's descriptions to "thinking", "presenting" and "measuring"). There is a great deal of fluidity in the use of each. For example, the informality suggested by the word "sketch" might place it more firmly in the territory of a thinking tool for the designer's use only,

but sketches are sometimes made quickly in a client meeting to convey a point, whereby they become presentation devices. They may also be dimensioned, becoming tools for conveying measurement. Similarly, "rendering" suggests a level of finish associated with presentation, yet rendered drawings appear in designers' sketchbooks and are not always shown to clients. So as not to get lost in semantics, we must concentrate upon what the intention of the expression is, rather than what we choose to call it.

FREEING THE MIND

In the past, we might have thought of drawing for design as being a series of one-way actions to represent what is in our heads on paper. We think about the design, do one drawing, wait until another idea comes into our heads, draw that and so on. Our drawings record the process and free our mind from holding their images. The writer W. Somerset Maugham once commented that characters haunted him until he could write them satisfactorily into a story. Once he had done this, he was free to forget them and this was a great relief. Drawing may provide a similar release to the designer. Particularly in complex projects, to hold all of the elements in one's head and consider how they might interrelate becomes difficult or impossible.

As was discussed in 3.1 The elusive design process, obviously when we draw to develop design ideas, we aren't thinking about lines on paper, but rather about what we are designing. Once pen touches paper, we are appraising what the drawing expresses. Hence many designers' sketchbooks are filled with half-finished sketches, some drawn over one another indicating that part way through the drawing it was decided that another form, another idea, was preferable. One of the great advantages of drawing over other methods

Fig. 1 Sketches from the second-prize-winning entry for the New Bus for London Design Competition (2008) by a consortium consisting of three companies: Miñarro García, Héctor Serrano Studio and Javier Esteban This montage shows the range of ideas explored quickly through sketching by Enrique Miñarro and Joaquin García.

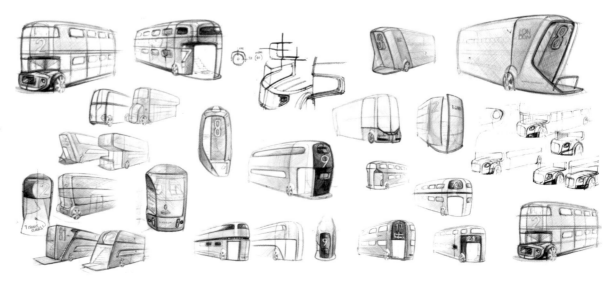

of expression is its immediacy. It can almost keep up with the speed at which the designer thinks – the speed with which he changes his idea of what he wishes to visualise.

SLIPPING INTO PRESENTATION

By contrast, the act of presentation drawing (by hand or computer) is more laboured and self-conscious. We might think of it as a separate activity and it can be. However, a design sketch can slip into being a presentation drawing simply with a lapse of concentration. When the designer becomes aware of his drawing as a set of lines on paper with an aesthetic of their own, he is liable to try and improve that aesthetic rather than improving the design they express. The drawing becomes a presentational device and stops being a thinking tool; light, shade and line weight take over from assessing the design itself. Self-satisfaction at reaching a particular stage can get the better of us as we start titivating the drawing in celebration of our success. In design education, the assessment of sketchbooks, without clear guidance, exacerbates this problem. Students are inclined to justify the unthinking rendering of design sketches because they feel they must give in a "presentable" body of development work. Experienced tutors will, of course, be more impressed by the evidence of the manipulation and interrogation of the object and its relations within the project. Presentation drawings have their place in the decision-making process, especially when feedback from others is required. But the difference is, they are done in preparation for a decision upon their completion rather than as an aid to thinking during the drawing process.

DRAWING IS GENERATIVE

What is not often recognised is the way in which drawing, beyond being a visual bookmark showing where we have got to in the design process, plays an active role in prompting new ideas. This happens because, as was mentioned early in this chapter, what your drawings express will always, to a lesser or greater extent, be different from what you try to make them express (that is, the drawing will not precisely represent what you had in your head). Only by making the drawing and seeing what it expresses, can we recognise this difference and be prompted to make a decision. Do we like what the drawing has expressed or shall we try again to express something different? Seeing drawing as an active participant in the decision-making process justifies its continued relevance in design. Technology now enables us to sketch into a computer, but whatever the medium, the speed and directness must be maintained in order for it to prove effective.

Not all designers feel the same attachment to drawing. As a device for refining and pre-determining the made object, it favours those who prefer studied, calculated action rather than spontaneous, impulsive decision-making. In design for industry, there is generally no option but to show drawn solutions, because the decisions as to what will be made must be signed off and because the making itself will be done by someone else. In craft or designer-maker activity, these mediators are removed. The notion of pre-planning the end result can be discarded in favour of letting the mind react directly with the expressions made by the materials during the making of the final work. Martino Gamper (whose 100 Chairs in 100 Days project is pictured on page 70) works directly with found furniture, cutting it and re-assembling it to create one-off pieces.

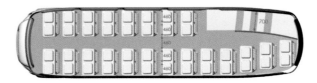

Fig. 2 Cross-section and floor plans for a new bus for London by Miñarro García, Héctor Serrano Studio and Javier Esteban These computer drawings are to scale and are dimensioned to show the size of the vehicle as well as the layout of seats.

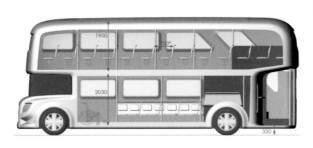

[2.]   -
Picci, F. 2008. "Gio Ponti
translated by Martino Gamper".
'Domus 911', February

[3.]   -
Gamper, M. In: Picci, F. 2008.
"Gio Ponti translated by
Martino Gamper". 'Domus
911', February
                       -
[4.]   -
Dormer, P. 1990. 'The Meanings
of Modern Design'. London:
Thames & Hudson
                       -
[5.]   -
"The workmanship of risk"
and "The workmanship of
certainty" are phrases coined
by David Pye in his seminal
book The 'Nature and Art of
Workmanship' (1968).
                       -

According to Gamper: "Drawing is an intermediary process: you have an idea, you transcribe it onto paper, then you translate it (have it translated) into reality, which means there are two extra steps [between idea and made object]". (2) "I like to draw, I like to make sketches...[but] even if you do drawing after drawing and define everything down to the last detail, you might still be disappointed with the end result...I'm more interested in the moment of creation itself, because while you are doing it you understand where you want to go; you can change direction, find more ideas...The cut is always a clean break. There's no going back." (3) Gamper could, of course, sketch out many possibilities for how to cut and assemble his found ingredients, and then choose the most desirable result, but this would slow him down. More importantly, it would turn the process of making into one of following a series of instructions rather than one of creation itself (of course such a set of instructions is exactly what industrial production requires from the designer, but that is not Gamper's context). The inherent risk Gamper sets up by not using an intermediary process like drawing is what allows the result to be seen as a virtuoso performance. In the words of Peter Dormer: "At the heart of the workmanship of risk, is the thrill of avoiding failure." (4) Drawing for design can be seen as an aid to the opposite – the workmanship of certainty – whereby risks are reduced by visualising the many options and choosing those least likely to fail. (5)

COMPUTER-AIDED DESIGN

Although advancing all the time, three-dimensional computer-aided design (CAD) software is yet to provide the fluency of interface needed to allow designers to think through their ideas in "virtual" three dimensions with the stream-of-consciousness fluency they can achieve on paper. Most CAD software was designed primarily for engineering or rendering and animation purposes, and has been co-opted by designers for use during the design process. As a result, such software requires the inputting of dimensions or the creation of geometry using various tools that divert the mind away from consideration of the design and into "driving the software". How an object is made on-screen requires its own bank of knowledge that driving a pen does not. Attempting to develop design ideas early on in a project using CAD can be problematic because the software sometimes requests the setting of precise dimensions before this level of detail is needed by the designer. General impressions are often what are required at an early stage – the exploration of layouts, proportions and scale. If set with CAD, these can become resistant to being questioned at a later stage. The design becomes "determined" to a level that may discourage other branches of enquiry. As a consequence, the hyper-reality of a CAD model can give the impression of a finished product when in fact the design process may have only just begun. Computer renderings present a clinical completeness, while a sketch is a suggestion that allows us to fill in the detail with our own imagination. Watching a CGI fantasy film as compared to reading the book of the same story generates the same dichotomy. However, even when meeting the client early on in a project, fewer and fewer designers have the confidence to show sketches and instead turn to the computer rendering for its seductiveness.

Although the process of using CAD has the same generative capability that drawing has, in the sense that it results in expressions that enable comparisons, if used on its own, it does not leave a paper trail that can be easily reviewed later on. CAD modelling is done by modifying the object on-screen. Unless the operators studiously save each step, the ability to compare current and past steps is relegated to what they can remember.

-          -

Fig. 3   **Presentation rendering of a design for a new bus for London by Miñarro García, Héctor Serrano Studio and Javier Esteban** A three-dimensional computer model of the final design has been rendered and set in context for the final presentation.

APPROPRIATE EXPRESSION

Once aware of drawing as a generative process, designers can consider what kinds of expressions (drawing or otherwise) will be most useful to them at various stages of the project. They can try to match the set of relations being investigated with a means of expression that shows them clearly. Hence, if we are chasing a flamboyant, sinuous form, large-scale freehand sketching is likely to be more effective than tight, precise drawing, or CAD. Likewise, if we are trying to understand scale and proportion in relation to the human body, the sketchbook must be given up for full-scale drawings or models. There are even some, such as the architect Will Alsop, who use large-scale canvas painting as part of their design process.

Notwithstanding the reservations expressed regarding its use too early in the design process, there comes a point in many projects where the computer becomes invaluable. With rapid prototyping (6) becoming more prevalent in mainstream product design practice, a rigorous design process becomes possible, whereby representations of a product pass freely from two dimensions to three dimensions, from virtual to real and back. Data is inputted to enable computer models to be "printed" in three dimensions and those models are then considered and altered – first by sketching and physical modelling, then by altering the computer data. Despite the slow speed of inputting this data compared to sketching, its advantages are revealed in the quality of representation, especially when that representation becomes three-dimensional. This holistic use of the computer greatly increases its importance in the design process over its role simply as a rendering or manufacturing tool.

[6.]
Rapid prototyping encompasses a number of methods of building objects from computer files created using three-dimensional modelling software (see 3.7 Maquette and model-making).

THE PARADOX OF PERFECTION

By offering up hyper-realistic representations, computer renderings make the designer responsible for delivering the results that such images suggest are possible. When presentation drawings were done by hand, they could be more ambiguous, and hence allow more room for manoeuvre. However, even these became highly sophisticated, developing into an art form with its own language of seduction. Rather than being still-lifes, the marker pen and pastel techniques of late-twentieth-century product designers gave a nod to reality but concentrated upon selling the beauty of the objects' form and surface. This art has now passed from drawing board to computer. Whereas photo-realism was once the holy grail of three-dimensional CAD users, designers soon realised that dynamism and flair were more compelling than reality.

RENDERING INTEGRITY

With the increasing competition in some sectors of the design industry, the rendering has become the currency young designers use to get noticed. Certain sections of the design press can be found printing renderings of designers' work before any concrete evidence of its ability to function or be producible has been shown. Such processes reduce design to a purely visual pursuit and denigrate its conceptual and technical aspects. Designers, clients and the media have a role to play in ensuring the integrity of the design process does not get sold for the price of a quick rendering. Designers must resist the temptation to overstate the maturity of quick ideas and clients must resist the seduction of the image, seeing it not as a page in their next catalogue but as the first step in a process that may lead to a multitude of different outcomes.

Fig. 4 Rear view of a new bus for London by Miñarro García, Héctor Serrano Studio and Javier Esteban The three-dimensional model is rotated to show one of the bus's innovative safety features: a rear platform that lights up as the bus is about to pull away.

Fig. 5 Interior view of a new bus for London by Miñarro García, Héctor Serrano Studio and Javier Esteban Here the three-dimensional model is seen from inside the upper deck and shows the seats with their removable upholstery pads.

MAQUETTE AND MODEL-MAKING

The craftsperson or designer-maker, should they choose, is able to define and refine each object as it is made, exerting their control during the act of making. The designer for production has relinquished that role, their craft skills instead being applied to embody their intentions prior to manufacture, particularly through drawing and models. Product design could be done without model-making but it is hard to conceive of a single project where its influence might not be of benefit. Even when a model simply confirms the efficacy of a preceding drawing, it has done its duty in allowing a fuller preview of the finished product.

This section examines the uses of maquette and model-making and attempts to identify their value. Like the drawing chapter, it is not a "how to" guide to techniques but instead studies why and where the process can be of benefit to the designer.

THE VALUE OF THE MODEL

Models come in many forms and serve many purposes. They can be the final stage or the starting point of a project – about capturing a rough impression or the complete picture. They may be real or virtual. Like "sketch", "drawing" and "rendering", the terms "maquette", "model" and "prototype" suggest three different levels of speed and refinement, and a gradual increase in sophistication as the project unfolds. All may be used as tools for process or presentation but, like drawing, the vital consideration on the part of the designer is "What am I making this model for?" or rather "What is it that I am looking to analyse and what effect do I want it to produce?"

Katherine Hearn and Anthony Quinn run the BA(Hons) Ceramic Design course at London's Central Saint Martins College of Art and Design and have researched and written about the use of maquettes and models in product design. They argue that: "The maquette, the point where the idea and its three-dimensional representation inhabit the world without recourse to manufacturing or market limitations, could be said to encompass the essence of design activity. When you see somebody in a department store, thoughtfully holding a fork and testing its balance, it is at this point that the consumer's act of enquiry exactly mirrors the investigations of the designer." (1)

Through an exhibition at The Aram Gallery in London, its curator Daniel Charny expressed a fascination with models and prototypes in their own right: "These objects ...hold a rare charm; there's an increased closeness to the designer's imagination, and a directness to the making that often changes when manufacturing and marketing forces are fully integrated. The objects may be characterised by a technical or material discrepancy, compared to the final product, due to a lack of access of the designer to technology at the process stage. It's a stark contrast to the current wave of limited editions – which has made for the unique to be diluted by multiples and for the production piece to be restrained in order to increase the value of singular pieces." (2)

Quinn and Hearn have found evidence that the general shift towards a less making-based culture, exacerbated by children growing up with largely screen-based entertainment, is having an effect in design schools. "As educators of designers we have become increasingly frustrated by the lack of manipulative making skills and tenacity in the physical working in 3D of these

[1.]
Quinn, A and Hearn, K. 2006.
'Blueprint'. December

[2.]
Charny, D. 2008. Press release
for exhibition, Prototypes and
Experiments, the Aram Gallery.

[3.]
Quinn, A and Hearn, K. 2006.
'Blueprint'. December

[4.]
Grcic, K. In: Bohm, F. 2005.
'Konstantin Grcic Industrial
Design'. London: Phaidon

Fig. 1   **Chair One model-making** Konstantin Gcric's Chair One seen on page 56 was modelled full size in cardboard. These images show the chair's development from an early model (left) to the final design (right).

potential designers...Our hypothesis is that the spirit of endeavour in trying to transform the ethereal idea into its first rudimentary physical representation is the hidden or forgotten craft of design." (3)

However, despite the decline in skills, most practitioners underline how important model-making is for designers. "The modelling phase represents the first real test for a design", says Konstantin Grcic. "All the models [in our studio] are built to full scale, so that they provide an opportunity to engage with the actual substance of the design (fig. 1, page 182)." (4)

The products of high-tech industry that Grcic designs take hundreds of thousands of pounds' worth of tooling to produce, yet they have the humblest of origins. Many of his models are made from cardboard, wire or anything that will allow for the quick expression of a design. They are not necessarily for showing to clients but are primarily for him and his team to move the project forward, testing pre-conceived assumptions and pinning down essential information.

MODEL AS SKETCH

For this kind of sketch modelling or maquette making, speed is of the essence. Like drawing, ideas flow fast and a process is required that allows the design to appear in three dimensions quickly in order to be seen, analysed and another response made. Whereas in a fully working prototype all aspects of the design must be proven in one model, at the beginning of the process many models may be made that fulfil only one or two criteria each, but collectively provide all the required information. For example, a model that tests proportions and visual appearance may intentionally ignore criteria such as structural strength. For his design for a wooden chair, Stefan Diez created a sketch model using a simple ribbon of cardboard and tape (fig.

2, page 183). The model requires a pile of magazines to be "sat on", yet it serves its purpose perfectly. Another model may do the opposite, testing the strength of the material without labouring over the precise detail of the form.

A common mistake is to try and jump from early sketches to a final facsimile model that requires considerable effort or expense to make. After the money and time have been spent, the result is almost always a piece that contains fundamental flaws that could have been discovered quickly and inexpensively through sketch modelling. Initial models may trial vastly different layouts or formats while later ones often concentrate upon almost imperceptible differences, such as exploring the precise contouring of a surface or setting a radius on an edge.

Material choice will depend upon the focus of the project and access to equipment. If a key part of the project is about exploring material properties, and you have access to the material concerned, then naturally, getting hands-on with it will be the first step. However, if you are yet to define the final material choice, are designing for an involved, time-consuming process (for example ceramic slip casting) or one that you do not have access to (such as plastic injection moulding), fast sketch modelling techniques will be beneficial. Designers co-opt whatever is to hand, but commonly keep stocks of materials such as paper, card, foam, wire or plaster available in their studios. Ready-made objects can also help leapfrog lengthy modelling processes early in the project. For example, £1 shops or their equivalent offer a multiplicity of hollow plastic forms (from plates and bowls to laundry baskets) that may be cut up and re-formed, to create parts that would otherwise need vacuum forming, a process that often requires time-consuming tool making. It is easy

Fig. 2   Friday **Chair models by Stefan Diez** A model need not test all aspects of a design at once. Here, Stefan Diez uses card modelling to quickly explore the chair's lines, proportions and dimensions, yet these models will not hold a person's weight without assistance from a pile of magazines.

[5.]
Kelley, D. In: Moggridge, B.
2007. 'Designing Interactions'.
Cambridge, MA: MIT Press

to dismiss materials such as card and paper, yet with techniques such as layering, cross-halving, skinning or using papier-mâché, a broad range of organic forms is also possible. Inexpensive, readily available modelling materials enable designers to work without a restricting sense of preciousness; to feel that each model need not be the last, but one of many that, through comparison and failure, will help refine the end result.

PROTOTYPING EXPERIENCE

While designers can use models to personally analyse their ideas, they offer the important potential of allowing other people to experience them. Expanding this notion, the model-making process finds itself transcending the boundaries of the singular object and becoming the vehicle to test services. This has given rise to some additions to the traditional set of materials and processes of the design studio. IDEO's David Kelley says of his Stanford D-School students: "We used to design objects, and we had machine shops to prototype them. We still need machine shops, but if you're going to design experiences and services, you have to have new prototyping tools to explain to people what it would be like if we had this new technology. Now we're using storytelling. My students are taking improv classes and acting things out. They all know how to use some kind of quick and dirty video process so they can tell a story; they are becoming cartoonists so they can do quick storyboards." (5)

The techniques of creating sets, props, performances and films stretch the skill base of the designer but can prove very effective, alongside direct engagement with the object. Whichever method is used, prototypes can become user research tools to establish whether a proposed approach is worth developing further.

The same techniques are being adopted by designers wishing to present scenarios as provocations (see 2.12 Design for debate).

RAPID PROTOTYPING

As most design projects evolve, there is a call for models with a higher level of sophistication than is provided by maquettes and sketch models. The various criteria the product must fulfil eventually need to be tested in one unified object to ensure they do not conflict (the final prototype of Stefan Diez's Friday Chair is shown in fig. 3, page 184). Such models used to be the province of highly skilled craftsmen, but to a large extent they have been superseded by the arrival of computerised rapid prototyping techniques. Rapid prototyping (RP) is the umbrella term for a number of methods of generating objects from computer files created using three-dimensional modelling software. RP machines use a variety of processes and materials with which to build models, all of which work by treating the three-dimensional form as a series of horizontally-sliced layers. The machines subsequently build these up in the following ways:

>   Solidifying liquid resin
>   (Stereolithography (SLA))
>
>   Fusing particles of plastic or metal
>   (Selective laser sintering (SLS) and
>   Electron Beam Melting (EBM))
>
>   Solidifying a plaster-like powder using a
>   liquid binder through ink-jet print heads
>   (3D printing (3DP))
>
>   Squirting a directed flow of molten
>   plastic through a nozzle (Fused
>   Deposition Modelling (FDM))
>
>   Cutting and laminating layers of
>   heat-bonded paper (Laminated Object
>   Manufacturing (LOM))

Fig. 3   **Friday Chair**
final prototype Bent wood
is used in the final prototype,
replicating the process that
would be used to manufacture
the chair.

[6.]
Levien, R. 2008. [Personal communication]. 26 March

The techniques vary greatly in price, possible materials that can be used and the properties of the models that emerge (SLA, SLS, EBM and FDM being generally higher end and consequently more expensive than 3DP and LOM). As it has advanced, RP technology has become able to mimic mass production materials with increasing precision. Using these techniques, designers are able to shorten model-making time and get a better appreciation of the end product before committing their clients to expensive tooling. In addition, three-dimensional modelling software is able to carry out many calculations such as stress analysis to predict how manufactured components will physically behave. This combined with RP technology and product renderings have enabled the designer to show clients, in ever-greater detail, the results of their process. As less and less is left to chance, the designer takes on greater responsibility for the effectiveness or otherwise of the end product.

With computers opening up these new methods of form creation, designers and craftspeople are beginning to explore the characteristics intrinsic to the computer as making tool. What was once reserved for prototyping has become a manufacturing method in itself. In addition to these RP technologies, the computer numerically controlled (CNC) cutting of sheet materials, solid blocks and the bending of wire has emerged as useful tools for prototyping and fabrication.

Students and practitioners face a bewildering array of software programs to allow them access to these technologies. In such a fast-moving market, it would be dangerous to make recommendations here as they would soon become outdated, but the safest advice is to be aware of the intended goals (different software has different advantages – rendering / animation / engineering drawing output / CADCAM (computer-aided design and manufacture) and RP compatibility) and consult an academic or practitioner. A recent development is the appearance of inexpensive student licences and freeware software such as Google's SketchUp that, while crude compared to professional tools, still offers useful basic functionality.

COMPUTE WITH CAUTION

However, just as drawing for design can easily slip into a presentation exercise, side-tracking the designer away from the analytical process, the computer offers a similar trap. It is all too easy to retreat into a self-satisfied world where every design looks beautiful as it floats in a virtual world. Careful consideration is needed as to whether time is best spent on the computer or in actual physical modelling that can give tangible feedback. Even when working towards a rapid prototype, the computer model seduces in a way that the sketch model does not; therefore, the idea that emerges as being valid from sketch modelling does so despite, not because of, the polish of its presentation, and hence may contain a deeper, more resonant value.

Despite its increased use, there are drawbacks to RP. Relatively few design studios have machines on-site, meaning there may be some delay between the creation and analysis of the model. More importantly for ceramics designer Robin Levien, the process itself contains none of the latent possibilities that modelling by hand does (6). Although they use computer modelling, the designers in his studio are all able to make highly accurate hand-carved models in foam and plaster. The act of carving, like drawing, is a cyclical process of expression, interpretation and response. Although designers may be working towards a predefined form, each intermediate step is an expression that triggers ideas that they are able to compare with what they were intending to make. These thoughts can offer valuable new directions within a project or starting points for new ones.

04 Context

[1.]
Arad, R. 2008. 'Design Products Yearbook'. London: RCA

[2.]
Sottsass, E. In: Bayley, S. and Conran, T. 2007. 'Intelligence Made Visible'. London: Conran Octopus Ltd

4.1

EMPLOYMENT

This chapter is concerned with the working contexts of designers. The assortment of terms that designers use to describe themselves tends not to give clear pictures of defined spheres of activity. What, for example, constitutes the role of a "freelance designer?" Do they work alone or within a team, for themselves or in a design office, to their own agenda or on projects directed by others? The answer can be all of these, and the range of fields in which their work may end up is broader still. Instead of attempting to focus the blurred edges of such terms, it is clearer to define context by the way in which the designer is engaged, project-by-project. We can do this with only three terms. A designer is either employed, has been commissioned, or is working speculatively.

This section therefore discusses the experience of working in-house for corporations, manufacturing firms or design consultancies. "Commission" examines the notion of operating as an independent designer or building a team under your own control, and looks at the nature of client relationships. "Speculation" looks at the context of working without a client – with the intention of bringing one on board at a later point – or not, choosing instead to engage directly with the public.

These contexts are not exclusive career paths. Designers operate across more than one, yet each project will be rooted somewhere, and this will affect the specific circumstances and the range of possibilities it generates. They ought therefore to be seen as different lenses through which the approaches to design in Chapter 2 would be viewed.

CONSIDERING EMPLOYMENT

Ron Arad, maverick designer and Professor of Design Products at the Royal College of Art in London, once declared (mischievously and with pride) that "my students are unemployable" (1), meaning not that they were unfit for employment but that they had developed personal agendas, incompatible with entering the corporate establishment. These were postgraduate students, yet ask most undergraduates studying design if they want to get a design job on completing their courses and the likely response will be "yes". The process of postgraduate education quite rightly lays out a critical landscape enabling the student to understand more fully the nature of their profession and form opinions on how it ought to change. Healthy though this critical distance is, a perhaps unintended side-effect can be to instil students with a sense of pessimism towards the possibility of effecting change by working within the corporate world. This, combined with media hype that increasingly focuses upon designers as personalities, has resulted in a rise among graduates of individualism and the desire to remain self-contained.

Another potential influence on this trend could be that members of the generation of designers who witnessed the decimation of the manufacturing industry in the UK throughout the 1970s and '80s, and a lack of interest in their work from what little of it remained, are now teaching. Their responses – turning to designer-maker activity or to freelance work in Europe – have been observed by the current generation of students and a certain romance has grown up around them. With this background, graduate designers are apt to feel alienated from industry rather than go knocking on its doors for employment. Ettore Sottsass, a man with extensive experience of corporate employment (with Olivetti) and avant-garde activism (with Memphis) once said "industry should not buy culture, industry should be culture" (2), and who, if not designers, are going to be the ones to "cultivate" industry from within?

The premise that finding a "design job" is difficult depends, in part, upon how narrowly one defines the term. As industries died out, the typical in-house designer, using craft-based skills to shape the products of the firm, will naturally have been swept away with their departure, but skills have a habit of being adapted to new contexts by the most observant, and new ones developed.

While being aware of the danger of reinforcing stereotypes and making generalisations, it is nonetheless worth ruminating about what designers are usually best capable of. Doing so might enable us to promote those that were taken for granted and see which are most suited to being adapted for use in different fields. Most are good at breadth – being aware of and collecting snippets of knowledge about many subjects, recognising differences, categorising and mapping them. Their creativity relies, in part, upon their ability to make often random but useful connections between these, spotting opportunities that others with more blinkered outlooks may miss. They are good at dealing with ambiguity – being faced with more than one possible solution. Designers learn to use their intuition, make educated guesses and test the outcomes. They are, of course, good at making tangible previously intangible thoughts, ideas, concepts and, obviously, objects. They are good at working within constraints and recognising boundaries, while still being prepared to question them. (3)

Frustratingly, one of the things a lot of designers are worst at is recognising what they're good at, and applying these skills in non-traditional ways. Market forces mean that more are looking for unusual employment opportunities, as they see the extent of the competition in the glamorous product and furniture design sectors, yet their training usually hasn't helped them to be versatile. Many design schools are yet to fully embrace the strategic potential of design, sticking to the craft-based model of teaching that emerged from the Bauhaus. While both are needed, design management experts predict that the growth area will be in designers influencing the strategies, structures and services, not just the physical products of businesses and the public sector.

CHANGE FROM WITHIN

Ultimately, finding meaningful employment is about finding a way for our distinct sets of values to feed rather than be eclipsed by an organisation's culture. For this to happen, that culture must at least be receptive to being fed. Yet it need not necessarily entirely match our own ethos; it need only avoid too painful a clash. Whether working within a manufacturing industry or a design consultancy, projects will land on a designer's desk that they will not be given the option to refuse. Hence, an awareness of the ethical content of likely projects and a sense that there is at least some common ideological ground is vital.

While it would be unwise to speculate which has greater social and cultural value – the external influence of avant-garde voices, or the Trojan Horses within organisations – both offer valuable contributions – it is clear that working to effect meaningful change from within is an "active" rather than "passive-aggressive" position. If global corporations, rather

[3.]
McCullagh, K. 2009. 'Riding the Flux: Design is changing in myriad ways. Are you?' [online]. [Accessed 27th January 2009]. Available from World Wide Web: <http://www.core77.com/reactor/07.07_flux.asp>

[4.]   -
Mama, J. 2008. [Personal
communication]. 4 July

[5.]   -
'Philips website'. 2004–2008.
[online]. [Accessed 27th
January 2009]. Available
from World Wide Web: <www.
design.philips.com/probes>
              -

than individuals, are most immediately able to tackle some of the world's toughest social divides and environmental challenges, being at the boardroom table, or having the ear of somebody who is, could be far more effective than working externally.

-               -
EXPERIENCING EMPLOYMENT

Engaging with large corporations, by working in-house, or consulting for them, greatly multiplies the scope and complexity of the projects that designers are able to participate in, compared to acting individually. The trade-off is that while your contribution in itself may be important, it will represent a small portion of the whole project. A suppression of ego is therefore required in handing over ownership of your ideas to the team. The designer must be able to glean sufficient satisfaction from the knowledge that he or she has played a contributory rather than leading role in the project, and that these contributions lead to products that may be enjoyed by many people.

Personal independence offers a seductive alternative, yet the individualists occasionally give the sense that they believe working within a corporate design team is a safe and unchallenging option: a place to hide rather than to make a difference. Such conclusions are comprehensible if derived from looking only at products rather than having knowledge of the reality of the work behind them. Many corporations that would be judged as conservative by their product output have extensive design research facilities where working life is anything but mundane. The challenges differ from working independently, but are nonetheless demanding when fully accepted. Whether working in research or on products for impending release, pressure is exerted on employees' ability to communicate effectively on a daily basis. Team working skills are central. Ideas need to be engagingly and persuasively presented to get various stakeholders on board, to convince managers to allow particular lines of enquiry, or to allocate investment to new projects. Like any area of design, extra commitment is needed when deadlines draw near. A 9–5 job it ain't.

For those working in design research exploring future directions for business, the results of all this effort go unseen by the outside world, glimpses only appearing years down the line as they filter into the products of the day. However, some companies, like Royal Philips Electronics, do disclose the results of this endeavour to invited opinion leaders, collaborators and the media, enabling it to enrich and influence the current market. Jack Mama, Creative Director at Philips Design currently working on the Probes Programme, gives an example of how the company's New Nomads projects about wearable technology led to collaborations with Levi's and Nike that resulted in products that hit the high street. "We're there to provoke the company to think about new business opportunities", he says. "Although we are informed about technologies, we start with looking at sociocultural trends. We start with people. It's about trying to anticipate what people's lives are going to be like in the future based on what the research says the economic, social, cultural, political and environmental concerns will be." (4) Research environments, design consultancies and manufacturers working across product genres offer a diverse range of projects for their designers to get involved in, puncturing another myth that employment means designing the same product over and over.

Although there are relatively few organisations that support internal research to the extent that Philips does – employing a permanent team on projects that look forward 20 years into the future (5) – the fact that they exist at all ought to help dispel another deep-rooted myth: that employment excludes opportunities for provocative, conceptual design. While this may be true in the majority of firms where the focus is restricted to products for current marketability, departments for research and strategy provide exceptions.

HOME TRUTHS

It is also tempting to be drawn into the notion that corporate structures offer high job security. While the overall risks may be lower than working in a consultancy (where they must bring in new work to stay afloat) or as an individual freelancer (where you must bring in new work), design services, particularly research, are often the first to experience cuts when recession strikes. Arguing "the case for design" to others within the corporate hierarchy may well become an intrinsic part of the job.

In doing so, it is not unheard of to find employers with a limited and, occasionally, warped sense of what a designer does. Just as common ground regarding ethos is important, so is a basic level of respect for the activity of design itself. Firms regularly advertise for designers when the positions they wish to fill are not creative ones, involving only the manual labour associated with design. One graduate told of an interview for a junior design position with a lighting firm, in which it was explained that the role would not involve designing lamps, but rather to produce technical drawings derived from camera-phone pictures of lamps taken in high street stores. Even companies that are more scrupulous than blatantly to copy are known

to frequently form their design directions by hashing together seasonal trends from magazine cuttings instead of setting their own agendas that embody discernible values.

It is also not uncommon for those who find work in the creative industries to discover a soul-destroying hierarchy that reserves the creative aspects of projects for those who have "served their time". All design involves "the perspiration part" that is not to be shied away from. However, making this the sole preserve of new recruits shows extreme short-sightedness from bosses who miss out on harnessing "untainted" creativity. The "naïve" questioning of entrenched methods that fresh minds bring is often precisely what is needed to open up new creative directions. Experience, it could be argued, is more desirable at the delivery stage.

Allied to this, a pernicious practice of non-payment for internships (work experience) prevails and conspires to make young designers dramatically undervalue their labour. While they may be prepared to work for free in exchange for what they hope will be valuable insights into the workings of the industry and a well-known name on the CV, employers who make this trade need to consider carefully the experience that will be provided. What other professions are able to get away with the custom that the employee's presence is a luxury they themselves should subsidise? However, if instead both parties look at experience as encompassing the full range of skills a designer may possess (as described above) rather than focusing solely upon computer software aptitude or years chalked up working elsewhere – a model that places most graduates on the bottom rung – both are likely to enrich their partnership.

[1.]
Woodgate, T. 2007. [Personal
communication]. 17 December

[2.]
Bayley, S. 2000. 'General
Knowledge'. London: Booth-
Clibborn Editions

4.2

COMMISSION

This section looks at the circumstances of being assigned work by a client, either as an individual or heading up a team. There is, therefore, some crossover with the context of the design consultancy, where external clients "commission" the firm to undertake projects, but here we consider this scenario from the perspective of the individual in charge rather than the employee. It examines independence as a means of enabling choices of who to work for and how to engage with them.

THE CHOICE OF INDEPENDENCE

"There is a certain joy to being the master of your own destiny", says designer Terence Woodgate, "I just do projects that I want to do, for the people I want to do them for." (1) Woodgate is one of many who choose to plough their own furrow in the world of product design. Considering that the frequency of decisions regarding what projects to take on as an independent designer is greater than the frequency at which those in employment change jobs, it is safe to argue that the former has greater control over the work they choose to pursue. The amount of influence they have therein, however, may differ dramatically.

Whereas the very title "designer" used to identify somebody who collaborates with clients and industry, those with critical voices who do not insist that they also have a rightful claim to the term, and are forcing the revision of this definition. Design historian and journalist Stephen Bayley proposes that: "The entire history of painting after, say, 1830 can be understood in terms of the dilemma faced by painters: whether to be society"s picture makers or to be misunderstood visionaries." Bayley tells us that: "Dostoyevsky described this as the choice between lofty suffering and cheap happiness" (2). Under this new broader definition, designers now face a similar choice (although the suffering may be somewhat less harsh than in 1830). The options between forming and following a personal ideology still exist– making money at the points where it happens to intersect with market demand – or consciously seeking out that demand and working to fulfil it. Of course, the degree to which one can be said to have "sold out" has a lot to do with the nobility of the demand that one chooses to serve, not to mention who is doing the demanding. It's hard to shake off the perception that "you are who you work for". The principles of client and customer tend to rub off, even if designers' work attempts to confront them.

TYPES OF COMMISSION

The range of work for which product designers may be commissioned is vast, and hence there is a necessity for them to define areas of aptitude, if not specialism. What are the skills and services being tendered and on what terms? Are designers prepared to "plug in" to projects being run by others – freelancing for companies or consultancies (in effect, undertaking short-term employment) – or is the idea to be at the helm? While there are those who go it alone from the start, there is a long-established model of others who "cut their teeth" in employment, observing, learning and subsequently leaving to set up shop, occasionally taking as many clients with them as they can.

The situation whereby the product or industrial designer establishes a strong, discursive relationship with a client that leads through a process of close collaboration until the release of the product is, to many, the most rewarding path to pursue.

However, other models of "offer" have augmented this, such as providing a menu of services, which may or may not include the design of a product (brand analysis, trend forecasting, lifecycle analysis, market research, ethnographic (user) studies and so on).

Alongside these come more making-based models of work, where the designer is responsible for both the design and production of one-offs or batches of objects. Here the designer may have a more or less "hands-on" aproach, either literally getting involved with the making of objects, or contracting it out to third parties. Alongside traditional designer-maker activity, the recently emerging field of "design-art" occupies this ground, with galleries commissioning designers to produce extraordinary objects at extraordinary prices. Similarly, many product designers, including some of the most renowned, have, as a core part of their business, undertaken the design and construction of exhibitions and trade fair stands, overseeing the sub-contracting of components and project managing their installation.

As mentioned in the last section, designers are being encouraged to see their skills as transferable and look for ways in which they can be applied in non-traditional ways. For those wishing to be commissioned, this means developing an awareness of emerging markets for their talents. Tim Brown from IDEO has noted that the commissioners are no longer who you might expect: "The people we are working for and are designing

[3.]
Brown, T. (CEO of global design consultancy IDEO) speaking at Intersections conference, The Baltic Centre, Gateshead, 25 October 2007

[4. 5.]
McCullagh, K. 2009. 'Riding the Flux: Design is changing in myriad ways. Are you?' [online]. [Accessed 27th January 2009]. Available from World Wide Web: <http://www.core77.com/reactor/07.07_flux.asp>

with are changing. This is the way I used to think of the world: businesses produced, people consumed, governments regulated and NGOs [non-governmental organisations] advocated…Now we are in a much more interdependent world where people are both creating and consuming, NGOs are funding businesses, businesses are funding NGOs and governments are investing in NGOs. It's incredibly more complex than it used to be. One result of that is that all kinds of new participants and entrepreneurs have emerged…We need to evolve. We can't necessarily rely on the processes we'd developed before." (3)

Brown is not the only voice suggesting that designers broaden their horizons for their own good. Kevin McCullagh, head of product strategy company, Plan, and a former director at industrial designers Seymour Powell, describes a bleak outlook for those who focus solely upon designing objects: "Globalization has reduced the number of manufacturers to a small number of behemoths, and multiplied the number of designers pitching for jobs. The era of product design as practiced by a small band of gurus in Milan, London, Munich and New York is long gone. There are now thousands of competent product designers around the world able to give good form. Design as 'styling' or 'form-giving' has become commoditized, and competing at this level is already a tough, low-margin slog… If we shed the blinkers and see the world differently there are many positive shifts, like the mainstreaming of design in business and the public sector, which offer glimpses of a chance to drastically expand the frontiers of design." (4)

As China up-skills, a portion of its workforce is training as designers. Already, those who have established themselves are able to dramatically undercut Western design businesses. McCullagh recalls:

[6.]   -
Mari, E. In: Burkhardt, F.,
Capella, J., Picchi F. 1997.
'Why Write a Book on Enzo
Mari?' Milan: Frederico Motta
Editore
                  -
[7.]   -
Grcic, K. In: Bohm, F. 2005.
'Konstantin Grcic Industrial
Design'. London: Phaidon
                  -
[8.]   -
Woodgate, T. 2007. [Personal
communication]. 17 December
                  -
[9.]   -
Hecht, S. 2008. [Personal
communication]. 24 January
                  -
[10.] -
Berge, S. 2007. [Personal
communication]. 11 December
                  -

"A Shanghai-based designer paid me the backhanded compliment, 'Your work is very good, but we do nearly as good for a tenth of the price!'" (5) While the objects themselves may be the central point of interest for many product designers and the idea of branching out, unappealing, they at least need to consider what will make their designs have more value than those of their competitors. Perhaps they will embody a more acute understanding of the market, or can be delivered through a supply chain of exemplary quality and provenance. Whatever the method of differentiation, the product designer of today is going to have to work much harder to find and maintain their niche than in years gone by.

-           -   -
THE RULES OF ENGAGEMENT

On top of these global business challenges, the designer starting out as an independent without prior experience faces a bewildering array of variables and the "rules of engagement" are often unclear. Hammering home the need for these to be thoroughly discussed and understood, Enzo Mari once declared that "95 percent of the project is words." (6) The very first ones – those with which the designer must interest the client – are the first hurdle and can be among the most difficult. The problem with the rules of engagement is that they are fluid: different cultures, product sectors and companies have different protocols for engaging with designers, different expectations of deliverables, different methods of paymentand so on. The first step is to find out how (and if) the client company wants to deal with an external, independent designer. If all goes well, a chance to assess compatibility will be set up, which could be anything from an informal chat down the pub to an intense show-and-tell of past work. Part of this process of investigating a possible working relationship, beyond establishing mutual respect, will be to ensure mutual understanding of the designer's, and indeed the client's, role in any ensuing project. The same applies if the company has approached the designer. Both must reach a clear understanding of why the other wishes to work with them and what it is they believe the other has to offer. Many projects break down at a later stage when differences in expectation come to the surface. Was the client primarily after a famous name, a house style, a pair of hands to direct, or do they see in the designer's thinking something that chimes with their own? Regrettably, the kinds of robust conversations that uncover such things can be tough to initiate and hence do not always take place. Yet they should be an intrinsic part of any project. "Design is always a two-way process, the result of a dialogue between the designer and the person commissioning the work", says Konstantin Grcic. "It's like a game of ping-pong: an exchange of knowledge, ideas and arguments, which only becomes exciting when both parties are equally strong players." (7)

Particularly difficult to establish prior to the design process getting underway is the extent to which the client feels they may impinge upon the designer's craft. "Once, early in my career, I let a client move my pen for me," recalls Terence Woodgate, "and I swore I would never let that happen again. They can give me constructive criticism on why something won't work, and ask me to go back and reconsider. And I'm quite happy to do that. [But the design] has to please me in every way, shape or form, use of material, the production, the ethical issues…you have to be guided by your principles." (8) Woodgate knows as well as anyone that design is about fulfilling constraints, but he is also keenly aware that the designer must be given space to do what he does best. Sam Hecht sheds additional light on the situation by offering that: "The difference between a constraint and a compromise is in when the information is given", (9) explaining that, if provided early on, it forms part of the design brief (a constraint) and it is therefore the designer's duty to accommodate it. If the client suggests a change, it risks unbalancing a concept tailored to the initial requirements and resulting in a compromise.

The design process takes as much or as little time as its protagonists feel necessary – from a scribbled sketch on a napkin to years of full-time commitment. Settling upon the scope of the project is key. A watch manufacturer might work with a designer on the future direction of their product ranges right down to the effect of a fraction of a millimetre difference in the radius running round the bezel of one of their watches. Being clear about the areas in which their expertise is being sought is essential. Some designers argue that it is their duty to challenge the boundaries of the brief, especially when clients appear to have conservative goals. However, wilfully delivering solutions beyond the scope of the client, no matter how innovative, is to fail them. "You can always find a creative angle to whatever you are doing", advises Sebastian Bergne. "You have to identify where the room for movement is, and within that space, how far you can go; what you propose will be accepted." (10)

Once the territory of the project has been determined, the forms in which it will be delivered can be discussed. Again expectations often vary, not least regarding the number of alternatives that the designer ordinarily presents. Is it the designer's duty to give the client a selection of product concepts or should it be their role to synthesise the problem well enough so that one solution stands out? The context of the individual project will produce different requirements, but it is perhaps worth proposing a rule of thumb. To the unenlightened client, volume of ideas represents good value. Yet the best designers will filter out, through experience and elimination, the ideas that do not fit, and have no wish to let the client pick from among them. On this point, Milan-based designer Perry King explains that the dialogue and consequent understanding of the problem from both parties prior to the presentation of any ideas meant that when the (singular) idea was presented, the client knew it was the right one. It is therefore the designer's role to communicate effectively the rigorous process that they have gone through, and to illustrate that all the points raised during consultation have been addressed.

An analogy may be made to the clothes retailer and the tailor. The tailor discusses your requirements at length, getting to know your preferences and needs and only suggests fabrics and cuts that are right for you. Having identified these, he will present one garment, but with the understanding that a fitting will take place to allow modifications. The retailer lines up choices in the hope of covering a range of tastes, but these rarely fit as precisely as the tailored garment. One is a time-consuming and, hopefully, rewarding process for both parties. The other is a gamble that may or may not pay off. It is worth remembering that the

[11.]   -
Bierut, M. 2007. '79 Short
Essays on Design'. New York:
Princeton Architectural Press
          -

way a product idea is presented can be fundamental to how well it is received. Hence, the same idea, dismissed when presented on-screen in an email, may be welcomed when presented in person supported by a verbal rationale of its context along with drawings and a model.

Aware of the competitive nature of the profession, some of the more sought-after clients have changed their practices. Rather than building deep-tailored relationships with designers they know and respect, some have resorted to a pitching process where designers are encouraged to send in speculative ideas. Like spoiled children, the most oversubscribed firms are instantly gratified by picking from the many projects pitched to them every week. Yet with each piece of work receiving such scant attention – most being sent by email rather than presented in person – there is insufficient time for the designer to explain any depth of meaning and the process becomes dangerously similar to that of a beauty contest.

While many young designers are happy to spend time on such work, the "hit rate" is extremely low and encourages a scattergun approach. Designers who work this way – detached from clients, firing product ideas at them "on spec" – may be able to predict some of the company's requirements based on existing ranges, but they cannot know their plans for the future. For the businesses concerned, it is a way to shortcut the payment of fees for ideas development, which designers must try to offset through other income. Ultimately, designers have a choice as to whether to take part in such a process or instead attempt to establish more meaningful links from the start. What is more important is that once any selection process is out of the way, the relationship is allowed to deepen so the project can be developed harmoniously, rather than at arm's length.

In the case of working with product manufacturers and distributors, another key contrast occurs in the extent to which the client has the capacity to undertake parts of the development process themselves. It must be established in early meetings, whether the designer is charged with defining the object in relation to the subcontracting of manufacture or if they must respond to specific existing facilities. Either way, they must determine where their role ends and the company's begins – a sketch, a model, a technical drawing, a CAD model, or drawings of tooling for manufacture? Companies with in-house engineering designers will be able to take drawings and models and cover the necessary engineering of the production process themselves. If this becomes part of the external designer's role, it can represent a considerable increase in the amount of technical knowledge required to complete the project.

-                    -

THE MYTH OF THE PERFECT CLIENT

Designers are forever moaning about clients who appear to take no interest in the finer points of what they are trying to achieve, focusing only on the bottom line. They long for enlightened clients to whom they feel they can relate. Yet as Michael Bierut points out (11), these "perfect clients" have at their helm, or in positions of power, individuals with a personal passion for design that they choose to bring to work. This is, Bierut says, the kind of passion that one might have for wine or music, and it becomes company strategy as opposed to emerging from it. Furniture magnates Giulio

Cappellini, Eugenio Perraza of Magis, Rolf Felbaum of Vitra, and, of course, Steve Jobs of Apple, are the most well-known examples of the company director immersed in the concerns of his designers. The output of all four firms typifies innovation and it is through this commitment that they have become the most respected names in modern design. These extremely rare and special cases are held up as the standards to which designers should aspire.

Looking at the issue another way, it can be argued that designers shouldn't expect manufacturers to have the same level of interest, enthusiasm or knowledge about design as they do. After all, a plumber wouldn't expect a householder to be interested in the finer points of u-bend specification. However, it is perhaps not too much to expect the client to engage with why the job needs doing, what a good (as opposed to mediocre) result will achieve and how this will be recognised.

–   –

SPECULATION

Designers work speculatively for a diverse set of reasons, the most obvious being simply for the pleasure of it. Although focused by constraints and deadlines, the creative mind need not require a client brief to propel it into action. Indeed, for those normally in search of one, the lack of a brief can be the impetus to set their own. Competitions offer other starting points (although with some asking for a large amount of work, the time investment needs careful consideration). What starts on a whim or as a "pet project" may be shown to a client at a later stage, once the designer has satisfied himself that it has potential. Like panning for gold, for some there is the hope that one day they will "strike it lucky" when one of their ideas is adopted by an industry in exchange for a lucrative royalty contract. Outside of this there are a number of contexts in which maintaining complete independence from industry is considered desirable and still others where it is inevitable.

Speculative work is rarely all a designer does. If well received, a project is likely to lead to commission or employment. Otherwise, it may intentionally be maintained alongside more commercial practice as an outlet for particular expressions.

IN LIEU OF A CLIENT

"When you start out...you're just happy to do anything that comes along," says Sebastian Bergne, "and if things don't come along you tend to make up projects using technologies that are accessible, with low investment." (1) Bergne, who now runs a successful design office covering industrial design, furniture and accessories, achieved early success with just such a project – a

design for a lampshade made from acid-etched stainless steel (fig. 1, page 198). Bergne could order batches of the piece, their flat-pack design enabling them to be easily posted.

As well as acting as a stop-gap between client projects, self-production can be an effective means of promotion, a "business card" that gives weight to graduate folios that may otherwise be stocked with unrealised concepts. By exploring available manufacturing technologies speculatively, experience can be gained that is usefully transferable to later client projects.

PRODUCTION ON THE EDGE

Some may argue that this designer-maker activity is more akin to craft, and yet it is discussed here because it is a route that many product designers are taking in order to get their ideas to the market. It is particularly common when the product in question does not fit the conventional rules of the market, yet the designer believes it will be well received. Constantin and Laurene Leon Boym followed this line of thought when they started their in-house label, Handy. Their Buildings of Disaster series (fig. 2, page 199) – small bronze models of buildings that had befallen a natural disaster or become major crime scenes, intended not to celebrate, but as cathartic reminders – were controversial enough for the Boyms to recognise immediately that they would have to produce the pieces themselves. "The bottom line for Handy is that the project should be crazy enough so that it's useless to approach any manufacturer with it", says Constantin Boym. "The Buildings of Disaster, for example, would be kicked out of the door by a manufacturer." (2)

Daniel Weil, now a partner in multinational consultancy Pentagram, designed and made a series of radios after leaving college in the 1980s. Intrigued by the postmodern theories being applied in Italy at

[1.]
Bergne, S. 2007. [Personal communication]. 11 December

[2.]
Boym, C. In: Hall, P. 2002. 'Curious Boym'. New York: Princeton Architectural Press

[3.]
Sans, M. 2008. [Personal communication]. 24 June

[4.]
David Report, Issue 7 June 2007, <www.davidreport.com>

Fig. 1   **Lampshade by Sebastian Bergne manufactured by Radius Gmbh** Bergne's acid-etched clip-on lampshade can be inverted to provide direct or indirect lighting. As a one-piece, single-process product, it allowed its designer to begin production cost-effectively.

the time, Weil used the radios as a means of exploring an alternative product language and lampooning British middle-class taste (fig. 3, page 200 and fig. 4, page 201).

Products like Weil's radios and the Boyms's Buildings of Disaster show that there is a role for designer-makers in filling niches considered dangerous or insufficiently profitable by mainstream industry, and in doing so spicing up the often bland range of products available to us. Although neither of these examples sold in vast quantities – this was not their aim – in producing them in series they take on the gravitas of "real" products as opposed to concepts that remain out of reach. Despite their expense (and consequent cult status) this availability ensured greater interest from both press and public alike.

The wilful rejection of industrial collaboration opens up the conceptual space that Boym, Weil and many others have entered. It allows for speculation as deviancy – a chance to pervert the norms of client projects. Michael Sans reflects that "this kind of work happens because designers don't have clients. Perhaps there is bitterness which manifests itself in dark humour." (3) For German-born Sans, his controversial work redesigning bullets and using taxidermy in domestic products is about rebelling against the typical strictness expected of German designers, while providing an ironic take on design and a chance to have fun.

-                          -
DESIGN-ART

Designer-maker editions can often prove financially unsustainable due to the high manufacturing costs of small batches and the low number of people prepared to invest in these special objects. However, a small branch of the practice has morphed into what has become known as "Design-Art". The term, coined by

auctioneer Alexander Payne of the Phillips de Pury chain of auction houses, has come to describe one-off or limited edition works by designers for galleries, art fairs and the auction market. Whereas the price of designer-maker editions, with the exception of a handful of star names, remains within bounds, Design-Art has established its own territory where prices have been pushed up to those associated with (if not quite that of the Grand Masters), artwork of considerable pedigree. Marc Newson's Lockheed Lounge chaise-longue, for example, allegedly sold for just under $1m. Characterised by Swedish design entrepreneur David Carlson in his influential David Report as "Vulgarism for the Nouveau-super-riche" (4), the design world is split between those prepared to embrace this new development and others, like Carlson, who see it as a dangerous distraction from design's more worthy goals.

Of course, this is not the first time that designers have been accused of financial elitism. When it happened previously, such as with the design group, Memphis, in the 1980s, some dodged criticism by ensuring the work had a clear intellectual rationale. Despite doing so through exclusive design objects, in challenging modernism's blandness and intellectual elitism the work of Ettore Sottsass and his cohorts placated many who might otherwise have lambasted it. To many, the rationale behind the work of the latest band of Design-Artists, such as Studio Job, Marcel Wanders and Jaime Hayon, is less comprehensible.

-                          -
ACADEMIA

Design education is, by its nature, a speculative space. However, in attempting to prepare students for work in industry by emulating its contexts, the full freedom of this space becomes constrained. While some courses encourage the plurality of approaches this book illustrates, the narrow industrial orientation of others channels them towards serving, rather than

Fig. 2 Federal Building, Oklahoma City from the Buildings of Disaster series by Constantin and Laurene Boym Self production has allowed designers such as the Boyms to deal with sensitive subject matter likely to deter most clients. Their Buildings of Disaster series aims to aid remembrance rather than celebration, of the tragedies that had befallen the locations they depict.

challenging, the status quo. A pretence is maintained that the circumstances of industry can be accurately re-created within academia. Yet beyond so-called "live" projects, students rarely encounter a "real" client and, though tutors try to predict appropriate responses, mismatches are inevitable. Tutors, many being designers themselves, are aware of many different potential outcomes. They are torn between advocating creativity and compliance with conventional thinking in the form of industrial constraints. Clients are liable to be more dispassionate, looking at proposals and seeing if they fit their needs.

In the light of this, design courses could do worse than polarise their projects into those that are genuinely "live" and those that use the speculative space available to explore specific issues without recourse to pseudo-industrial constraints.

As many reading this will be aware, the structure of most undergraduate degree courses in product or three-dimensional design is broadly similar, with much or all of the first two years spent learning skills within brief-led projects and the third, self-directed. This requires students to be capable of setting themselves a worthwhile project in the final year that has a clearly understood context, a subject that they are passionate about, and that is of a scope that can realistically be brought to a conclusion. The choice of what to investigate can be seen as an indication of the concerns of those students. Sadly, too few appear to engage with the issues and challenges facing design and the world beyond, instead retreating into introspective projects that investigate little beyond their own self-interest in specific objects.

RESEARCH

Rigorous practice-based design research is rarely possible within the time and financial constraints of commercial design projects. However, design research work that does not need to bring an immediate return is vital. Just as chemistry explores the effects of substances independently from the search for cures (chemistry's equivalent of the design brief), design research can investigate the nature of materials, processes, forms and behaviour outside of the brief of applying these to objects. Despite the financial pressures, some quarters of industry do regularly undertake research outside of the design process, which turns up invaluable discoveries that spark new projects and feed our culture.

THE CONSCIENCE OF DESIGN

Led by the need to give shareholders a return on their investment, many buisnesses have no in-built incentive to behave philanthropically. The design that it commissions must first and foremost serve this financial bottom line and the compromises this presents diminish the potential of many products. As we have seen, this background has motivated some designers to avoid the pressures and dogmas of entrenched business and marketing methodologies and go in search of more vibrant and humane alternatives. Speculative work, although constrained by individual circumstances, offers the opportunity for a truly independent voice – for designers to express their values through the design of objects, either as optimistic presentations of what they ideally want or as cautionary tales of where we might be heading. A mature understanding of today's design culture must embrace the fact that design has transcended its roots as a service industry and has expanded to become a tool for independently expressing personal and political standpoints. Speculative work is therefore the conscience of design and may be seen as a barometer of the prevailing concerns of designers.

Fig. 3   Radio in a **Plastic Bag by Daniel Weil** Weil's radios were curious, quirky objects likely to baffle manufacturers yet demonstrated insights such as the desire for transparency, that would later become mainstream. This example sets the components as a graphic composition inside a clear plastic bag.

Fig. 4   **Small Door radio by Daniel Weil**
Weil argued that it was only tradition that boxed up radios and restricted their visual language. This response places the components in a cage behind a door and covers the speaker with chintz fabric, alluding to the backward-looking tastes of middle class Britain.

05 Sources

BIBLIOGRAPHY

The following list gives a selection only of the works consulted. For more information, see individual margin notes.

Ambasz, E. 1972. Italy: the New Domestic Landscape'. New York: MOMA

Antonelli, P., Aldersey-Williams, H., Hall, P., Sargent, T. 2008. 'Design and The Elastic Mind'. New York: MOMA

Bakker, C. and van Hinte, E. 1999. 'Trespassers'. Rotterdam: 010 Publishers

Ball, R. and Naylor, M. 2005. 'Form Follows Idea: An Introduction to Design Poetics'. London: Black Dog

Barrow, J.D. 1997. 'The Artful Universe: The Artful Universe'. London: Penguin Books

Barthes, R. 1957. 'Mythologies'. Paris: Editions du Seuil

Bayley, S. and Conran, T. 2007. 'Intelligence Made Visible'. London: Conran Octopus Ltd

Bayley, S. 2000. 'General Knowledge'. London: Booth Clibborn Editions

Bierut, M. 2007. '79 Short Essays on Design'. New York: Princeton Architectural Press

Bohm, F. 2005. 'Konstantin Grcic Industrial Design'. London: Phaidon

Bovier L. 2003. 'ECAL Design Industriel / Industrial Design'. Lausanne: ECAL

Boym, C. 2002. 'Curious Boym'. New York: Princeton Architectural Press

Braungart, M. and McDonough, W. 2002. 'Cradle to Cradle: Remaking the Way We Make Things'. New York: North Point Press

Bürdek, B. 2005. 'Design: History, Theory and Practice of Product Design'. Basel: Birkhäuser

Burkhardt, F., Capella, J., Picchi F. 1997. 'Why Write a Book on Enzo Mari?' Milan: Frederico Motta Editore

Chapman, J. 2005. 'Emotionally Durable Design: Objects, Experiences and Empathy'. London: Earthscan

Cummings, N. (ed.) 2003. 'Reading Things'. London: Chance Books

Dormer, P. 1990. 'The Meanings of Modern Design'. London: Thames & Hudson

Dunne, A. 1999. 'Hertzian Tales: Electronic products, aesthetic experience and critical design.' London: RCA Computer Related Design Research

Dunne, A. and Raby, R. 2001. 'Design Noir: The Secret Life of Electronic Objects'. Basel: Birkhäuser

Dreyfuss, H. 1955. 'Designing for People'. New York: Simon and Schuster

Gaver, W. 'The Curious Home'. 2007. Goldsmiths University of London

Fiell, C. and Fiell, P. 2001. 'Designing the 21st Century'. Colgne: Taschen

Fiell, C. and Fiell, P. 2007. 'Design Now'. Cologne: Taschen

Fletcher, A. 2001. 'The Art of Looking Sideways'. London: Phaidon

Flusser, V. 1999. 'The Shape of Things: A philosophy of design'. London: Reaktion Books

Forty, A. 1995. 'Objects of Desire'. London: Thames & Hudson

Fukasawa, N. 2007. 'Naoto Fukasawa'. Phaidon Press

Gaver, W. 2007. 'The Curious Home.' London: Goldsmiths, University of London

Gershenfeld, N. 2005. 'FAB: The Coming Revolution on your desktop-from personal computers to personal fabrication'. New York: Basic Books

Hecht, S. and Colin, K. 2005. 'Product as Landscape'. London: Industrial Facility

Hecht, S. and Colin, K. 2003. 'Things That Go Unseen'. London: Industrial Facility

Heskett, J. 1980. 'Industrial Design'. Oxford: Oxford University Press

Jencks, S. and Silver, N. 1973. 'Adhocism – The Case for Improvisation'. New York: Anchor Books

Julier, G. 2000. 'The Culture of Design'. London: Sage Publications

Lidwell, W, Holden, K, Butler, J. 2003. 'Universal Principles of Design'. Gloucester, MA: Rockport Publishers Inc.

Moggridge, B. 2007. 'Designing Interactions'. Cambridge, MA: MIT Press

Morrison, J. 2002. 'Everything but the Walls'. Baden: Lars Muller Publishers

Norman, D. 2002. 'The Design of Everyday Things'. New York: Basic Books

Papanek, V. 1970. 'Design for the Real World: Human Ecology and Social Change'. New York: Pantheon Books

Pipes, A. 2007. 'Drawing for Designers'. London: Lawrence King

Polano, S. 2001. 'Achille Castiglioni'. London: Phaidon

Potter, N. 2002. 'What is a designer?' London: Hyphen Press

Pye, D. 1978. 'The Nature and Aesthetics of Design'. London: A & C Black

Ramakers, R. and Bakker, G. (eds). 1998. 'Droog Design: Spirit of the nineties'. Rotterdam: 010 Publishers

Redhead, D. 2000. 'Products of Our Time'. Basel: Birkhäuser

Smith, C. 2008. 'Design for the Other 90%'. New York: Cooper Hewitt National Design Museum

Sudjic, D. 1989. 'Ron Arad: Restless Furniture'. New York: Forth Estate/Wordsearch

Thackara, J. 2005. 'In the bubble: designing in a complex world'. Cambridge, MA: MIT Press

Van Hinte, E. (ed.) 1997. 'Eternally Yours – Visions on Product Endurance'. Rotterdam: 010 Publishers

von Vegesack, A. 1996. 'Thonet: Classic Furniture in Bent Wood and Tubular Steel'. London: Hazar Publishing Ltd

Williams, G. 2006. 'The Furniture Machine: Furniture Since 1990'. London: V&A Publications

PICTURE CREDITS

Introduction

P8, fig. 1 Courtesy of Dyson Ltd

P8, fig. 2 Image courtesy of Ron Arad Associates

P9, fig. 3 Courtesy of Inflate

P9, fig. 4 Client: IKEA, Advertising Agency: Kamarama, Campaign: Van den Puup, Photograper: Henrik Halvarsson. With thanks to Curtis Brown.

P10, fig. 5 Courtesy of Inga Knoelke

P11, fig. 6 Courtesy of Morrison Studio, Walter Gumiero/Magis

P12, fig. 7 TAKEO PAPER SHOW 2004 "HAPTIC"/Juice skin. Photo by Masayoshi Hichiwa/(hue amana group), courtesy of Naoto Fukasawa Design

P12, fig. 8 Courtesy of Edward Goodwin and Richard Hartshorn

P13, fig. 9 Courtesy of Dunne and Raby

01 Perception

P16, fig. 1 Courtesy of Alessi

P18, fig. 2 Courtesy of Wedgwood

P18, fig. 3 V&A Images/ Victoria and Albert Museum

P19, fig. 4 Courtesy of Apple

P19, fig. 5 DIGITAL IMAGE © 2008, The Museum of Modern Art, New York/Scala, Florence

P20, fig. 6 Photograph by Ben Kelway, courtesy of Intersection Media

P20, fig. 7 Photograph by Kay Adams

P21, fig. 8 Photograph by Ivan Coleman, courtesy of Amos Field Reid

P21, fig. 9 Photograph by Ivan Coleman, courtesy of Jessica Corteen

P21, fig. 10 Photograph by Ivan Coleman, courtesy of Rhian Jones

P22, fig. 11 Courtesy of Auger–Loizeau

P23, fig. 12 Courtesy of Jai Redman/UHC Design Ltd

P23, fig. 13 Heatwave (2003) Designer: Joris Laarman, Manufacturer: Hot water version Jaga The Radiator Factory <www.jaga.be>, Electric version Droog Design <www.droogdesign.nl>

P24, fig. 1 Mods on scooters. 31st March 1964: Mods on scooters at Clacton. (Photo by Terry Disney/Express/Getty Images) Photograph © 2007 Getty Images

P25, fig. 2 Rockers, British youths into scruffy clothes, motorcyles and leather, tearing along road in convoy. (Photo by Terrence Spencer//Time Life Pictures/Getty Images) Photograph © Terrence Spencer, courtesy of Time & Life Pictures/Getty Images

P26, fig. 3 Courtesy of Freeplay Energy

P26, fig. 4 Courtesy of Freeplay Energy

P27, fig. 5 Image © Olinchuck

P27, fig. 6 Anna G corkscrew. Design Alessandro Mendini, Alessi S.p.A.

P29, fig. 7 Photograph by Tim Parsons

P31, fig. 8 Photographs by David Sykes, courtesy of Zaha Hadid Architects

P32, fig. 1 DIGITAL IMAGE © 2008, The Museum of Modern Art, New York/Scala, Florence

P33, fig. 2 Courtesy of Ettore Sottsass for Memphis

P35, fig. 3 Illustration by Tim Parsons

P35, fig. 4 Courtesy of Alessi S.p.a.

P36, fig. 5 DIGITAL IMAGE © 2008, The Museum of Modern Art, New York/Scala, Florence

P37, fig. 7 Photograph by Tim Parsons

P38, fig. 8 Courtesy of Robin Levien and Caroline Aston/ Studio Levien

P39, fig. 9 Courtesy of Sam Hecht/Industrial Facility

P40, fig. 10 Photographs by James Bartlett

P41, fig. 11 From the series: 'Making Do and Getting By'. Courtesy of Richard Wentworth and Lisson Gallery

P41, fig. 12 Pablo Picasso, Tete de taureau. Realisee a partir d'une selle et d'un guidon de bicyclette. 1942. © DACS 2008. White Images/Scala, Florence

P42, fig. 13 Courtesy of Antonio Cos

P43, fig. 14 David Gresham, American, b.1956 (Designer), Martin Thaler, American, b.1954 (Designer), Model for Book Computer, 1985, Plastics, 20 x 32 x 32cm, collection of Cranbrook Art Museum, Bloomfield Hills, Michigan, Gift of David Gresham and Martin Thaler through Design Logic. With thanks to Professor Bernhard E Buerdek

P43, fig. 15 Collection of Cranbrook Art Museum, Bloomfield Hills, Michigan. With thanks to Lisa Krohn

P44, fig. 16 Design: Sander Mulder; Photography: Niels van Veen, Sander Mulder

P44, fig. 17 Photograph by Patrick Gries, courtesy of Matali Crasset

P45, fig. 18 Courtesy of Established & Sons and Zaha Hadid Architects

02 Motivation

P52, fig. 1 Image © Kodak

P52, fig. 2 Image © Kodak

P53, fig. 3 Image © Paul Linnell <www.simplyswitchon. co.uk> Photo: Jon Linnell

P54, fig. 4 A map of the Paris metro at Bastille station, circa 1950. In the foreground is an art-nouveau entourage designed by Hector Guimard. (Photo by Gabriel Hackett/ Hulton Archive/Getty Images)

P54, fig. 5 DIGITAL IMAGE © 2008, The Museum of Modern Art, New York/Scala, Florence

P55, fig. 6 Photo by Luigi Colani/Colani Trading AG

P55, fig. 7 Courtesy of Bernhardt Design

P56, fig. 8 Courtesy of KGID office/Magis S.P.A.

P57, fig. 9 Illustration by Emmi Salonen

P58, fig. 10 Courtesy of Braun and Daniel Nelson

P59, fig. 11 Courtesy of Apple

P60, fig. 12 Courtesy of Sam Hecht/Industrial Facility

P61, fig. 13 Courtesy of Sam Hecht/Industrial Facility

P62, fig. 1 Jasper Morrison Ltd. Product: Flower pot table, produced by: Capellini, photo credit: Morrison Studio

P62, fig. 2 Knifeforkspoon. Design Jasper Morrison, Alessi S.p.a. Photograph by Andre Huber

P63, fig. 3 Courtesy of Morrison Studio

P63, fig. 4 Socrates corkscrew. Design Jasper Morrison, Alessi S.p.a.

P64, fig. 5 Courtesy of Association Marcel Duchamp

P64, fig. 6 Courtesy of Massimo Varetto

P65, fig. 7 Courtesy of Zanotta SpA - Italy/Studio Museo Achille Castiglioni

P65, fig. 8 Courtesy of Zanotta SpA - Italy/Studio Museo Achille Castiglioni

P67, fig. 9 Courtesy of Sam Hecht/Industrial Facility

P67, fig. 10 Courtesy of Sam Hecht/Industrial Facility

P67, fig. 11 Courtesy of Sam Hecht/Industrial Facility

P68, fig. 12 Plusminuszero/A4 light Photo by Hidetoyo Sasaki, courtesy of Naoto Fukasawa Design

P68, fig. 13 Photograph by Tim Parsons

P69, fig. 14 Courtesy of Zanotta SpA - Italy/Studio Museo Achille Castiglioni

P70, fig. 15 Photograph by Angus Mills, courtesy of Martino Gamper

P71, fig. 16 Courtesy of KGID office

P72, fig. 17 Photograph by Tim Parsons

P72, fig. 18 UNITED STATES - DECEMBER 12: Bands of light wrap the Guggenheim Museum at night, New York, New York (Photo by Bates Littlehales/ National Geographic/Getty Images)

P72, fig. 19 Muji/CD player Photo by Hidetoyo Sasaki, courtesy of Naoto Fukasawa design

P73, fig. 20 Plusminuszero/Sole bag Photo by Hidetoyo Sasaki, courtesy of Naoto Fukasawa design

P73, fig. 21 Photograph by Patrick Gries, courtesy of Matali Crasset

P74, fig. 22 Photograph by Patrick Gries, courtesy of Matali Crasset

P74, fig. 23 Photograph by Patrick Gries, courtesy of Matali Crasset

P75, fig. 24 Courtesy of Bouroullec

P75, fig. 25 Photograph by Tim Parsons

P76, fig. 26 Courtesy of William Warren

P76, fig. 27 Courtesy of William Warren

P77, fig. 28 Photograph by Tim Parsons

P77, fig. 29 Courtesy of William Warren

P78, fig. 30 Courtesy of William Warren

P78, fig. 31 Courtesy of Richard Hutten

P79, fig. 32 Photograph by Nigel Haynes/randomproduct.com

P80, fig. 33 Courtesy of Studioball and Ligne Roset

P80, fig. 34 Courtesy of Michael Marriott

P80, fig. 35 Courtesy of Michael Marriott

P81, fig. 36 Courtesy of Ian Roberts

5.3

ACKNOWLEDGEMENTS

Like any design process, a book is greatly influenced by the relationships that occur during its creation, both personal and professional. I am eternally grateful for the boundless support, patience and contributions of Jess Charlesworth and my parents David and Dorothy Parsons. I am also highly indebted to my friends, whose vigorous discussions and debate formed many of the ideas expressed herein.

I would like to thank all those connected to the Design Products course at the Royal College of Art who sowed the seeds that led to this book. Many of the ideas took shape while teaching at Manchester Metropolitan University and latterly, at Camberwell College of Arts. I would like to thank Ian Roberts and the staff of the Three Dimensional Design programme at MMU/Manchester School of Art for their friendship and encouragement, David Crow for his kind recommendation, and Stefan White for his valuable insights. Thank you to Karen Richmond at Camberwell and to students past and present for their energy and inspiration.

In the delivery of the book, I would like to express my gratitude to all of the designers who contributed images of work and in particular, to those who gave up their time to be interviewed. I would like to thank Emmi Salonen for the design and layout of the book itself and her help with illustrations. I am very grateful to Leafy Robinson, Caroline Walmsley, Leonie Taylor, Lucienne Roberts, Helen Stone and Brian Morris at AVA for their hard work and patience. Thanks to Edward Goodwin, Alke Groppel-Wegener and David Parsons for their assistance with proofreading.

Interviewees:
Michael Marriott
Terence Woodgate
Anthony Dunne
Tim Brown
Sam Hecht
Deyan Sudjic
Robin Levien
Sebastian Bergne
Jeremy Myerson
Roger Coleman
Stefan White
Jack Mama